A VERY SMALL INSURANCE POLICY

Glen Barclay is associate professor of International Relations at the University of Queensland. He is vice-president of the Queensland branch of the Australian Institute of International Affairs and reviews editor of *Australian Journal of Politics and History*. Author of *Commonwealth or Europe* (1970), *History of the Pacific* (1978), and *Friends in High Places* (1985), Dr Barclay is currently writing a history of the diplomacy of Australian disengagement from Vietnam.

A VERY SMALL INSURANCE POLICY

THE POLITICS OF AUSTRALIAN INVOLVEMENT
IN VIETNAM, 1954–1967

Glen St J. Barclay

University of Queensland Press
ST LUCIA • LONDON • NEW YORK

First published 1988 by University of Queensland Press
Box 42, St Lucia, Queensland, Australia

© Glen St J. Barclay 1988

This book is copyright. Apart from any fair dealing for the
purposes of private study, research, criticism or review, as
permitted under the Copyright Act, no part may be reproduced
by any process without written permission. Enquiries should
be made to the publisher.

Typeset by University of Queensland Press
Printed in Australia by The Book Printer, Melbourne

Distributed in the UK and Europe by University of Queensland Press
Dunhams Lane, Letchworth, Herts. SG6 1LF England

Distributed in the USA and Canada by University of Queensland Press
250 Commercial Street, Manchester, NH 03101 USA

Cataloguing in Publication Data

National Library of Australia

Barclay, Glen St. J. (Glen St. John), 1930–
   A very small insurance policy.

   Bibliography.
   Includes index.

   1. Vietnamese Conflict, 1961–1975 — Participation,
   Australian. 2. Australia — Military policy. I. Title.

959.704'3394

British Library (data available)

Library of Congress

Barclay, Glen St. John, 1930–   .
   A very small insurance policy.

   Bibliography: p.
   Includes index.
   1. Vietnamese Conflict, 1961–1975 — Australia.
   2. Australia — Foreign relations — Vietnam.
   3. Vietnam — Foreign relations — Australia. I. Title.

DS558.6.A8B37   1987   959.704'33'94   86-27284

ISBN 0 7022 2069 8

For Elizabeth

Contents

Illustrations   *ix*

1 The Australians Must Be Terribly Excited (1954)   *1*
2 To Get Some Share of the Credit (1954–1962)   *14*
3 These Australians Could Share in Our Casualties (1963–1964)   *35*
4 The Americans Needed Stiffening (1964)   *58*
5 We Must Pursue the Tough Line (1965)   *79*
6 A Mark of Appreciation of a Good Ally (1965–1966)   *106*
7 The PM Has Been Mesmerized (1966–1967)   *134*
Conclusion   *165*

Notes to the Text   *170*
Glossary   *184*
Bibliography   *186*
Index   *193*

Illustrations

Photographs following page 118

Dean Rusk and Sir Robert G. Menzies
Sir Keith J. Holyoake, Sir Robert G. Menzies and Sir Garfield Barwick
Sir Keith Waller and Lyndon B. Johnson
Harold E. Holt
Hubert H. Humphrey, Harold E. Holt and Arthur A. Calwell
Lyndon B. Johnson and Harold E. Holt
Lyndon B. Johnson, Park Chung Hee, Ferdinand E. Marcos, Imelda Marcos and Nguyen van Thieu
Sir Harold Wilson, John McEwen and Sir Paul Hasluck
Sir Paul Hasluck

1

The Australians Must Be Terribly Excited (1954)

Australian Ambassador to the United States, Sir Keith Waller, could never quite remember whether Australia "ever got a specific request for a combat unit" in Vietnam, "or whether we offered it without that request having been made. I know," he told interviewer Joe B. Frantz, "we started originally with one battalion and ended up with three. I know with the second and third there was no request. Whether there was for the first, I don't remember."[1] Actually this was not quite the case. There had in fact been a most embarrassing absence of any request for the first battalion and repeated and increasingly insistent appeals, virtually amounting to requests, for the third. One might have expected Ambassador Waller to remember the latter circumstance in particular as he had been the channel through which most of these appeals had been relayed to Canberra. But the truth is that almost all the circumstances of Australian military involvement in Vietnam were so utterly confused that even those most directly concerned at the time could be excused for not being sure afterwards who exactly had done what, when or why.

Prime Minister Sir Robert G. Menzies was sure, however. "It took us not five minutes," he told Frantz, "to decide that when this thing came to the point of action, we would be in it, if invited by the government of South Vietnam . . . we had no hesitations, no doubts, and I've never had any regrets."[2] It would of course be unwise to take Menzies's words too literally. Rhetorical exaggeration was the dominant characteristic of the style of the founder of the Liberal Party of Australia. So was obfuscation. People who asked Menzies a direct question were not always entitled to believe that he had returned them a direct answer. One would certainly like to imagine that the ministers responsible for committing Australian military forces to Vietnam had given serious consideration to other possible courses of action before settling for that particular option. A few regrets might not have been out of place, in retrospect, either.

They had certainly had plenty of time to ponder alternatives. Military involvement in Indochina had been a prospect before the minds of Australian politicians and their advisers for more than ten years. It had had its genesis in a lighting flash of inspiration experienced by United States President Dwight D. Eisenhower on 3 April 1954. He and Secretary of State John Foster Dulles had been reflecting on the desperate position of the French at Dien Bien Phu — beseiged by Viet Minh forces superior in both numbers and firepower. It was a crisis for which, according to the official historian of the United States Army, "Washington policymakers, accustomed to reports of 'steady progress' ", were totally unprepared.[3] Dulles suggested to the president that "the feeling was that Congress would be quite prepared to go along on some vigorous action if we were not doing it alone. They want to be sure the people in the area are involved too." Eisenhower "did not blame the Congressmen for this thought. They agreed that the stakes concern others more than us." He added with typical realism that "you can't go in and win unless the people want you". Dulles commented that it was the attitude of the British that the legislators were really thinking about. "It is hard to get the American people excited if they are not," he told the President. He accordingly suggested that Eisenhower write personally to British Prime Minister Sir Winston Churchill to try to elicit some positive response from London. But Eisenhower's mind was already running along other lines. He wondered aloud "if ANZUS, as a base, would ask us to consult — then", his secretary recorded, "he interrupted this thought and said the Australians must be terribly excited. The Sec. said the Australian and New Zealand Ambassadors were coming in Monday. The President said why not suggest to them consultation with Britain, Thailand and the Philippines."[4] Allied intervention in Vietnam had just been put on the strategic agenda of the United States.

Dulles acted at once. He called what he termed "a sort of an ANZUS Meeting at his house Sunday" before the scheduled session with the ambassadors.[5] He also cabled US embassies in Paris and London regarding the importance of "a strong coalition (U.S., France, Associated States [Laos, Cambodia and Vietnam], U.K., Australia,

New Zealand, Thailand, Philippines) who will recognize threat to their vital interests in the area and will be prepared to fight if necessary".[6] National Security Council (NSC) advisers were reserved in their prognoses for the success of this *démarche*. They warned that the United Kingdom, "apprehensive of the possiblity of war with Communist China, would approve U.S. intervention only if convinced that it was necessary for the prevention of further expansion of Communist power in Asia". Australia and New Zealand would, however, "fully support such a U.S. action, and Canada to a lesser extent". Nationalist China and the Republic of Korea would positively welcome US intervention in Indochina, but for the rather unsatisfactory reason that "both hope that this would lead to general war between the United States and Communist China". South Korean President Syngman Rhee had indeed "offered, without solicitation, to send a Korean Army element to Vietnam to assist in the war against the Communists. This proposal was . . . relayed to the Department of State where it was promptly turned down." Thailand would probably permit the use of its territories and facilities, the report continued, "if assured of U.S. guarantees of adequate performance". The Philippines was also likely to support US intervention.[7]

It would be the response of the British and French, however, which would determine finally if the enterprise were to be undertaken or not. Dulles complained to Eisenhower on 7 April, that he still had had no reaction from London or Paris. Eisenhower accordingly sought to inspire the allies into activity by providing the most memorable if also the most misquoted image of a collective peril demanding a collective response. He told a news conference later that day about:

> the broader considerations that might follow what you might call the "falling domino" principle. You have a row of dominoes set up, you knock over the first one, and what will happen to the last one is the certainty that it will go over very quickly. So you could have a beginning of a disintegration that would have the most profound influences . . . But when we come to the possible sequence of events, the loss of Indochina, of Burma, of the Peninsula and Indonesia following, now you begin to talk about areas that not only multiply the disadvantages that you would suffer through loss of materials, sources of materials, but you are talking about millions and millions and millions of people. Finally, the geographical position achieved thereby does many things. It turns the so-called island defense chain of Japanese, Formosa, of the Philippines and to the southward, it moves in to threaten Australia and New Zealand. It takes away, in its economic aspects, that region that Japan must have as a trading area or Japan, in turn, will have only one place in the world to go — that is, toward the Communist

area in order to live. So, the possible consequences of the loss are just incalculable to the free world.[8]

All this might well seem to add up to the "worst possible case" for the West in anybody's eyes. It was no doubt intended to have that effect. But Eisenhower could think of something still worse. He had in fact been presented with an even more horrific scenario along these lines by the NSC in January 1954. His response then had been to tell a news conference that he could not personally "conceive of a greater tragedy than to get heavily involved in an all-out war in any of these regions, particularly with large units".[9] He had not changed his mind. Indeed, he immediately followed up his exposition of the falling domino principle with the caution that "this is the kind of thing that must not be handled by one nation trying to act alone".[10] The dominoes would just have to fall if other Western-aligned governments with the appropriate qualifications were not prepared to help Washington prop them up.

Australian Minister for External Affairs Richard G. Casey had no doubt that this actually was Eisenhower's position. He had been advised of "Washington's latest thinking on Indo-China: they won't go in alone, and if we and others don't respond they may change their South-East Asia attitude". His particular problem was that the Australian government was very unwilling to respond. Menzies and most of his other ministers were anxious to "avoid commitment in respect of troops, or in warning Communist China — as a 'warning was a commitment' ". Casey was, however, uncomfortably aware that "this desire to avoid commitment conflicted with our desire not to appear to the Americans to be dragging our feet on the occasion of the first instance when the Americans had asked us to join with them in action to repel what is the obvious menace to us for the future".[11] Even Casey apparently had no doubt at this stage that the obvious menace was Chinese-directed communist expansionism in Southeast Asia and the Pacific, with Australia as the ultimate target, or at least victim. The concern of the coalition government to preserve peace did not, in Michael G. Birgan's words, involve "any questioning of the basis of American assumptions, but rather a desire to avoid involvement in a dangerous and unwinnable war".[12] Casey did indeed modify his perceptions of Chinese intentions considerably over the next few years. His cabinet colleagues never did.

What finally decided the course of action to be followed by the Menzies government in 1954 was the course of action followed by the British government. Dulles had fancied that he and British Foreign Secretary Anthony Eden were for once "pretty well agreed" when Eden told the House of Commons on 13 April that the British government was "ready to take part, with the other countries principally concerned, in an examination of the possibility of establishing a collective defence, within the framework of the Charter of the United Nations, to assure the peace, security and freedom of Southeast Asia".[13] But if ever two people were separated by a common language, it was Dulles and Eden. Neither seemed able to comprehend at any time what the other was really getting at. Dulles immediately called on the British, Australians, New Zealanders, and the Philippines to hold preliminary discussions with the United States. Eden, however, instructed British Ambassador Sir Roger Makins on 18 April to inform the Secretary that the British government would not be participating in any such discussions. Dulles drew the obvious conclusion. "Nehru has howled," he told Senator H. Alexander Smith of New Jersey, "and Eden is trying to compromise as Nehru threatens to get out of the Commonwealth." Then he flew off to London to try to "bring the British position into the clear".[14]

Their experiences during the Korean War had conditioned Americans to see the influence of Delhi in every move by London to equivocate or compromise on the hard issues of Cold War confrontation. But Casey also thought that the Indian Prime Minister's attitude towards the problems of Indochina was "too simple and uninformed to thought out some method of handing Indo-China to the Communists on a silver salver, they could not have evolved any more effective plan . . . Nehru," he concluded, "had so many complexes and inhibitions working inside his mind, that you never knew what answer to any particular problem might emerge."[15] It was Nehru's views that were shared by other Commonwealth leaders, however. Casey told Eden and Canadian minister for External Affairs Lester B. Pearson that he was personally interested in Dulles's notion of intervening by mass air attacks to interdict Chinese assistance to the Viet Minh. Air and sea operations of this kind have a natural appeal for politicians in being faster, more dramatic, more impersonal and less likely to result in embarrassing casualties to one's own forces than the use of ground troops. However, Eden and Pearson told Casey flatly at lunch on 20 April that they just did not see how it could be done. Ottawa was even less in favour of US intervention in Indochina in any form than the NSC had supposed.

6 A Very Small Insurance Policy

Casey was in a delicate position. Dulles reminded him that "you only had to look at a map to see the relative importance of Indo-China to Australia and to the United States. It would be more understandable if we (Australia) were pressing the United States than for them (the United States) to be pressing us."[16] Casey lived to see the day when Australia would indeed be pressing the United States to intervene in Indochina. But Menzies was looking for a way out in 1954. Casey explained to Dulles that there was to be a federal election in Australia in May. Nobody could expect an Australian government with a theoretical life of only a few weeks to commit the nation to military intervention in Indochina. Dulles could appreciate this. He did not in consequence make "our active intervention a condition of their (American) intervention".[17]

The fact of the matter was that the Americans were not going to intervene anyway, for the same reason that the Australians were not going to intervene; namely, that the British were not going to intervene. Dulles told Eden on 23 April that "major combat action by US forces in Indochina would need the consent of Congress, but that Congress would be more amenable if assured that Britain agreed to participate in unified action".[18] Eden told the Secretary in reply that Churchill, the British Cabinet and their Chiefs of Staff, as well as himself, were all totally opposed to becoming directly involved in the war in Indochina in any way, although they were "prepared now to join with the United States in a secret study of measures which might be taken to defend Thailand and the rest of Southeast Asia if the French capitulate".[19] Eisenhower noted contemptuously that Eden had "apparently gone to the Geneva Conference under strict instructions to press earnestly for a 'cease fire' in Indo-China, possibly with complete indifference to the complex decisions that the French and the Viet Namese will have to make". But what interested him far more was the notion that this attitude of the British government "is bitterly resented by Australia and New Zealand. It is entirely possible that these two countries will approach the United States separately to request that in company with them — and possibly with the Philippines, Thailand, France and Indo-China — we form a coalition to the complete exclusion of the British. This would be a very tough one for us, but I think that I would go along with the idea because I believe that the British government is showing a woeful unawareness of the risks we run in that region."[20]

It was a remarkably accurate prophecy. A coalition would indeed be formed over the next twelve years for the purpose of military intervention in Southeast Asia. France would not be participating, but the United States, Australia, New Zealand, the Philippines, and part at least of Indo-China would be. The British would be excluded, albeit entirely by their own choice. Eisenhower was less accurate in his appreciation of the situation with which he was actually dealing in 1954, however. Neither Canberra nor Wellington had the faintest intention of becoming involved militarily in support of the French. Casey's concern had been to conceal this resolve from the Americans under an appearance of sympathetic understanding, while at the same time evading any attempts by Dulles to entrap him into a commitment. This seems to have led to some confusion all round. Eisenhower noted that he had been "informally told, at the time, that both Australia and New Zealand were ready to listen to any proposals the United States Government might make to them for collective action for entering the Indo-China war".[21] They would always be prepared to listen to American proposals for anything. Acting on them was a different matter. Dulles similarly was affirming as late as 29 April that there was "a fair chance of Australia and New Zealand coming along", if France and the United States could agree on a plan to "withdraw present forces to defensible enclaves in deltas where they would have U.S. sea and air protection", although he did not indicate any grounds for this belief.

Even Dulles admitted, however, that it was "unlikely that the UK would initially participate and would probably use its influence to prevent participation by Australia and New Zealand".[22] Practically speaking, there was no chance of Australia and New Zealand entering an enlarged Indochinese war. They would of course always be ready to listen to any proposals that Washington might suggest, in the assurance that London would provide a completely satisfactory excuse for not acting upon them. Casey had been most successful in his attempts to convey the impression that the Australian government would have been only too willing to participate but for the obstinacy of the British. A warning from Undersecretary of State General Walter Bedell Smith that "Australia and New Zealand had withdrawn from their original position favorable to united action" thus seemed to Eisenhower merely to provide further evidence of British sabotage. He told Smith to go ahead and call a meeting of the ANZUS partners in Geneva anyway, as he was "not at all sure that merely because the

8 A Very Small Insurance Policy

British had turned down our invitation to join a regional group we should abandon the whole effort".[23]

Smith's summons inspired Casey with the gravest apprehensions. He had already been told by Eden that there was no way that the British would fight for or in Indochina, although it would be a different matter if Thailand were threatened. He had also been given to understand that New Zealand, presumably under British pressure, had resolved not to join in any military action at all except under United Nations auspices, which would clearly be impossible with communist states having the power of veto in the Security Council. Casey was not looking forward to trying to explain all of this to John Foster Dulles. He was indeed convinced that the Secretary had called the meeting expressly "in order to stand us up against the wall and ask what we were going to do". Nothing of the kind happened. Dulles, to Casey's amazement, "spoke as if the United States had not ever had an intention of intervening with air assistance, which we know they had, if the United Kingdom would have co-operated".[24] Dulles, as a lawyer, was of course capable of saying very different things at different times, according to the exigencies of the case. But Eisenhower's own vision of US policy had been considerably more complex than foreigners, especially the British and Indians, were inclined to suspect. He told his old navy buddy Captain E.E. ("Swede") Hazlett later that "you are somewhat wrong in your statement, 'I know that at one time you contemplated some really drastic action in Indo-China'. What I really attempted to do was to get established in the region the conditions under which I felt the United States could properly intervene to protect its own interests. A proper political foundation for any military action was essential. Since we could not bring it about (though we prodded and argued for almost two years), I gave not even a tentative approval to any plan for massive intervention."[25]

Eisenhower, as Stephen Ambrose points out, had been regarded by two of the greatest generals in US military history — Marshall, whom he revered, and MacArthur, whom he detested — as being quite simply the best staff officer in the US Army. It is precisely the role of a staff officer to identify all aspects of a situation, to determine what can be done, what cannot be done, and above all what must be done, and express this in words that other people can understand. Eisenhower had no reason to doubt that this was what he could do as well as anybody else around at the time. He also had no reason to doubt that Anthony Eden could not, after receiving the foreign secretary's proposal that the United Kingdom, United States, France, Australia, and New Zealand should participate immediately in an examination of all aspects of Southeast Asian defence. Eisenhower told the Joint Chiefs of Staff flatly that the United States would not agree to "a 'white man's party' to determine the problems of the Southeast Asian nations . . . the U.S. would never intervene alone". There had to be "an invitation by the indigenous people and . . . there must be some kind of regional and collective action".[26] He was in no mood to respond favourably to any proposition put up by Eden, whom he described with chilling venom as "a man known by the company he keeps; a man known by the excuses he makes".[27] Nor was he feeling any more sympathetically disposed toward the French, who, as he told NATO Commander General Alfred M. Gruenther, had never made "a single effort to meet the conditions that we have insisted upon for three years as constituting the only sound basis on which any European government could be fighting in South East Asia". On the other hand, "Thailand, the Philippines — and in a more clandestine way — Australia, have all shown far more statesmanship and have all recognized the basic requirements of a cooperative effort more than our principal European allies, France and Britain".[28]

It is not difficult to be statesmanlike in words when one knows that there is no danger of having to match those words with actions. Casey was in fact still afraid that the Americans were "intent on injecting themselves, physically, into the area, which might well bring Communist China in and lead us all into a third world war". His apprehensions were shared by all save a couple of his cabinet colleagues who held that "the U.S.A. is our only standby in this part of the world, and that we should follow them whatever they did".[29] It was a view that would be held more widely in Canberra in a few years' time.

Casey was careful to conceal these misgivings from the Americans. The New Zealanders had even stronger misgivings, which they did not conceal. They asserted that US ideas on a Southeast Asia Treaty Organization to contain communism in the region after a settlement in Indochina were in conflict with British views and consequently "would not be understood by NZ public opinion". Dulles reacted characteristically by asking New Zealand Ambassador Sir Leslie K. Munro "if they want us not to act if there is overt aggression. We would," he remarked ominously, "take that into account." Furthermore, he added, "the interests in that area are not immediately ours — they are more those of the UK, NZ and A."[30] Casey attempted to mollify the Secretary by insisting that there was no real problem of divided loyalties involved. He was certain that "our relationship with Britain was such that it was inconceivable that we should be belligerent in any trouble whilst the United Kingdom was not — and I thought the reverse held too". He reflected privately that there might even be an "appreciable advantage in Australia's being poised rather delicately between the U.S. and the U.K. in respect of international affairs. By keeping outselves so placed, we are in a position to exercise some influence on each."[31]

There was unfortunately no evidence whatever that this was actually the case. Australia was not poised between the United States and the United Kingdom so much as clinging desperately to both. It was a relationship of double dependency, which by definition excluded any possibility of the dependent partner's being able to exert significant influence on either of its desired protectors. Australia's freedom of choice consisted in following the directions of one protector, at the risk of offending the other. It was following a British lead in 1954. This indeed had the effect of influencing United States policy, but the Americans knew perfectly well that the influence was being exerted by London, not Canberra.

Casey was all too well aware himself of Australia's inability to exert real influence in its region. He came close to resigning on 28 July over the refusal of his cabinet colleagues to approve spending on either national defence or foreign aid at a level commensurate with Australia's standard of affluence. It was, he considered, frankly humiliating that the United States should be contributing $1.90 per head of population on aid to Southeast Asia alone, Canada $1.80, New Zealand $1.40, and Australia only 80 cents. Defence spending had meantime fallen from a peak of 5.2 per cent of Gross National Product at the end of the Korean War to 3.9 per cent, and was still declining. The result was, he observed gloomily, that "there is inadequate equipment to enable our forces to be sent outside Australia in case of emergency — which means something quite unpleasant — and this is known to, at least, the Americans. I believe they are very conscious that we have a 40-hour week, that we are constantly reducing taxation, and that the period of training of our young men is for three months and not eighteen months or two years as is the case in Britain or America. Bearing in mind that our survival depends on our retaining the confidence of the U.S., this isn't very good."[32] So much for Australia's being able to exercise influence on its great and powerful friends.

What might have made the situation even more embarrassing was Menzies's readiness to accept obligations which Australia would be quite incapable of fulfilling in practice. The decisive battle for Australia, he informed federal parliament, "may be fought far away, in Malaya, over the great oceans, over the cities and fields of England ... We must," he proclaimed, "by armed strength, defend the geographical frontiers of those nations whose self-government is based upon the freedom of the spirit."[33] Apart from the fact that it would have been difficult to identify which nations in the region were supposed to fit that description, these were surprising words from the leader of a nation incapable, in the opinion of his own minister for External Affairs, of sending any significant forces overseas in the event of even a quite unpleasant emergency.

Casey's apprehensions about American regard for Australia were about to be realized in the most humiliating fashion. Dulles had reached the end of his patience with the allies. He had, he told Assistant Secretary of State for British Commonwealth Affairs, Livingstone Merchant, "great reservation about the [SEATO] Treaty — whether it will be useful in the mood of the participants — whether we are not better off by ourselves". The Secretary was particularly incensed by the "running away from the world Communist". The allies "seem to have no desire or intention to hold the balance in Indochina. By going into a treaty of this sort," he complained, "we limit our own freedom of action. Once we sign, then we have to consult re action. They are more concerned with trying not to annoy the Communists than stopping them."[34] The implication was perfectly clear. What Washington was interested in was international support for US policies. The allies were to show their flags where Washington told them to put them. It was not the role of the allies to provide suggestions, unless these happened to coincide with what the Americans had decided to do anyway. It was an attractive theory, assuming that only Washington in the whole Western system had any ideas worth considering. Eisenhower and his advisers had obviously come to the conclusion by August 1954 that this was very likely to be the case.

Dulles was certainly not interested in any ideas that Australia might have had to offer. He unceremoniously deleted from the draft of the treaty establishing SEATO every reference that Casey sought to introduce regarding regular consultation among the members, insisted on the right of the United States to sign with a reservation to the effect that its own obligations would apply only in the case of specifically communist aggression, and flatly refused to concede the right of Australia or anybody else to sign with a similar reservation. Such a *démarche* by Australia, the Secretary told Casey, would "set off a chain reaction and the signing of the Treaty might be indefinitely delayed". Furthermore, "the whole psychological effect of unity reflected by this Conference might be lost. He said that it would be taken as 'indecision' on the part of Australia and that he could not overestimate the effect of such indecision on public and governmental opinion in the United States, the consequences of which to Australia might be 'disastrous'. Actually," Casey recalled, "Dulles said a good deal more than this in which he used the terms 'catastrophic' and 'calamitous' . . . It was clear that if Australia signed with the same sort of reservation as the United States was to make, Australia would forfeit the goodwill of the United States, which is so vitally important to us to maintain for the future."[35]

It was a difficult situation for Casey. He had been instructed by Menzies that he was to "sign the Treaty with a reservation similar to the American reservation", unless he were "completely convinced that such action by Australia would stop the Treaty being signed at all. In that case he should sign 'subject to the right of the Australian Government to introduce a reservation on the lines of the American reservation prior to ratification of the Treaty' ." It was not at all clear why it should be so utterly unacceptable for Australia to do just what the United States was doing. But it was unambiguously clear that Dulles was determined to find it utterly unacceptable. Casey found a typically ingenious way out. He signed as demanded by Dulles, without reservations about communism, but wrote about his signature that he signed "subject to the right of the Australian Government to review the Treaty prior to ratification, in accordance with Australian constitutional practice. The real purpose of the Treaty is to present a concerted front against aggressive Communism . . . Our own defence policy is directed to this dominant purpose."

Casey was entitled to congratulate himself on a finesse genuinely diplomatic in the conventional sense of the word. Menzies, however, cabled him the following day "expressing surprise at what had happened and instructing him to re-open the matter with the other signatories".[36] This was fortunately impossible, as Dulles had flown off to Taipei immediately after signing the Treaty, thereby demonstrating again the low regard he felt for SEATO and everybody connected with it. It was easy for Americans at perhaps the highest peak of their postwar dominance as the world's number one superpower to feel that allies were in practice more of a nuisance than they were worth. Dulles and Eisenhower had already had more reason than they needed to share this view. But the paradox was that there were still things that Washington was not prepared to do without the support of its allies. It was, for example, already involved secretly in Vietnam, with the assistance of partners whose role could not possibly be recognized publicly, even if the American intervention itself had been less clandestine. Unmentionable allies were appropriate for unmentionable operations. But the United States would soon be looking for allies whom it need not hesitate to acknowledge publicly if it ever became necessary to intervene openly in Asian affairs again. Its choice could be severely limited. The most likely partners in such an exercise were in general the most undesirable, and the most desirable were almost without exception the least likely. Australia was the most conspicuous exception.

2
To Get Some Share of the Credit
(1954–1962)

Covert US intervention in Vietnam had begun almost as soon as the idea of open intervention had been abandoned. Colonel Edward G. Lansdale, United States Air Force (USAF), arrived in Saigon on 1 June 1954 to establish the Saigon Military Mission (SMM). His official duties were "to undertake paramilitary operations against the enemy and to wage political-psychological warfare". This involved initially rather low-intensity exercises like fabricating accounts of the rape of Viet Minh village girls by Chinese Communist soldiers, distributing fake leaflets purporting to originate from Viet Minh HQ depicting the dreadful penalties reserved for those failing to show proper respect for the communist conquerors, and attempting to contaminate fuel supplies for public transport buses in Hanoi. But Lansdale soon had the opportunity to expand his activities in a far more significant manner.

He was approached a couple of weeks after his arrival by Oscar Arellano, the Filipino Vice-President for Southeast Asia of the International Jaycees. Arellano suggested that Free World Asian countries might provide medical teams to assist and train the South Vietnamese in operating public health programmes. Lansdale was quick to perceive the counterinsurgency possibilities of this proposal. He advised Washington that "SMM would monitor the operation quietly in the background". The Americans then requested South Vietnamese President Ngo Dinh Diem to sanction the scheme by appealing for Free World assistance in the public health sector. Operation Brotherhood was born. So was the future pattern of allied intervention in Vietnam. Washington would decide what form intervention should take and would direct Saigon to ask for it.

Operation Brotherood's ostensible function was exactly what Arellano had proposed; namely, "to provide medical assistance to the hamlets and villages throughout the Republic". But it developed under the guidance of Lansdale and the CIA into what might be described more accurately as a programme of pest control. Filipino and "other Asian and European teams" coordinated their public health activities with "Vietnamese Army operations which cleaned up Vietminh stay-behinds and started stabilizing rural areas". Operation Brotherhood had thus become a clandestine counterinsurgency and pacification campaign under the direction of the Americans, with the assistance of Filipino mercenaries and certain other unidentified operators.

The International Jaycess had presumably no idea what they were starting. Operation Brotherhood was followed rapidly by other clandestine operations originating in the Philippines. There was, for example, the Freedom Company of the Philippines, described by Lansdale without any evident trace of irony as "a non-profit organization, with President Magsaysay as its honorary President". Executive director of the company was in fact Magsaysay's former Complaints and Actions Commissioner, "Frisco" Johnny San Juan, whose talents and experience were particularly suited to this new enterprise. It was, as Lansdale put it, "similar to an employment agency, with an almost untapped potential for unconventional warfare (which was its original mission)". Its specific function was to "supply Filipinos experienced in fighting the Communist Huks to help in Vietnam (or elsewhere) ... Philippines Armed Forces and government personnel were 'sheep-dipped' and served abroad". Freedom Company thus provided over the next few years "about 500 trained, experienced Filipino technicians to Governments of Vietnam and Laos ... They instruct local military personnel in ordnance, quartermaster, etc., maintenance, storage and supply procedures." They also, with their US partners, helped to "write the Constitution of the Republic of Vietnam, trained Vietnam's Presidential Guard Battalion, and were instrumental in founding and organizing the Vietnamese Veterans Legion".

Another Filipino-based support agency for the South Vietnamese was the Security Training Center operated overtly by the government of the Philippines and covertly by the CIA as "a counter-subversion, counter-guerilla and psychological warfare school", with a capacity of twelve instructors. Its mission was to "counter the forces of subversion in Southeast Asia through more adequate training of security personnel, greater cooperation, better understanding and maximum initiative among the countries of the area".

Assistance of a more orthodox kind was also provided by the famous General Claire Lee Chennault — former leader of the Flying Tigers and longtime lover of Mme Chiang Kai-shek. Chennault and a dozen or so ex-Tigers formed an allegedly commercial airline, misnamed Civil Air Transport (CAT), on Taiwan in 1946, to provide air support for the defeated Nationalist Chinese. It was taken over in 1950 by the CIA, using secret funds through a Delaware holding company entitled Airdale Corporation. CAT, in Lansdale's estimation, had "some notable achievements" to its credit, such as "support of the Chinese Nationalist withdrawal from the mainland, air drop support to the French at Dien Bien Phu" (when twenty-four CAT Pilots had heroically flown USAF C-119 *Flying Boxcars* to drop supplies by parachute to the beleaguered garrison), and "numerous overflights of Mainland China and Tibet" to deposit or uplift Nationalist secret agents. CAT also carried out in 1954 "a secret evacuation to remove some of the Nationalist Chinese who had set themselves up as opium dealers in Southeast Asia after the Communists expelled them from their own country". Those who are in the business of unconventional warfare are liable to find themselves in strange company at times. CAT also supported "covert and clandestine air operations" through the "procurement of supplies through overt commercial channels and the maintenance of a fairly large inventory of transport and other type aircraft under both Chinese and U.S. registry".[1]

Two aspects of Lansdale's report seemed to call for comment. One was that it was disturbing that the South Vietnamese should have needed to be trained by foreigners to conduct counterinsurgency operations against their own people, and surprising that the Filipinos should have been considered the people best qualified to give them such training. The other was that the best efforts of Lansdale himself, "Frisco" Johnny, CAT, and the rest could only be marginal at the most. South Vietnam was beset with problems far too massive and complex to be set right by the covert activities of a handful of soldiers of fortune.

Most urgent of these was the Army of the Republic of Vietnam (ARVN) itself. United States observers reported in 1954 that it had "experienced a complete breakdown of combat capabilities since the ceasefire and the stopping of supplies from the United States". This was hardly to be wondered at. The ARVN, according to the official

US military historian, had been "created originally as a kind of combat auxiliary to the French Expeditionary Corps", and had almost no logistical capability of its own.² It certainly acquired logistical capability over the next few years, but distinguished Australian journalist Denis Warner wondered if this might not have been a positive disadvantage. "Whether even this is a sufficient army, or the right army," he wrote in December 1959, "is open to doubt . . . It suffers from the handicaps of a Western-type army (dependence on roads for movement and air drops for field supply) . . . we seem to have forgotten the lessons of the Indo-China war."³

One quality of a Western-type army which the ARVN had disastrously not aquired was professionalism. "Insubordination," the US official historian recorded, "was rampant; orders were freely disobeyed, and senior officers were reluctant to punish subordinates who might have powerful political connections." Senior officers also "routinely supplemented their income by selling on the black market, embezzling official funds, exploiting prostitution and dealing in drugs. The lower ranks committed extortion and sometimes even outright robbery against the local population, particularly in outlying districts. In those remoter areas, regional commanders occasionally attempted to establish themselves as local warlords, in some instances even trying to collect taxes." The officer corps in general was "riddled with favoritism and corruption. Officers who failed to manifest personal loyalty to the President often fell victim to secret denunciations by jealous or ambitious rivals." And the Department of National Defense, he considered, "appeared designed primarily to increase confusion with conflicting, duplicating chains of command and communication and . . . various major agencies . . . installed in widely separated areas so as to hamper coordination, rapid staff action and decision making".⁴

It was a description of an army programmed for defeat. But the ARVN was of necessity merely a reflection of the inherent weaknesses of South Vietnamese society itself. President Diem's regime was in fact a racket rather than a regime, with the exception of Diem himself; and his conscientiousness was hardly less fatal to good government than the criminality of his relations. A Vietnamese friend told Warner that Diem was "not a priest . . . A priest at least learns something of the world through the confessional. Diem is a monk living behind stone walls. He knows nothing."⁵ He preserved this state of ignorance by immersing himself for up to eighteen hours a day in the minutiae of administration, thus ensuring that he would have no time left for study or reflection. He also discouraged attempts by foreigners to enlighten him by subjecting visitors to monologues of six hours or more, which left them neither the opportunity nor the patience to tell him anything. His brother the Archbishop of Hue was involved in dubious dealings in real estate in Vietnam and Australia. Another brother, Ngo Dinh Can, operated a smuggling ring that shipped rice to the communist enemy, North Vietnam, as well as a drug ring functioning in his episcopal brother's archdiocese of Hue. These activities naturally involved Can in extortion and murder as well. An even more sinister brother, Ngo Dinh Nhu, Diem's chief political adviser, ran a private secret police force and was implicated in "illegal lotteries, drug traffic, waterfront rackets, exchange manipulation and the extortion of Chinese business leaders".[6]

There could hardly be more promising conditions for a successful revolution. United States Army Chief of Staff General Matthew B. Ridgway had insisted in 1954 on certain essential conditions that had to be fulfilled before the United States should assume responsibility even for training the South Vietnamese defence forces, let alone doing their fighting for them. First of these was "a reasonably strong, stable, civil government in control. It is hopeless," Ridgway declared, "To expect a U.S. training mission to achieve success unless the nation concerned is able to effectively perform governmental functions."[7] This the Government of the Republic of Vietnam (GVN) was obviously unable to do.

A logical course would therefore have been for the United States to write off South Vietnam and concentrate on holding the line against communism on the borders of the more defensible states to the west and south. But it was not so easy to decide to write off South Vietnam. It was the essence of the falling domino principle that the defence of Vietnam was critical to the defence of the rest of the region — and some credible evidence was accumulating in support of that principle. It was evident by 1959 that the threat of communist insurgency would not confined to Vietnam. Laos was also in turmoil. Then in May the Central Committee of the North Vietnamese Communist Party publicly announced its intention to "smash" the government of Ngo Dinh Diem. It was a direct challenge. The United States response was virtually automatic. One hundred and twenty Special Forces troops were flown from Fort Bragg in South Carolina the following month to Laos to assist the Meo tribespeople against the communists. The NSC reported in February 1960 that it might be necessary similarly to manifest US readiness to assist "Free Viet Nam, in accordance with the SEATO Treaty, to defend itself against external aggression".[8] But there was a technical problem — US Military capability at the time consisted almost entirely in its expertise in waging orthodox war at the highest level of technology. What was needed in South Vietnam was counterinsurgency capability. And counterinsurgency, the official historian recorded, "was little studied or understood" in the United States Army of the 1950s. The term itself "was almost unknown at the time . . . Few officers or enlisted men had had any practical experience in actual counterguerilla operations. Whereas the conduct of guerilla warfare was a specialized skill restricted to U.S. Army Special Forces units, the Army considered counterguerilla training to be adequately covered in the four hours of instruction provided for all troops."[9]

There were people available to whom the Americans might have turned for assistance in this area, had they been so inclined. The assorted training camps for mercenaries in the Philippines were admittedly in the business of producing assassins and saboteurs rather than elite counterinsurgency units; but the French had just completed a murderously successful counterinsurgency campaign in North Africa, which suggested that they had learned some useful lessons from their bitter experiences in Indochina. General feeling in Washington was, however, that the United States could not possibly have anything to learn about the art of war from the French, on the grounds that France had not won a war since 1815 and the United States had never lost one. The argument was of course as irrelevant as it was inaccurate. What was relevant was that the French had probably more experience of counterinsurgency operations than any other great military power and the Americans had less. But it was difficult for Americans in those first exuberant postwar decades to believe seriously that they had anything to learn from anybody.

They did not even believe that they had anything to learn from the British, who had undeniably been on the winning side in a few wars since 1815, and were just then in the process of winding up counterinsurgency campaigns in Cyprus, South Yemen, Kenya, and Malaya. Some of these operations had admittedly been less satisfactory than others, but the Malayan Emergency at least had been a model of what could be achieved in an Asian context with administrative rigour, political sophistication, good intelligence, and thorough professionalism, none of which unfortunately was much in evidence in

South Vietnam. Diem himself was sufficiently impressed to fly to Malaya in early 1960 for a personal briefing by British security experts. They invited him to send some ARVN officers to attend a course at the Malayan Jungle School, but the experiment "proved to be short and unhappy. The first class of Vietnamese officers . . . made a marginal showing and returned to complain that the British 'treated them like colonials'." This was unlikely to have been the real problem. The British had a long experience of training officers from their own colonies. They did not treat them like colonials. They treated them like British officers. And the standards of performance required of infantry officers in the British Army differed ominously from those of the ARVN. Training sessions at the Malayan Jungle School were too much like hard work for people whose interest in actually fighting in the jungle was limited at best.

Lansdale did not think that the experiment was worth perservering with. He considered that the British experience in Malaya was not relevant, because it had been "sharply different, in many areas", from the situation in Vietnam. This was undoubtedly true, but the actual tactics of anti-terrorist warfare were equally applicable in both instances. There was also the ominous angle that the British might have been able to succeed in Malaya precisely because the situation there was so different from Vietnam. Maybe nothing could succeed in Vietnam. But Lansdale had a more fundamental objection to enlisting the support of the British in this area. It was that there could be "a subtle sapping of the American character in this trend toward reliance upon others".[10] It was not so much that the allies had nothing to teach. It was that the Americans had no need to learn, except from their own mistakes.

The South Vietnamese could hardly be left to learn from their own mistakes. Eighteen leading political figures in Saigon demanded Diem's resignation on 26 April 1960. Diem had them all arrested. United States Ambassador Eldridge Burrow warned in July that internal security had become the number one problem for the regime "as a result of intensification of Viet Cong guerilla and terrorist activities, weaknesses apparent in the GVN security force and the growth of apathy and considerable dissatisfaction among the rural populace". The monthly assassination rate among local officials had risen to 96 in January 1960 and to 122 in February; anti-guerilla training for the ARVN was manifestly inadequate; and the peasants were becoming even more alienated by "improper actions by local officials such as torture, extortion and corruption", than by the terrorism of the Viet Cong.[11] It was really only a choice of terrorism, and the activities of the government, as Denis Warner pointed out, were troubling more people than those of the Viet Cong.

Nor was it only in Vietnam that the situation was desperate. Laos appeared about to fall by the spring of 1961. And the collapse of Laos would expose SEATO member, Thailand, as well as Vietnam. The falling domino principle was looking all too credible. President John F. Kennedy consulted with British Prime Minister Harold Macmillan at Key West in Florida in March 1961 about the possibility of joint intervention under the terms of the Manila Pact. Macmillan did not dispute the strategic importance of Thailand; but he was appalled, as he put it, by "the danger of being sucked into these inhospitable areas without a base, without any clear political or strategic aims and without any effective system of deploying armed forces or controlling local administration".[12] His misgivings were all too wellfounded. CINCPAC (Commander in Chief Pacific Fleet) Admiral Harry D. Felt was nonetheless warned by the Joint Chiefs of Staff (JCS) that London and Paris might "subsequently be requested to support a request from Royal Laotian Government for intervention by SEATO within 48 hours if an effective cease fire is not quickly obtained".[13]

Secretary of State Dean D. Rusk was wondering who else might be induced to take part in such an enterprise. The Pakistanis, he thought, "could be relied upon if we paid for them and . . . a few Malays, New Zealanders and others would help".[14] It was not a very convincing list. Kennedy decided not to risk the unforeseeable consequences of trying to engineer a SEATO intervention in Laos at that stage. But this made it all the more important to keep South Vietnam viable. Even Lansdale thought that it would be appropriate to count on allied support there. The United Kingdom, he claimed, "has already expressed a strong interest in cooperating to help the Vietnamese stop the Communists. It has offered to provide training personnel with years of experience in Malaya. It has also offered financial support. Other like-minded countries, notably the Philippines and Australia, have a capability and a possible interest in this regard."[15]

It remained to be seen just how far the allies might be prepared to translate these capabilities and interests into practical support for the Saigon regime. There were in any case two practical problems to be resolved first. One was to determine just what kind of support was going to be most useful. The other was how to get it there without breaching the Geneva Accords too blatantly. Kennedy sent Vice President Lyndon B. Johnson to Saigon on 9 May, to report on the situation directly. His assessment could not have been less ambiguous. "The battle against Communism," he advised the president, "must be joined in Southeast Asia with strength and determination to achieve success there — or the United States, inevitably, must surrender the Pacific and take up our defenses on our own shores." Vietnam and Thailand were "the immediate — and most important — trouble spots, critical to the U.S. . . . The basic decision in Southeast Asia," he considered, "is here. We must decide whether to help these countries to the best of our ability or throw in the towel in the area and pull our defenses back to San Francisco."

This was the falling domino principle stated in its most uncompromising form. But Johnson was as convinced as Eisenhower has been that nothing that might happen in mainland Asia could justify unilateral military intervention by the United States. Any assistance to less developed nations to secure and maintain their own freedom "must be part of a mutual effort. These nations cannot be saved by United States help alone." American troop involvement in Vietnam in any event, he insisted, was "not only not required, it is not desirable". Asian leaders did not want American troops "involved in Southeast Asia other than on training missions". But he also affirmed that there was now "no alternative to United States leadership in Southeast Asia. Leadership in individual countries — or the regional leadership and cooperation so appealing to Asians — rests on the knowledge and faith in United States power, will and understanding. SEATO is not and probably never will be the answer because of British and French unwillingness to support decisive action."[16] It naturally remained to be seen how far the SEATO allies would be prepared to follow United States leadership in the region. American power and will had never been in doubt. American understanding still remained to be demonstrated.

There was also a technical problem, as Durrow's successor in Saigon, Frederick E. Nolting, Jr., pointed out. The amount of additional training personnel and equipment needed by the South Vietnamese would far exceed the limits acceptable to the International Control Commission (ICC) set up to monitor the Geneva Accords. But Washington had a friend at court. Canada was a member of the ICC, along with India and Poland. It was not an easy relationship. It was made worse by the fact that the Canadians were keeping Washington ever more fully informed of the proceedings of the Commission as their relations with the Indians and Poles deteriorated, which of course helped to make them deteriorate still faster. The Canadians naturally realized that "if it became generally known that we are passing information to the United States concerning the activities of the International Commissions it would have very serious repercussions for our representatives on the Commission", as the Canadian Department of External Affairs reminded cabinet. But they kept on doing it. CIA agents continued to visit Ottawa regularly "specifically to talk with returning ICC members".[17]

The Canadians were prepared to go much further. Their representatives on the ICC approaches US officials in Saigon soon after Johnson's arrival there, seeking a frank discussion of press reports that the Americans were contemplating actions which would involve serious violations of the Geneva Accords. The Americans very frankly told them that that was exactly their intention. The Canadians consulted with Ottawa. They then returned to the US embassy on 20 June to tell Ambassador Nolting that they had received "purposely general" instructions from their government to pursue discussions on increased US programmes of assistance to South Vietnam in violation of the Accords. They emphasized that Ottawa was in complete agreement with the general idea and that their only concern was to ensure that the ICC did not create any difficulties. They had a number of practical suggestions to this end. American personnel could, for example, be introduced into Vietnam in the guise of civilians on commercial aircraft, or alternatively on unscheduled flights by military aircraft arriving and departing at times when ICC teams would not be on hand, or in areas where such teams did not operate anyway. Canadian representatives on the Commission would be able to keep the Americans advised of appropriate times and places. Supplies of material could similarly be introduced at ports not controlled by the ICC or put ashore in infrequently patrolled coastal areas. Major problem items might be represented as "credit based on French outshipments which since not controlled by ICC not included on ICC war materiel register. This would permit Canadians to stall questions for year or more." Things would be confused even more satisfactorily, the Canadians pointed out, if the Americans were to combine overt and covert introduction of personnel and materiel.[18]

There was a quality of North American sophistication about the Canadian *démarche* that Washington must have found very reassuring.

But it was becoming all too evident that the Diem regime could be salvaged only operations too massive to be concealed by any degree of clandestine manoeuvring. Viet Cong strength was mushrooming. Insurgency cadres had been built up to seventeen thousand by mid-1961, nearly six times the figure estimated twelve months earlier; and Laos was on the brink of collapse again. Kennedy approached selected SEATO governments once more to explore the "possibility of an enlargement of SEATO Plan 5", for the concentration of US forces in Laos in response to an overt communist threat.[19] Macmillan was just as appalled at the prospect of armed intervention as he had been in March. He told Kennedy that any provisional agreement they might have come to at Key West had since lapsed and that fresh cabinet approval would be required for any United Kingdom consent to such a proposal; and he had no intention of seeking cabinet approval. He indeed warned Queen Elizabeth that he was convinced that "part of the State Department and Americans on the spot" were deliberately trying to sabotage the success of proposals for a neutral Laos. "We are thus," he told her, "threatened with the possibility of being asked to intervene militarily in the Far East, just at the time when the European crisis is deepening."[20] Johnson had been right in warning Kennedy about British unwillingness to support decisive action. The British might also have been right in not supporting it.

United States planning proceeded on the assumption that decisive action might be invoked and that it would receive allied support. Admiral Felt told a SEATO conference in Bangkok on 1 October that plans being evolved for every eventuality included using American troops to check the communist advance in the region. The Joint Chiefs advocated eight days later "a concentrated effort in Laos which would, at the same time, protect Thailand and protect the borders of Vietnam . . . Forces available", they advised, "will be the British Commonwealth Brigade, Pakistan, Philippine, and some US forces and limited amount of Thai forces", numbering some 22,800 in all.[21] One might hope that Kennedy himself had some idea how unlikely it was that almost any of these units would actually be available. He agreed, however, to "consultation with our SEATO allies, principally the British and Australians, regarding SEATO actions in support of the deteriorating situation in Vietnam".[22] He also decided to send Military Representative to the President, General Maxwell D. Taylor, to Saigon to bring back "an educated military guess as to what the situation that the government there faces. Then we can come to conclusions as to what is best to do."[23]

Kennedy was looking for more than just a military guess. He told Taylor that he "should bear in mind that the initial responsibility for the effective maintenance of the independence of South Vietnam rests with the people and the government of that country. Our efforts must be evaluated, and your recommendations formulated, with this fact in mind. While the military part of the problem is of great importance in South Vietnam," he reminded Taylor, "its political, social, and economic elements are equally significant, and I shall expect your appraisal and your recommendations to take full account of them."[24] It might well seem that Kennedy was looking for positive reasons for not getting involved further in Vietnam. Taylor was not going to give him any. Everything that the military representative encountered on his visit convinced him that an unambiguous US commitment to the region was both required and expected. The United States Mission met with Thai leaders in Bangkok on 25 October. The Thais expressed the view unreservedly that US troops were necessary in South Vietnam and that "military action should be taken by unspecified parties to block the Ho Chi Minh trails in Laos". Taylor mentioned the possibility that "we might send logistics troops to help with the flood in the delta". Thai Prime Minister Sarit Tanarat "replied that he thought that would be a good idea but growled *sotto voce* to his interpreter, "Damnit, I want to know if they will send fighters' ".[25] Johnson had apparently been mistaken in supposing that Asian leaders did not want US troops in the region except on training exercises.

What Taylor believed he was confronted with was nothing less than a crisis of confidence throughout the region, amounting in South Vietnam to a literal "collapse of national morale . . . the thought", he recalled, "was always with us that we needed something visible which could be done quickly to offset the oppressive feeling of hopelessness which seemed to permeate all ranks of Vietnamese society".[26] Nothing could be more visible than US troops on the ground. Taylor accordingly proposed that Washington should allay doubt that the "U.S. is determined to save Southeast Asia" by providing a "U.S.A military presence capable of raising national morale and of showing to Southeast Asia the seriousness of the U.S. intent to resist a Communist take-over". Such US forces, he further advised, should be prepared to "conduct such combat operations as are necessary for self-defense and for the security of the area in which they are stationed".[27]

Taylor's report evoked the gravest misgivings among some of Kennedy's advisers. One obvious implication was that feelings of hopelessness were so widespread in Vietnam simply because the situation in Vietnam was hopeless. Nothing could be done to save Vietnamese society against any credible challenge. His military proposals were also disturbingly open-ended. It was not certain how large a force would be needed for self-defence or how wide an area it would be necessary to secure. Undersecretary of State George W. Ball warned Kennedy that within five years the United States would have " 'three hundred thousand men in the paddies and jungles and never find them again. That was the French experience.' 'George,' " the President explained, " 'you're just crazier than hell. That just isn't going to happen.' "[28] Ball was in fact an impressively accurate prophet. There would be 391,000 US troops in Vietnam by the end of 1966. And the military would be asking for 542, 588 for the following year.

State Department was meanwhile initiating the usual approaches to the usual selected allies seeking support for this "new and more dynamic phase of American military participation in the struggle to preserve the independence of South Vietnam".[29] First on the line was Australia. Ambassador Sir Howard Beale was informed as early as 17 November that the United States was "considering increasing its assistance to the Republic of Vietnam, although this assistance would be in the form of equipment, transport, training and advisers rather than combat forces". An "indication of Australia's view and willingness to assist was requested." This new American approach was just as inconvenient for the Australian government as its predecessor had been in 1954, and for the same reason. Menzies was again planning to hold a federal election. He accordingly replied on 26 November that he was "examining the possibility of increasing Australian assistance to the Republic of Vietnam and hoped to be able to make a decision after the coming Federal election". But the solicitations from Washington continued. Beale sent a further cable on 5 December 1961 that he had been given to understand that "demonstrable Australian support for the Republic of Vietnam would make a very favorable impression on the United States administration and suggested that Australia might supply counter-insurgency training personnel, small arms and ammunition".[30]

Taylor had meanwhile persuaded Diem to write a letter to Kennedy pleading that the communist forces arrayed against South Vietnam were "more than we can meet with the resources at hand. We must have further assistance from the United States if we are to win the war now being waged against us."[31] Secretary Rusk told a press conference the following day that the United States was "now taking steps to help South Vietnam develop the military, economic and social strength needed to preserve its national integrity. It is our hope," he added significantly, "that other nations will join us in providing assistance until such time as the Communists have halted their acts of violence and terror."[32]

Australia, however, was in no position to join in any foreign involvements with unpredictable implications. Menzies's coalition government had received a devastating setback in the federal election. Its share of the popular vote had fallen from 46.5 to 42 per cent. That of the Labor Opposition had risen from 42.5 to 48 per cent. The government's majority in the House of Representatives had crumbled from twenty-two to two, giving a working majority of one, after the appointment of a speaker. It was not the time to seek a mandate for adventures in which Australian military personnel could get killed. But the Americans were moving already. Thirty-three *Shawnee* helicopters with four hundred Marine aviators to fly and maintain them arrived in Saigon on 11 December. It was for the Americans, as British Prime Minister Harold Macmillan put it, "the beginning of their long and painful experience" in Vietnam.[33] Former Chief of Naval Operations Admiral Arleigh S. Burke reflected later that Kennedy may well simply not have known what he was doing; for example, he never "realized he was comitting U.S. troops". He did not appreciate that the helicopters would be committed to combat and that the US military of the time "had gotten into the habit . . . of thinking that if they were to do certain things the logical next step would be taken, too. Inevitably. And it wasn't."[34] One could hardly blame them for making such an assumption. But it was unfortunate that they had not explained to the president what they were assuming that he would be doing next, so that he could have told them that he would not be doing it. There was a particular quality about Vietnam, however, which seemed to make it extraordinarily difficult for anybody involved in it to be completely honest with anybody else.

Menzies thought it appropriate to make some cautiously sympathetic responses to the importunings Beale was relaying to him from Washington. He directed External Affairs Minister Sir Garfield Barwick to circulate to other United Nations members copies of letters, received from Saigon, protesting against communist infiltration from the north;[35] and he advised Washington on 13 December that Australia might be able to supply some small arms and ammunition, although only "a token contribution in training";[36] but there was one area in which even a token advisory contribution from Australia might have been particularly welcome. United States observers had long been disturbed by the ineptitude of the ARVN for jungle warfare. Combined Studies Group expert Gilbert Langton thought that the problem was that the Vietnamese were "not jungle people. They're village people and town people."[37] But the North Vietnamese did not live in the jungle any more than the South Vietnamese. In fact, none of the people who were very good at jungle warfare did actually live in the jungle. The British did not. Neither did the Gurkhas nor the Rhodesians. Nor did the Australians, who had developed an international reputation for expertise in that area. This was one field in which Australia could make a highly relevant contribution with a minimal effort.

Ambassador Anderson put the offer to the newly formed United States Military Assistance Command (MAC) in Saigon. He was told bluntly that they did not want any token Australian assistance, either personnel or materiel. Rusk intervened hastily to retract this rebuff to the only ally who had actually offered anything, be it ever so little. The United States Military were compelled to agree grudgingly that Australia should be asked formally to provide counterinsurgency and jungle warfare instructors. Beale assured Canberra that it would make Australia's mark with the Kennedy administration if even a handful of instructors could be sent to Vietnam. Military utility was evidently not the real issue here. Gestures of solidarity were what Secretary Rusk was looking for.

He had in fact received a very discreet but potentially very significant one already. Macmillan had dispatched the former Director of Operations and Co-ordinating Officer, Security, during the Malayan Emergency and subsequently Permanent Secretary for Defence in Malaya, Sir Robert G. Thompson, to establish a British Advisory Mission in Saigon, with up to six other "skilled counterinsurgency and police officers". Thompson had plenty to suggest to the Americans, on both the theoretical and practical sides. He told them, for example, that his experience in Malaya had shown that the emphasis in counterinsurgency "should always be on quality rather than quantity of forces and to achieve this, training, organization and discipline are the first requirements. The emphasis in Vietnam has always been on quantity ... if 600,000 troops are undertrained, badly organized, ill-disciplined and some poorly equipped, then 900,000 will be worse and the confusion greater ... The conventional structure of the South Vietnamese Army," he warned, "also made it completely ineffective, except for a few elite units, in counter-insurgency operations."[38] His practical suggestion was to implement a Strategic Hamlet Program, integrating "various economic and social programs into an effective campaign to re-establish [the government's] influence in the heavily populated Mekong Delta". This campaign should "lead by stages to a reorganization of the government machinery for directing and coordinating all action against the communists and the production of an overall strategic operational plan for the country as a whole".[39] It was how the British had coped successfully with the Emergency in Malaya. This might not mean that it would be appropriate or practicable in the Vietnam situation. But nobody had yet won a counterinsurgency war any other way.

Menzies had meanwhile been delaying on the critical step of sending Australian military personnel overseas again. Minister Assisting the Minister for External Affairs, Senator John G. Gorton, told Federal Parliament on 30 March 1962 that Saigon had made some requests for "strictly military assistance" from Australia, but alluded only to "such things as barbed wire to enable the villages to be ringed in order to protect them from sudden attacks by armed guerilla bands. We have also," he added, "provided some communications equipment."[40] What he did not mention was that Washington had repeatedly been soliciting Australia to send military personnel as well.

It was becoming increasingly difficult to go on obfuscating and equivocating. Diem appealed the very next day to the heads of government of ninety-three non-communist states, naturally including Australia, for "increased military assistance and support from Free World countries" to help his regime from being "overwhelmed by massive subversion from Communist North Viet Nam, backed by heavily increased support from the Communist bloc".[41] Menzies consulted with his military advisers. They told him that it would be possible to release ten officers and some NCOs for service as instructors in Vietnam. Menzies made this hardly lavish offer to Admiral Felt at an ANZUS Council Meeting in Canberra during 8-9 1962. It was not much, but it was the only direct response that the Americans received to an appeal for military assistance, and it was coming from the kind of country they were most anxious would show its flag in Vietnam —

an unimpeachable representative parliamentary democracy. Felt did not want instructors. He told Menzies that a couple of patrol boats or transport aircraft would be of more use.

Menzies's position was doubly awkward. It was inconvenient enough that Felt did not want to have what Australia was in a position to offer; it was even more so that Australia was not in a position to offer what Felt wanted to have. Menzies explained that as far as he knew Australia had no patrol boats or aircraft to spare. But he was prepared to send up to thirty combat instructors. Rusk intervened again to avert a further rebuff to the only ally who had so far shown any wish to send anything. Felt was persuaded to accept Menzies's new offer. Secretary Rusk stressed his gratitude in a speech at the end of the meeting in which he alluded to certain allies who "seem to think that we have some magic mountain out of which we can shovel gold that makes no difference to anyone", but added that he "did not need to say this to you people who are 'putters in' in this business".[42] Barwick nonetheless seemed to find it necessary to obfuscate about exactly what Australia was putting in and why, when he was asked some months later in federal parliament just what requests the Secretary of State had made of the Australian government during the ANZUS meeting "with respect to — (a) the number and type of personnel for service, and (b) the quantity and type of materiel for use in Vietnam". His reply was that the Secretary "did not make any requests of the Australian Government, during the ANZUS Meeting, with regard to assistance for Viet Nam".[43] Rusk had indeed not made any requests during the meeting, but he had made appeals before the meeting and he had intervened during the meeting to persuade Felt to accept an offer which Menzies had made in response to those appeals. He had not made a request because he had not needed to make a request. Barwick did not need to have one of the most astute legal minds in the country to know that the Members could not reasonably be expected to come to that appreciation of the situation from what he had been telling them.

Menzies informed Diem on 14 May that he could "be assured that your efforts to maintain the integrity and independence of the Republic of Viet Nam will have the full support of the Commonwealth of Australia".[44] It was also decided that any Australian assistance to South Vietnam should be represented as being in accord with or within the context of SEATO, even though Diem had never invoked SEATO but had instead appealed for help to the non-communist world in general, after the Americans had told him what help they would be giving him. But the issue was complicated suddenly by a genuine appeal for assistance under the terms of SEATO. The Office of the Prime Minister of Thailand on 15 May described the collapse of government forces in Laos as constituting "a threat to the Kingdom of Thailand and the safety of the Thai people". United States and Thai officials had in fact already agreed that five thousand US Marines should be dispatched to Thailand. Kennedy declared that the action had been taken "in order that we may be in a position to fulfil speedily our obligations under the Manila Pact of 1954".[45] He then sought support from the other SEATO allies. British Prime Minister Macmillan thought that "the objective is to show as many flags as possible in Thailand", and decided to "send a more or less token force into Thailand, should we be asked to do so by the Thai Government. A squadron of *Hunters* of the RAF," he reflected," could go back. They have recently been in Thailand on an exercise. But I have my doubts as to whether the Thais really want us."[46] Macmillan was clearly not impressed with any sense of urgency. He was however prepared to make a gesture of support on behalf of Thailand which he had not been willing to make for Vietnam. Thailand was a viable if not exactly stable polity; it was a genuine SEATO ally; and its strategic relevance could not be doubted. Vietnam was something else.

The Menzies government was also prepared to send assistance to Thailand. It sent assistance first to Vietnam, however. Defence Minister Athol Townley told the media on 24 May that "up to 30 Australian Army personnel would be sent to provide instruction in jungle warfare, village defence and other related activities such as engineering and signals. Colonel F.P. Serong, formerly Commandant of the Jungle Training Centre at Canungra, would shortly visit Saigon to ascertain on the spot the most effective way in which the Australian instructors could be fitted into the defensive measures against the Communist activities."[47] Diem was informed the following day of the assistance that Washington had agreed that Canberra should send him.

Colonel Serong arrived in Saigon on 6 June for discussions with Commander US Military Assistance Command General Paul D. Harkins, Sir Robert Thompson and Diem. Serong was obviously an excellent choice for the mission. "Confident, innovative and highly individualistic," as Ian McNeill described him, he was "suited for the special combination of military, political, sociological and economic warfare being waged in Vietnam."[48] But the first conflict he had to face in that theatre was predictably with his own allies. Diem wanted the Australians concentrated in the province of Quang Ngai, four hundred kilometres north of Saigon, where they might hopefully be wiped out by a Viet Cong thrust, which Diem expected to "spark off an 'avenging military intervention' from Australia". Thompson thought that they should be deployed in the Mekong Delta to assist in the pacification of this vital area through the Strategic Hamlet Program, involving the clearance of insurgents from an area and the establishment of a secure rural hamlet government. United States General Harkins was concerned mainly with the absurdity of having "all Quang Ngai an Australian province ... and Quang Tin a New Zealand province", and wanted the Australians "pepper-potted throughout South Vietnam, filling individual American manpower slots". Serong disagreed with all these views. He did not want his team to be stranded in Quang Ngai as bait for the Viet Cong. He did not want to "see Australians, trained and equipped for jungle conditions, exposed to the endless swamp and rice paddy terrain that existed in the Mekong Delta". Nor did he want them spread so thinly as to lose "the concept of an identifiable Australian presence".

This was the real problem. There would be only some 30 Australians in Vietnam, as against about 11,300 Americans. It would be all too easy for such a miniscule Australian presence to be swamped and its public relations effect lost. Serong's solution was "for the team to be divided into a number of identifiable groups to operate within the American advisory structure in Vietnamese training establishments. Of four separate locations chosen, three were in the northern provinces of South Vietnam, and one was near the central coast."[49] It was a practical way of coping with the inherent problem of attributing significance to an essentially insignificant effort. But the whole contretemps had revealed a number of disturbing factors. Most ominous was the complete disagreement among all the parties principally concerned as to what kind of strategy or even tactics should be pursued. Another was the evident determination of the United States Military to run the entire operation in their own way and the corresponding inability of the Vietnamese to assert any kind of rational direction of their own. It is not encouraging to get into a war in partnership with people who do not know what they are doing or cannot agree among themselves what to do.

Serong had no doubt what the Australians should do. They were there as experts in jungle warfare, whether anybody else wanted to fight in the jungle or not. "Conventional soldiers", he told reporters at Saigon airport when he returned with his team on 31 July, "think of the jungle as being full of lurking enemies. Under our system, we will do the lurking."[50] Thompson had been willing to let the Viet Cong lurk in the jungle to their hearts' content and to concentrate on securing the centres of population against their raids. The Americans had no intention of going into the jungle at all. They swept in with waves of helicopters, rigged up with .30-calibre machine guns and 2.75-inch rocket launchers, to drive the Viet Cong out into the open where they could be overrun by ARVN forces riding in newly supplied American Armored Personnel Carriers (APCs) under the direction of US military advisers.

It was a wholly American concept of war and it worked brilliantly at first. The tide of battle swung spectacularly against the VC for the first time in the autumn of 1962. But the new strategy created new problems. One was that, as Admiral Burke pointed out, "if you're going to stick to advising you have to stick to advising". The Marine aviators in the helicopters, however, were being used in a fully combat role — in support of ground operations. It was true that Washington had not yet committed ground troops to combat; but the distinction was wholly unreal. Combat is combat. It was clear in any case that allied support would eventually extend to ground troops as well as aviation, if a conventional war were to be fought and won in Vietnam. The ARVN was still hopelessly deficient by any standard of military professionalism. This was something on which Serong and Thompson were in complete agreement. It might, Serong reported to General Harkins in October 1962, be possible to win the war in Vietnam, given a sufficient number of years for the purpose, but it was certainly "possible to lose it, and quickly". The problem was the ARVN and the social system of which it was a reflection. Soldiers, Serong complained bitterly, were "neglected by their officers, inadequately paid and provided with a ration allowance 'no higher than that for a dog' ". Officers were "poorly trained, fearful of making mistakes, and constantly shifting initiative and responsibility to ever-higher levels of authority".[51] It was the kind of army that professional soldiers would be overjoyed to be fighting against. It was one that they would be appalled to have to fight alongside.

Serong's forebodings were soon justified by events. ARVN forces, supported by aviation, APCs and artillery, and accompanied by fifty-one US advisers, were repulsed by outnumbered and outgunned VC at Ap Bac, on 2 January 1963. Sixty-five ARVN and three US personnel were killed and five helicopters lost. Defeat had been due primarily to the refusal of ARVN commanders to take any action liable to provoke the defenders into retaliating. One ARVN armoured cavalry officer took three and a half hours to advance his APCs 1,500 metres against largely ineffective small arms fire. ARVN gunners delivered four rounds an hour when their US advisers called for a heavy barrage. The following week, the VC killed twelve ARVN guards and captured huge supplies of arms in Lien Giang province. These setbacks did not seem to concern President Kennedy, however. He proclaimed in a State of the Union Address on 14 January 1963 that the "spear point of aggression has been blunted in Vietnam".[52] Ambassador Anderson informed Canberra that US officials in Saigon had hinted that Washington might soon ask Australia to send a small RAAF contingent. He thought that such a request ought to be received sympathetically because "the Americans believed that they were winning the war and that it was time for Australia to make a contribution and get some share of the credit".[53] The timing could not have been more opportune. Canberra had suddenly become aware of reasons for cooperating with the Americans more compelling than any that had emerged since 1942.

3

These Australians Could Share in Our Casualties (1963–1964)

Barwick told the Foreign Affairs Commiteee of cabinet on 18 February 1963 that Australia had reached "a real turning point in our diplomatic history. Britain," he explained, "obviously will be unable to defend her 'sphere of interest' in Malaysia once she loses bases in Nairobi and Aden, whereas the USA will still not intervene as she does not regard this as part of her area." Australia would nonetheless still have to support Malaysia strongly herself, even "without much help from Britain and with the USA only in the background", because it was Australia's "only hope of a bastion against China".[1] None of the ministers nor their senior advisers seemed to have questioned the necessity for such a bastion. Traditional Australian fears of China had been reinforced by the communist victory on the mainland, by the experience of actual armed conflict with the People's Liberation Army during the Korean War, by the confrontations over the Offshore Islands in 1955 and 1958, and above all by the prospect of a Beijing Jakarta Axis emerging in the context of Indonesian confrontation with Malaysia. Desk officer for China Gregory Clark was soon made to realize by his superiors in the Department of External Affairs that they were not interested in any reports of his that "seemed to cast a less than totally hostile light on the nature of Chinese politics".[2]

This amounted virtually to a Pearl Harbor situation. The British would be withdrawing from east of Suez to the other side of the world. There would once again be nobody for Australia to look to except the United States. American protection should indeed have been assured under the terms of ANZUS, but it was the concern of the Menzies government that any potential threat to Australia should be checked as far away from their island continent as possible and there was some confusion in Canberra as to just how far north and west of the Australian mainland the Americans were prepared to accept obligations under ANZUS.[3] What would of course provide the ideal bastion against China would be an ongoing US commitment to the Republic of Vietnam. It was the best of all reasons for doing whatever was necessary to sustain the US involvement. If this meant augmenting the Australian involvement, it could only be a very small price to pay to secure Australia itself against the threat from Beijing.

The Australian involvement was in fact already creating problems. Serong complained to the chairman of the House Foreign Affairs Committee Sir Wilfrid Kent Hughes about "the elementary nature of the training in which the advisers were engaged. He explained the frustration which they felt at being denied the opportunity to provide specialist training in jungle frighting."[4] It was inevitable when Australia was supplying what the parties concerned did not want because of its incapacity to supply what they did want. And it arose again when the Americans submitted their anticipated request for a squadron of RAAF *Dakota* transports and sixteen pilots to operate them.

Menzies had to explain this time that the *Dakota* squadrons of the RAAF were about to be replaced by *Caribous*. Committing the existing squadrons overseas could create logistic problems. A more pressing concern was that the British were likely to call for Australian units to assist them in defending Malaysia against Indonesia. Menzies admittedly tended to be more concerned with hypothetical appeals from London than with real ones from Washington.[5] But the situation was vexatious for all concerned. It was particularly so for the Australians, as the New Zealanders, who had not even been asked for any support yet, were creating a very favourable impression with the Americans by sending one of their staff officers, Lieutenant Colonel Robert M. Gurr, to Saigon for consultations during 5–10 June. Gurr displayed an active interest which the Americans found most gratifying in "such categories of assistance as workshop teams, engineers, field medical elements, naval elements, and army combat elements . . . [He] pointed out that while his government was reluctant to become deeply involved in combat operations for political reasons, the New Zealand military was interested in gaining knowledge of Vietnam and experience in combat operations".[6]

It seemed at the time, however, that military operations were about to be wound down, rather than augmented. Thompson recommended that the United States should pull one thousand troops out by the end of 1963, with a view to the complete Vietnamization of all essential functions by 1965. This would certainly have been highly convenient for Kennedy who was preparing for re-election in 1964. But South Vietnam was beginning to fall apart. Government officials in the provincial capital of Hue had allowed Roman Catholics to fly flags in honour of the birthday of their archbishop, President Diem's brother, the international real estate operator. But they refused to allow Buddhists (eighty per cent of the population) to fly flags according to tradition on 3 June in honour of the birthday of Buddha. Twelve people, including three children, were killed in the ensuing disturbances. Riots flamed from Hue to Saigon. A Buddhist monk burned himself to death in Saigon on 11 June in protest against the religious policies of the Diem regime. Diem's sister-in-law, the beautiful but rather disconcerting Mme Nhu, spoke gleefully of a "bonze [monk] barbecue". Many foreigners thought this to be in bad taste. Then her criminal husband, the chief of the state security apparatus, unleashed raids on Buddhist pagodas, in the course of which another 30 monks were injured and 1,400 arrested. Undersecretary Ball warned Ambassador Henry Cabot Lodge that the "US Government cannot tolerate situation in which power lies in Nhu's hands", and advised Lodge that if, "in spite of all your efforts, Diem remains obdurate ... then we must face the possibility that Diem himself cannot be preserved".[7]

Even the Australian government was starting to feel concerned. Deputy Whip Peter Howson decided after a briefing on Vietnam that "we don't like Diem's policies", although he still felt that "any alternative seems to be worse".[8] This was not the American viewpoint. Ambassador Lodge told Washington flatly the following day that "there is no possibility, in my view, that the war can be won under a Diem administration".[9] He followed this up with the grim forecast that "if we undertake to live with this repressive regime, with its bayonets at every street corner and its transparent negotiations with puppet bonzes, we are going to be thrown out of the country in six months". He indeed considered that "at this juncture it would be better for us to make the decision to get out honorably".[10] This might have been the great missed opportunity of the Vietnam imbroglio. Kennedy found it easier at the time to take the advice of Taylor and McNamara, who proposed on 2 October that the United States should "take no initiative ... to encourage actively a change in the government", but should "seek urgently to identify and build contacts with an alternative leadership if and when it appears".[11] Alternatives were not slow in appearing. General Duong Van "Big" Minh advised a CIA agent on 5 October that the ARVN high command believed that a coup was necessary if the war were to be won. Kennedy told Lodge that he did not "wish to stimulate coup", but also did not "wish to leave impression that U.S. would thwart a change of government or deny economic and military assistance to a new regime if it appeared capable of increasing effectiveness of military effort, ensuring popular support to win war and improving working relations with the U.S."[12] That was sufficient encouragement. Minh and his supporters surrounded the presidential palace on the afternoon of 1 November after the seventh bonze had suicided by fire in Saigon, and while Mme Nhu was in New York on an informal visit. Diem and Nhu surrendered and were murdered while being taken to ARVN headquarters.

Washington could hope again. The decision was taken on 15 November to begin withdrawing US service personnel from Vietnam, in the expectation that the new regime would be able to enlist popular support which Diem had alienated. Even Kennedy's own assassination a week later did not halt the process of disengagement. General Harkins announced on 2 December that "on December 3 the first increment of approximately 300 U.S. military personnel will be withdrawn from the Republic of Vietnam. They will be followed during the next two or three weeks by another 700, making a total reduction in force of 1000 before the end of 1963."[13] It was what Sir Robert Thompson had proposed. But it necessarily depended upon the demonstrated capacity of the new regime to handle affairs better than its predecessors. It was already obvious that it was handling them worse.

A CIA report of 16 December stated that the situation in Vietnam "continued to be marked by a lack of forward motion on the part of the country's new rulers in getting on with the many-sided struggle against the Viet Cong". They had, for example, proceeded incontinently to replace provincial administrators appointed by Diem with ones presumably more loyal to themselves. But Diem's local appointees, the agency commented, "at least had some idea of what was expected of them and had the organization resources for implementing national policy in the countryside even though imperfectly and oppressively". The Viet Cong had naturally been "quick to move into this vacuum of authority and initiative ... most observers agree that the VC have made definite progress and that in some areas, the situation has deteriorated to a disturbing extent. Particularly hard hit has been the strategic hamlet program", which had been the chief index of success in the struggle against subversion.[14] It had also been the essential element in the counterinsurgency strategy proposed by the British Advisory Mission, because it had been the essential element in the success of their own campaign in Malaya. The difference was that the Program had been operated efficiently and intelligently by an honest administration in Malaya, under the leadership of a pragmatic and able fighting general who represented almost everything that Diem and his family did not. In Vietnam, by contrast, as the US Marines' official historian recorded, the Strategic Hamlet Program had been "mismanaged and poorly coordinated from the outset", and had "failed to fulfil even the most moderate of American and South Vietnamese expectations".[15] Denis Warner summed up the situation succinctly when he reported that "there is not a fully 'white' or Communist-free, hamlet in the province and few anywhwere in the delta".[16]

So nothing had worked. Defense Secretary McNamara reported to President Johnson that current trends in Vietnam, "unless reversed in the next 2–3 months, will lead to neutralization at best and more likely to a Communist-controlled state".[17] This forecast was supported by a further CIA assessment that there was "no organized government in South Vietnam at this time". It was, moreover, "abundantly clear that statistics received over the past year or more from the GVN officials and reported by the US mission on which we gauged the trend of the war were grossly in error. Conditions in the delta and in the areas immediately north of Saigon are more serious now than expected and were probably never as good as reported. The Viet Cong control larger percentages of the population, greater amounts of territory, and have destroyed or occupied more strategic hamlets than expected ... Revelation of factual data evidences a far greater problem for the GVN in arresting the unfavourable trend and recovering the situation that was thought." Furthermore, the VC were "receiving substantial support from North Vietnam and possibly elsewhere, and this support can be increased". Their appeal to the people of South Vietnam on political grounds "has been effective, gained recruits for their armed forces and neutralized resistance". By contrast, the political stability of Minh's regime was subject to serious doubt. In short, the report concluded, "there are more reasons to doubt the future of the effort under present programs and moderate extensions to existing programs (i.e., harassing sabotage against NVN [North Vietnam], border crossing, etc;) than there are reasons to be optimistic about the future of our cause in South Vietnam".[18]

This left Johnson with two logical options. One was to accept that South Vietnam was in fact indefensible for practical purposes — to cut his losses and to seek to contain the communist advance in more favourable positions to the west and south. The other was to embark on a quantum leap in United States involvement, with all the predictable and unpredictable hazards that this would involve. The CIA, at least, were trying to leave the president in no doubt as to what the real options were. They were telling him that he would have to get out or go to war. McNamara had seemed to be saying much the same. However, he suddenly became wildly incoherent, assuring the bewildered Johnson that "we can still win, even on present ground rules", but that in the eyes of Asia "and of key areas threatened by Communism in other areas as well, South Vietnam is both a test of U.S. firmness and specifically a test of U.S. capacity to deal with 'wars of national liberation' ". Moreover, "the stakes in preserving an anti-Communist South Vietnam are so high that, in our judgment, we must go on bending every effort to win", especially as, he concluded, "the American people are by and large in favor of a policy of firmness and strength in such situations".[19]

McNamara might have been trying to explain that the choice was not necessarily between disengagement and military intervention on a scale amounting at least to limited war. It might still have been possible to save the situation by upgrading the United States commitment far beyond its present level but still short of fullscale war. The distinction was necessarily arbitrary and probably unreal. And it was by no means clear exactly what "key areas threatened by Communism" regarded Vietnam as a test of US firmness and capacity. He could not, for example, have meant Japan, which had refused to become militarily involved, or Europe, which had not only refused to become militarily involved itself but was also almost unanimously opposed to the United States becoming involved. But McNamara, like many other advocates of intervention in Vietnam, seemed to think that the best way of resolving issues was to confuse them. He told the House Armed Services Committee that the war "a Vietnamese war, and in the final analysis it must be fought and won by the Vietnamese. To leave our advisers there beyond the time they are truly needed would delay the development of Vietnam's initiative." This could hardly sensibly be doubted. But he also insisted that "the survival of an independent government in South Vietnam is so important to the security of all of Southeast Asia and to the free world that I can conceive of no alternative other than to take all necessary measures within our capability to prevent a Communist victory". This could mean going far beyond merely providing advisers, many of whom, McNamara failed to explain, were actually flying on combat missions already.

The Secretary concluded his testimony with some really remarkable misstatements of fact. He admitted that the Diem government unfortunately "did not choose to follow the advice we offered". However, he insisted that he was confident that the "new government . . . has considerably more popular support that its predecessor and the Military Revolutionary Committee is beginning to take action to intensify military operations and improve civil administration. The strategic hamlet program which had been overextended in the delta area is now being built more solidly."[20] Three days later, "Big" Minh was deposed after a wave of strikes, mounting evidence of lack of popular support and increased VC activity. Ambassador Lodge bleakly asked new incumbent Major General Nguyen Khanh how he knew that " 'there isn't going to be another coup in about three months and it will be your turn to be in jail?' 'I am absolutely totally protected against another coup,' " Khanh replied. " 'It is utterly impossible for it to happen.' " He also assured Lodge that he intended " 'to go rather faster, and I must have someone who can keep up with me.' " Lodge told him that " 'nothing could please Americans more than the sight of an oriental head of state who wanted to go fast and did not hesitate to kick people in the rear end.' "[21]

The only way Khanh was going fast was downhill. CIA observers reported a fortnight later after this encouraging interview that the VC now controlled more than fifty to sixty per cent of the area in many provinces and as much as eighty per cent in some. "National level direction of all programs," they considered, "appears to be weak or non-existent." The Strategic Hamlet Program, which McNamara had told the House Committee was being built more solidly, was in fact "at a virtual standstill". Of fifty-two hamlets previously established in Hau Nghia, for example, only eight were not viable. On the hearts and minds side of the war, things could hardly have been worse. There was "no evidence of any particular GVN appeal to youth or students and as matter of fact GVN propaganda mechanism in toto is largely moribund". Hamlet militia were effective only in areas where they did not have to do any fighting. ARVN forces for their part were "outgunned as well as outmanned in a number of areas".[22] This was the more ominous in that the ARVN was being consistently worsted even in situations where it enjoyed superiority in numbers and materiel. Crack ARVN Rangers had encountered VC units only thirty-five miles from Saigon in a set-piece battle situation most favourable to conventional forces. The VC escaped because the Rangers refused to close with their less numerous and more lightly armed opponents. Then ARVN paratroops, supported by dive bombers and artillery, fought a pitched battle with the VC and lost, taking ninety-four casualties, their highest to date.

Assistant Secretary of Defense John T. McNaughton was already pondering a contingency plan. "If worst comes," he suggested, "and South Vietnam disintegrates or becomes abominable, it might be possible to 'disown' South Vietnam, leaving the image of a patient who died despite the extraordinary efforts of a good doctor."[23] It was a totally reasonable way of looking at things in the circumstances. But it was not the only way. Johnson sent McNamara and Taylor back to Saigon for a firsthand assessment. They reported back that things were indeed "unqestionably growing worse", but they insisted that disastrous consequences were "likely to follow should South Vietnam fall to the Communists". The United States must therefore make it unambiguously clear at all levels that "we are prepared to furnish assistance and support for as long as it takes to bring the insurgency under control".[24] There was no exit from Vietnam, such as McNaughton had been contemplating. It was of course very difficult to argue against a case resting entirely on necessarily unsupported assertions. And there was another intangible but equally compelling factor operating on Johnson himself. He had come to believe that "his predecessor's complicity in the overthrow of President Diem had been the worst error made by the United States during its involvement in Vietnam. The United States *became* responsible for the fate of successive governments in South Vietnam." Taylor himself argued that the "encouragement afforded the enemy by Diem's downfall found expression in a massive offensive, political and military, to exploit the removal of their mortal enemy". According to Head of the MAC, General William C. Westmoreland, it "morally locked us in Vietnam ... Were it not for our interference in political affairs of South

Vietnam and based on pragmatic consideration, we could in my opinion had justifiably withdrawn our support at that time in view of a demonstrated lack of leadership and unity in South Vietnam."[25]

It is all rather unconvincing in retrospect. After all, Diem was deposed and murdered by his own people. Washington had tacitly encouraged his removal because of the overwhelming evidence that it was impossible to win a counterinsurgency war under a regime as corrupt, incompetent and unpopular as Diem's. The Americans could logically have supported Diem only if they had actually wanted to make a communist victory inevitable, or in other words, if they had been looking for an excuse to disengage. Assisting the Vietnamese to get rid of a regime which had lost control of the situation could hardly create any commitment to support other regimes which could not control the situation either. It would have made more sense to argue that the Americans had given the South Vietnamese an opportunity to put their own house in order. They had failed to do so and could not reasonably expect any more assistance from anybody. But it was not a matter of making sense. It was, according to Taylor, a matter of choosing between accepting defeat or introducing American military forces. The United States was not yet accustomed to accepting defeat and no president was temperamentally less inclined to accept defeat than Lyndon Johnson.

The decision, however, was not as difficult as it might appear. American military forces had in fact been introduced and even committed to combat already. Any changes in that direction would be only changes of degree. More Americans would be involved and they would presumably engage in operations on the ground instead of giving close-in support to ground operations from the air. It might well seem that there were really no new policy decisions to be confronted in an option for increased intervention. It would merely be a matter of modifying policies which had been evolving over the past ten years or more. An option to disengage would however require a new decision. It was far easier for an administration in an election year to move forward than to move back. It was exactly as Macmillan had prophesied at Key West in 1961. The Americans were allowing themselves to be "sucked into these inhospitable areas without a base, without any clear political or strategic aims and without any effective system of deploying armed forces or controlling local administration".

Yet they had no intention of being sucked in alone. Johnson was determined not to commit the United States to further efforts in

Vietnam without the support of allies. And this meant allies possessed of suitable credentials as defenders of democracy. Potential allies unfortunately deficient in such credentials were offering their services already. Chiang Kai-shek, for example, suggested to Admiral Felt on 24 February 1964 that the United States should undertake joint planning with Taiwan for the use of Nationalist Chinese forces against North Vietnam. Chiang's Defence Minister Yu Tai-wei proposed that such planning should provide for an assault on the communist Chinese-held island of Hainan in the Gulf of Tonkin,[26] but Washington was not prepared to provoke a war with the People's Republic of China (PRC) at a time when it was still hoping to avoid going formally to war with North Vietnam.

Chiang then moved to enlist the support of the South Vietnamese for his dream of recovering the mainland. He suggested to Khanh that an Asian Anti-Communist Front be formed, comprising South Vietnam, Taiwan, South Korea, and possibly Thailand. Khanh passed the idea on to McNamara, who passed it on to Rusk. The Secretary was not in favour. He had already pointed out at a news conference that the United States was not "an ally of South Viet-Nam, Cambodia, Laos. These are three of the protocol states of the South-east Asia Treaty Organization."[27] He told Lodge that the United States "cannot and of course does not intend prevent GVN moves for closer cooperation with GRC [Government of the Republic of China (Taiwan)], or Korea, Thailand or other friendly countries". But Khanh should be "left under no repeat no misapprehension that U.S. would be willing to underwrite a military alliance of the three or four governments". It might, he thought, be possible to use "high-level GRC advisers in Vietnam", but, he emphasized for Lodge's eyes only, he saw "distinct disadvantage in overt alliance relationship as having effect of exporting the Chinese civil war to Korea, Saigon, Bangkok". He was in any case "doubtful that Thai would presently be interested or willing join any such arrangement". Khanh should have been aware that the United States continued to "regard SEATO as essentially viable and effective system for prevention and/or defeat of aggression in Southeast Asia", and that "reasons which have precluded Viet-Nam from joining defensive alliances in past retain, in our view, a certain validity for future and should not be disregarded".[28]

Johnson himself had told Kennedy that SEATO was unlikely ever to be effective for anything. What Rusk was really concerned about was the possible proliferation of Asian military arrangements not subject to United States control. He was accordingly disturbed to learn that South Korean Foreign Minister Kim Chong-p'il had also arrived in Saigon for discussions with Khanh. The Secretary could "see no significant military contribution ROK [Republic of Korea (South Korea)] could advisably make". However, he thought it possible that "ROK forces might have both practical and political impact in support or in special capacities in civic action field".[29] It was another American perception of East Asian realities that would not be validated by experience. Korean efforts in the civic action area tended to be more controversial than effective. Their military contribution was by contrast certainly the largest and perhaps the most combat-effective deployed by any of the allies, other than the United States itself.

Rusk's reservations about the Koreans and Taiwanese made it all the more necessary to start rallying support from less equivocal quarters. Initial approaches were made at the Ninth SEATO Council Meeting in Manila during 13–15 April 1964. A final communique expressed "grave concern about the continuing Communist aggression against the Republic of Viet-Nam", and declared that "the members of SEATO should remain prepared, if necessary, to take further steps within their respective capabilities in fulfilment of their obligations under the Treaty". They recognized further that "the defeat of the Communist campaign is essential not only to the security of the Republic of Viet-Nam, but to that of South-east Asia".[30] President Johnson suggested that the SEATO governments might start doing something practical to ensure the defeat of that campaign when he expressed the hope at a press conference on 23 April that "we would see some other flags in there ... and that we could all unite in an attempt to stop the spread of Communism in that part of the world".[31]

The only other flag in there at the time was the Australian blue ensign. Only Australian military personnel were visible in uniform besides the Americans and the South Vietnamese. Other governments were providing less conspicuous assistance. The British Advisory Mission was still there in civilian clothes as befitted their status as law enforcement officers. London had also supplied some agricultural equipment, medical supplies and English language teachers. Malaysia had sent a twelve-man advisory team to assist in training the Vietnamese Air Force (VNAF), a few native trackers and scout cars for the Vietnamese Civil Guard, as well as training over two hundred ARVN officers and NCOs at the Jungle Warfare School, however unsatisfactory this experience had been for all concerned. Korea had sent some instructors in taekwando; Germany had supplied machine tools and loans; Japan had sent construction materials and equipment; France had supplied industrial equipment and loans; New Zealand had sent surgical teams; and Canada had sent wheat and an entomologist.

Canada had of course also provided invaluable covert assistance by helping to sabotage the operations of the ICC. Canadian Prime Minister John G. Diefenbaker agreed on 30 April to allow the State Department to borrow the services of J. Blair Seaborn, the chief Canadian representative on the ICC, to "prevent United States views on the Vietnam war and the outlook for peace to the officials in Hanoi".[32] But Rusk was looking now for something more overt and tangible from people less delicately placed than the Canadians. He advised Lodge that the Philippines could, for example, contribute civic action personnel, guerilla warfare training teams, nurses and nurse instructors. Thailand could send C-47 pilots, border patrol police, special forces personnel, and marines and navy advisers to act in "indoctrination and orientation roles", as well as maintaining its current nursing program. New Zealand and the United Kingdom could assist with more C-47 pilots, as well as reconnaissance aircraft, air traffic controllers, air defence training units, medical and dental teams, and liaison personnel at every level. Military engineers, transportation and medical operational units "from any of the SEATO nations except France and Pakistan" should contribute actively in civic action programmes. Among non-SEATO countries, West Germany could contribute medical and dental teams, civil engineers of every kind and shipyard advisers. Japan could also supply agricultural experts and nurses. Korea could help with special forces advisers, although Rusk was insistent that Korea and Taiwan "for political reasons, should confine the nature of their contributions to efforts other than those of an expressly combat-type military nature".

Rusk had presumably written the French off because the government of President Charles de Gaulle was unreservedly critical of the expanding American involvement in Vietnam. But this did not mean that Paris was unwilling to be helpful. Assistant to the Assistant Secretary of Defence Thomas C. Thayer recalled that the French military attache in Saigon in 1964 had been "handpicked by the French Government because of his exceptional knowledge of the English language and his distinguished record in Indochina and Algeria. He was told to help the Americans in whatever way he could. During the first eighteen months of his assignment, the only American who visited him to ask about the war was an American defense contractor of French origin."³³ Washington was asking its allies for flags in Vietnam, not for advice.

All these governments, the Secretary advised Lodge, had been approached already, either informally or indirectly. He proposed to follow up these advances with bilateral discussions at the forthcoming NATO meeting in The Hague over 12–14 May. "The result desired," he explained, "is a voluntary approach by the Free World Governments directly to the Government of the Republic of Viet Nam offering assistance in a category of need and making direct arrangements between that Government and the Government of Viet Nam for the rendering of this assistance." It was naturally extremely important that the government of Vietnam should be appropriately responsive. Lodge was therefore directed to seek assurance from Khanh that "all such offers of assistance from Free World nations will be appropriately and gracefully received and seriously considered by the Government of the Republic of Viet Nam".³⁴

It was not part of Rusk's plan that Khanh should start making approaches of his own. Lodge reported, however, that the Vietnamese were planning to send a high level military mission to Manila, and that "plans have been drawn up send Phil[ippines] Special Forces Unit to assist in training SVG [South Vietnamese Government] military personnel". Ambassador William E. Stevenson's personal contact in the South Vietnamese Embassy in Manila was unable to confirm whether these rumours were true, or even whether the South Vietnamese actually wanted such assistance. The contact assured him nonetheless that "Phils in past appeared more than ready to make commitment". When asked if he meant "Phils were ready to assist with medical team, etc., he responded, 'No, with small unit of troops' ". Stevenson decided that his informant was trying to convey the impression that "Phils are ready, anxious made commitment of fighting force, while Vietnamese reluctant to 'internationalize' conflict in their country". Stevenson himself was aware of "no indication of any kind that GOP [Government of the Philippines] pressing to get involved militarily in Vietnam".³⁵ The US embassy in Manila believed in any case that the Philippines would not be able to provide a conventional fighting force. What they could provide would be "additional teams in support of rural development programs, field dispensary units and pioneer platoons with engineering construction experience". The real problem, the embassy considered, was "whether the US would be willing to finance all or any part of such effort. GOP has capacity to do so... Believe we should initially indicate that we expect them to do so. Further insistence on this point would depend upon degree of importance US attaches to Phil presence in South Vietnam."[36]

It was not very satisfactory. There was no way of telling what kind of games Saigon and Manila were really playing; it was on balance unlikely that any significant military contribution would be forthcoming from the Philippines; and it was very likely indeed that Washington would be expected to foot the bill for whatever assistance Manila might eventually decide to send. It must have been a considerable relief to Rusk to reflect that there was at least one ally which seemed to know exactly what it was doing, which had made a valuable military contribution already and which had never expected anybody else to pay its bills.

Lodge was unstinting in his praise of Serong and his team. He told the Secretary that the thirty Australian officers and NCOs engaged in advisory duties and "other semi-covert counter insurgency operations" were "technically highly qualified, strongly motivated and easily integrated into our MAAG [Military Assistance Advisory Group] and CAS [Chief of Air Staff] operations. In effect they are making valuable contribution and are likely and appreciated by GVN and our own military. We should," he considered, "have more of them." State Department should therefore try to persuade Canberra to commit a minimum of eighteen more advisers, an additional training cadre for corps centres, additional special forces personnel, a helicopter unit, fixed wing observation and liaison units, a fixed wing transport unit, and two or three surgical teams. What made an augmented Australian commitment particularly desirable, he told Rusk, was that "for the most part these Australians could replace MACV [Military Assistance Command (Vietnam)] personnel and share in our combat casualties".[37] There was really nobody else around who could qualify for that role.

Rusk was in full agreement with Lodge's proposals. He immediately directed US embassies in the Pacific region that "consideration should be given to high level approach to the GOA [Government of Australia] on expanded Australian assistance to her non-Communist neighbors", on the grounds that "the countries of Southeast and Southwest Asia are the first line of defense for Australia". Substantially larger Australian assistance in Vietnam, Thailand, Laos, Burma, and the Philippines could also "afford considerable relief to present and future demands for US assistance which could then be reoriented and concentrated in projects of a purely military nature". Furthermore, "a significant expanded Australian effort throughout Southeast Asia would provide concrete evidence GOA's sincere desire maintain political integrity and independence of these nations."[38]

Australia was, however, already committed to maintaining the political integrity and independence of a regional nation. This would make it very difficult for it to provide any additional combat assistance in Vietnam. Canberra had sent Defence Force units in April to the Federation of Malaysia against the threat of Indonesian confrontation. This threat became at least potentially alarming when Indonesian President Soekarno issued an "action command" on 3 May calling for twenty-one million volunteers to increase the vitality of the Indonesian Revolution and to help the peoples of Malaya, Singapore, Sarawak, Brunei, and Sabah to dissolve their own federation. It all sounded very much like a typical Soekarno fanfare, but Washington could hardly risk having its only militarily active ally in Vietnam tied down indefinitely defending the latest British experiment in decolonization against a non-communist challenge further south. Assistant Secretary of State for East Asia and Pacific Affairs, William P. Bundy, warned Soekarno bluntly that the United States might have to cut off all remaining aid programmes if confrontation were escalated. Ambassador Howard P. Jones assured the Indonesian president that Bundy was merely "stating facts of life ... Sukarno asked whether Bundy's statement meant that US was now defending Malaysia. I said if he meant by this militarily defending Malaysia, the answer of course was negative, although, I continued, escalation of the conflict would result in ANZUS treaty being involved. If he meant politically support Malaysia, he was aware that we recognize Malaysia and that we had welcomed its formation."[39] That should hopefully have been enough to deter Soekarno from taking any action which would materially affect Australia's capacity to increase its commitment to Vietnam. On the following day, the US embassy in Canberra presented Foreign Minister Paul C. Hasluck with Lodge's list of the various ways in which Australia might assist US efforts to hold the disintegrating republic together.

This approach received immediately the strongest support from the Australian embassy in Washington. Minister Alan P. Renouf urged that Canberra's response should be "both as positive and as prompt as possible", allowing for the physical limitations on what Australia could actually do. Renouf considered that his government's objective should be "to achieve such an habitual closeness of relations with the United States and sense of mutual alliance that in our time of need ... the United States would have little option but to respond as we would want". Vietnam, Renouf stressed, was an area "where we could without a disproportionate expenditure pick up a lot of credit with the United States". As a matter of tactics, Hasluck "could soon announce that Australia will respond positively to the approach made by the United States, but naturally cannot yet announce in which way (it would be admirable", Renouf added, "if Australia could be the first so to announce)".[40]

Australia's response could not have been more positive or more prompt. Prime Minister Menzies's recollection that it took not more than five minutes to decide and that there were no hesitations or doubts seems to have been literally true. Hesitation and doubt could not have been more strikingly absent from Hasluck's reply on 13 May to a "Dorothy Dixer" from Liberal backbencher Raymond H. Whittorn. Australia, the minister explained, was "closely associated with the United States in SEATO. We strongly support the United States in its various activities to safeguard the peace of this region ... I assure the House that there will be no holding back or unwillingness on our part to do what is within our capacity to do."[41]

Hasluck then directed Renouf on 14 May to inform the Americans that Australia was anxious to reply promptly and sympathetically to their suggestions. His assurance of support came at a peculiarly opportune time. Rusk was surveying the bleak results of the State Department's first efforts to enlist more flags for Vietnam. It amounted to a litany of apologies, interspersed with active discouragement. The US embassy in Brussels, for example, had not even dared to suggest that Belgium might make some military contribution "as there is no rpt no hope whatsoever she would do so", but they had asked Foreign Minister Paul-Henri Spaak if "Belgium would be able to make some contribution in civilian assistance field, possibly in cooperation with private agencies and could adequately publicize such action". Spaak, however, "commented sympathetically on terribly difficult situation we face in Viet-Nam but did not know what Belgium might be able to do". Chancellor Erhardt of Germany was not so much sympathetic as outspokenly critical. He gave the impression of being understandably far more interested in self-determination for the East Germans and suggested that the pursuit of detente might well be retarded by

Western involvement in Vietnam. He doubted in any event whether the "Viet Cong can be contained, or even pushed back". He was prepared to consider sending another medical team, "since it would have a peaceful appearance", but it would have to be a civilian unit, not a military one. It was significant that US Ambassador McGhee thought that this distinctly reserved response by the Federal Chancellor was positively encouraging in view of the "unenthusiastic, if not critical" attitude of the German press towards the idea of sending aid of any kind to Vietnam.

That was the consistent pattern. Public opposition in Canada had been very evident and no definite pledge of aid had been extended by Ottawa. The Dutch had been uncompromisingly negative. Reports from Oslo were "not particularly favourable" either. Thai Foreign Minister Khoman had said that it was "quite possible there were some things Thailand could do", but had not indicated what they might be. The Japanese had stated that they would not give military aid but would consider other forms of assistance. The Italians said that it could be assumed that they could give some medical help, but had not said how much or when. The Philippines "gave emphatically affirmative response" and stated that they "could extend meaningful help in technical assistance field", but Manila was notoriously swift to promise and slow to deliver. The British had agreed "to investigate possibility of providing additional counter-insurgency advisers and medical experts", but of course without any commitment at that stage. And New Zealand was considering sending the usual noncombatant unit.

Out of fifteen nations approached, only from Australia had the response been "wholly favorable. Australian government," the Secretary gratefully told his ambassadors, "now examining possibility of increased military training assistance as well as additional economic and technical aid with emphasis on village level. Public statements of support for our policy in Viet Nam have been made."[42] And Canberra moved quickly to give effect to its promises. It was announced on 29 May that Australia would be sending an additional thirty military advisers, an army dental team, engineers, mechanics, driving instructors and six *Caribou* transport aircraft. Moreover, Canberra had resolved that "the role of the army training team should be extended to permit its employment in the field at battalion and lower levels as advisers", even though it was "recognized that Australian casualties must be expected if the army training team were to be employed in this way".[43]

Australians would be sharing in American casualties, as Lodge had hoped they would.

There were nonetheless a number of aspects of the Australian government's response which might have given cause for concern in Washington. Chief of these was its uniqueness. There could only be something suspect about a policy which was supported unreservedly by not a single other democratic country in the world. There also seemed to be very serious limitations to what Australia could effectively do to assist. *TIME Magazine* ran a feature on the state of Australia's defences on the same day as Hasluck's announcement of increased Australian aid to Vietnam. It rather tactlessly referred to the RAN as obsolete and the RAAF as a memory and compared the figure of 2.65 per cent of GNP currently being expended by Australia on defence with the British figure of 7 per cent and the American one of 9 per cent.[44] Even more embarrassing to all concerned were a series of procedural problems. Rusk's original idea had been that countries proposing to show their flags in Vietnam should approach Saigon directly to reach agreement on the form their assistance should take. But the Australian decision had been reached after consultation with the Americans, and the Vietnamese ambassador in Canberra was informed only after the nature of the Australian response had already been determined. He agreed that the Australian government could announce that the increase in its commitment was being provided after consultation with both Washington and Saigon; but there had been no consultation with Saigon. There had not even been consultation with the US Military Assistance Command in Saigon, who objected that Canberra was sending them more dentists and driving instructors, which they had not asked for, instead of liaison and observation personnel and helicopters, which they had. They told the surprised Australians that they could keep their non-combatants and send more military advisers instead.

It had the makings of a diplomatic catastrophe. Wires ran hot between Saigon, Canberra and Washington. Ball warned that "Australian enthusiasm could be dampened by further delay" in resolving the issue. Ambassador Battle in Canberra had told him that the Australians were "poised to airlift $100,000 medical supplies to SVN [South Vietnam] and felt let down when it turned out this was not a requirement". Moreover, doubt was now being cast on the need for other items as well. "I cannot stress too strongly," Battle warned, "adverse feeling sure to emerge in GOA if we now indicate that many of the specific requirements we asked them to fulfil were not real."[45] It would indeed be extremely unfortunate if the only democratic government anxious to show its flag in Vietnam were to be rebuffed in this way. Rusk put the matter in its correct perspective in a directive to Lodge. He reminded the ambassador that "desire for QUOTE: more flags END QUOTE in Viet Nam results from desire by highest Washington authority that there be visible demonstration of Free World solidarity with struggle against Viet Cong. Short-term operational or administrative difficulties must not RPT not stand in way of realizing this important political objective."[46] "Actual value or utility of any aid contributions," he similarly told Ambassador McGhee, "is not RPT not primary object of this appeal, although we certainly do not want to impede war effort in Viet Nam with useless or frivolous QTE assistance UNQTE. Main idea behind this multilateral effort is to show Free World solidarity with Vietnamese in their struggle against Communist aggression from North — the same solidarity that has been of such benefit to all countries we now approaching."[47]

Public relations was still the main consideration in the war in Vietnam; and the Australians were about to enjoy what in the circumstances could only be regarded as a public relations coup. Defence Minister Shane Paltridge announced on 6 June 1964 that the number of Australian military personnel in Vietnam would be doubled to sixty. On the same day the first Australian soldier to be killed in Vietnam died when the Viet Cong attacked the Special Forces camp in Da Nang, killing two US advisers and fifty-five ARVN as well. Australia was the only "Free World" country so far to have made a military commitment to Vietnam, and the only one to have shared so far in American casualties there. There was no more convincing way of seeking to establish the sense of mutual alliance that Renouf had advocated.

Other "Free World" governments were still not manifesting any disposition to follow Australia's lead, however. "There is still not enough progress", Rusk complained to Johnson on 15 June. Public and press opposition were actually intensifying in Canada, although Ottawa was considering sending a medical or engineering laboratory to the University of Hue. German public opinion was also increasingly hostile. The Greeks were "nervous about any overt contribution". The Norwegians had flatly refused to send anything. So had the Dutch, although the Vietnamese Foreign Office had been advised to try giving greater publicity to the gift of a dredge made by the Dutch government for the Mekong River Project. It was possible that Japan would be asked to send one hundred thousand small radio receivers. The Koreans were still talking about field hospitals and signal corps support, but Rusk had warned the US embassy in Seoul "to give no encouragement to the Koreans" on the idea of sending combat units, although they should "push the idea of the Koreans contributing special forces advisers".

Washington naturally could not agree to anybody else sending combat troops to Vietnam when it had not yet committed combat troops officially itself. Apart from that, the Americans were all too glad to accept anything, especially from Europe. This might have seemed a rather indiscriminate way to organize an aid program, but it was difficult to be more precise in the absence of specific requests from the Vietnamese themselves. Rusk noted that it was "only within the past few days that we have had any indication that the Vietnamese Government was going to be able to produce an overall coordinated list of aid requirements".[48] One consequence of this was to encourage any governments interested in supplying aid to ignore completely the views of the Vietnamese. This in turn tended to cause some diplomatic inconveniences. Australian Ambassador Anderson told his government that he was "mildly embarrassed by successive instructions from Canberra to inform the Vietnamese of Australia's decision to provide additional aid, to ask the Vietnamese if these items were needed and then, having been assured that they were needed, to inform the Vietnamese that some of them would not be provided".[49]

The fact of the matter was that the Australian government was not primarily concerned with providing aid to Vietnam. What it was primarily concerned with was establishing a sense of mutual alliance with the United States. It was the gratitude of Washington that was being sought, not that of Saigon. Securing a viable, non-communist government in South Vietnam would not in itself necessarily solve Australia's security problems. Only securing an American military commitment in Vietnam, it was assumed, would do that, and this could best be achieved by sending the kind of assistance that the Americans wanted, whether the Vietnamese had asked for it or not.

There was indeed a sense in which Australian policymakers viewed what was actually happening in South Vietnam as irrelevant to their concerns, practically speaking. External Affairs Minister Hasluck had no doubt, after a tour of Southeast Asia, that "South Vietnam is absolutely vital for the peace and security of the whole Southeast Asian region . . . If there were any weakening in our determination to defend South Viet Nam, this could have dramatic and dangerous repercussions far beyond Southeast Asia." But that was not because of whatever the Vietnamese might be doing to themselves. It was not, he explained, simply a matter of "Annamite aggressiveness and the desire to dominate their neighbours", but rather of "the determination of China to establish Chinese hegemony throughout Southeast Asia, working in the first place through the agency of her North Vietnamese puppets".[50] It was the ultimate rationale of Australian involvement in Vietnam. The paradox was that this fear of Chinese aggression southward did not seem to be taken seriously anywhere else in the world except in North Vietnam itself. Canberra and Hanoi shared the same apprehensions about the intentions of Beijing towards their region.

This was of course why the more flags programme was failing. Nobody cared very seriously about South Vietnam. Australia cared very much about China, but its perception of Chinese intentions was not shared by other democratic governments. President Johnson desperately addressed a personal directive to US ambassadors in Tokyo, Bonn, London, Rome, Brussels, Ottawa, Copenhagen, Bangkok, Taipei, Karachi, and Athens. He advised them that he was:

> gravely disappointed by the inadequacy of the actions by our friends and allies in response to our request that they share the burden of Free World responsibility in Vietnam. It has now been nine weeks since the Secretary of State instructed your Embassy to seek assistance from the Government to which you are accredited. While the tenor of the Government's verbal response has indicated sympathy, the actual performance does not demonstrate that they recognize their share of this responsibility or that they realize how significant we consider it that they should discharge that responsibility . . . The American people should not be required to continue indefinitely alone and unassisted [forgetting about the Australians] to be the only champions of freedom in Viet Nam today . . . You should not hesitate to inform the Government that the American people and the American Congress, in observing the responses of our friends when faced with this test of determination in Viet Nam will be bound to wonder about the willingness of these same friends to react effectively in the defense of freedom anywhere. In the truest sense therefore the allied response to this request is a test of the merit of our alliances . . . There should be free men helping to build peace and freedom in Viet Nam . . . I hope to see evidence of your success in the very near future.[51]

It did not work. Democratic governments elsewhere in the world simply did not regard Vietnam as a test case for the defence of democracy. Ball recorded glumly on 10 July that there had been "little overall progress since last report". The South Vietnamese had still not formulated a shopping list of aid requirements or made suitable approaches to suitable governments, although they had agreed to send a mission to Argentina and it was all too evident that they were in active contact with Chiang K'ai-shek. The British were considering sending some fishing boat engines. The Japanese had not made up their minds about transistors. Nobody else had budged an inch.

Meanwhile South Vietnam was plummeting towards total collapse. An ARVN patrol was overwhelmed by the VC near Tay Ninh on 19 June. Sixty-three of the government forces were reported missing in action, including three US advisers. The camp at Kontum was overrun on 4 July. Sixty more ARVN troops were killed on 6 July, against forty-nine claimed VC dead. Another fifty-five ARVN, three Americans and an Australian were killed in action the following day. Then two hundred ARVN were killed in the bloodiest encounter of the war so far at Vinh Chio on 10 July. Khanh desperately called on 19 July for "mass attacks against the North". His appeal was promptly taken up by Vietnamese Air Force (UNAF) Commander General Nguyen Cao Ky, known to the media as "Captain Midnight" for his penchant for dramatic flying ensembles of black overalls relieved by mauve or yellow scarves, a style adopted also by his stunningly beautiful wife. Ky deliberately sought to embarrass the Americans by revealing that the South Vietnamese had been delivering covert air and sea strikes aginst the North with US assistance since the beginning of the year.[52] These had ranged from "flights over North Vietnam by U-2 spy planes and kidnappings of North Vietnamese citizens for intelligence information, to parachuting sabotage and psychological-warfare teams into the North, commando raids from the sea to blow up rail and highway bridges and the bombardment of North Vietnamese coastal installations by PT boats".[53]

They had obviously not achieved much. Khanh, however, at last did something of which the Americans could approve — appealing for assistance to the heads of government of thirty-four countries, including Australia, on 25 July. He expressed the hope that they would "kindly grant us all the support you deem possible and opportune in order to help us successfully fight the Communist aggression". There was no significant response once again, except from the Australians who began to ask themselves "what can we do if we have to move into Saigon",[54] and from the Americans, who send another three thousand combat advisers. Then something happened, or alternatively seemed to happen, which provided the opportunity for all concerned to escalate their commitments far beyond anything that could be represented as merely advice and support. The March of Folly was proceeding with giant steps.

4

The Americans Needed Stiffening (1964)

Three North Vietnamese torpedo boats closed with US destroyer *Maddox* in international waters in the Gulf of Tonkin on the afternoon of 2 August 1964. *Maddox* was not on innocent passage, as she had been carrying out an intelligence-gathering sweep for the South Vietnamese, so the North Vietnamese were justified in pressing their attack. They were fighting far out of their class, however. Two torpedoes missed *Maddox*, which responded with gunfire, leaving one of its assailants dead in the water and the other apparently damaged. CINCPAC ordered *Maddox* not to pursue. Four *Crusaders* were however dispatched from the carrier *Ticonderoga* to strafe the surviving PT boat with rockets. Hanoi announced the loss of both craft. President Johnson's immediate response was to double the patrols in the Gulf, introduce air cover and order the commanders of US ships and aircraft "(a) to attack any force which attacks them in international waters, and (b) to attack with the objective not only of driving off the force but of destroying it".[1]

This might be regarded as increased provocation after a highly intimidating reaction to a justifiable North Vietnamese response to initial US provocation. Chicken-and-egg arguments of this kind, however, are not much use as a guide to future action. The real question was whether the North Vietnamese were prepared to take the bait and give the Americans an excuse further to escalate the conflict in an area in which they enjoyed total superiority. It seems that Hanoi decided to swallow its pride, observe appropriate caution and live with the consequent loss of face. But it did not do it much good.

Maddox was sailing east in the Gulf again on the evening of 4

August accompanied by another destroyer, C. *Turner Joy*, when her radar operator reported five PT boats making toward the American ships. The destroyers opened fire, claiming two North Vietnamese boats sunk and two more damaged. The blips certainly disappeared from the radar screens. But no wreckage was subsequently found in the water and no evidence ever discovered to indicate that an attack had actually been made. The most reasonable supposition is that a North Vietnamese flotilla had observed the US ships, had approached them to investigate, and had withdrawn on orders from Hanoi as soon as they were fired upon. By that time the Americans were undertaking the appropriate evasive manoeuvres at speed, in the dark, and shooting at anything that appeared on their screens. This could very easily have been their own wakes. As Chairman of the Interagency Task Force on Vietnam, William H. Sullivan explained to Paige Mulhollan years later that the problem was "when you get in such a low profile target as a torpedo boat, particularly if you've got a ship that's moving with any speed and doing any turning, your radar signals get very, very confused".[2] It was an appropriate image for a great many things about the Vietnam War.

Johnson himself concluded a few days later, according to Undersecretary Ball, that, " 'Hell, those dumb, stupid sailors were just shooting at flying fish!' "[3] But this was after he had had time to examine the evidence, and the damage had already been done. His immediate action was to strike back at the presumed defiance of American power. He did indeed assure Canadian Prime Minister Lester B. Pearson that the retaliation would be " 'relevant' to the provocation and to the attack". Pearson replied that he "understood that they must feel strongly about the attack", but "expressed the hope that the retaliatory action would not be in excess of what the circumstances required; would be limited in scope".[4] It might indeed have seemed questionable whether any retaliation was required in the circumstances. The Americans had been carrying out espionage missions in support of the South Vietnamese; the North Vietnamese had responded to the provocation, had lost at least two of their own vessels without inflicting any damage or casualties on the US Navy and had apparently decided to desist. Washington had sufficiently demonstrated its capacity to do what it liked on the high seas off Vietnam.

Johnson's response might well have seemed savage and even excessive in any circumstances. Sixty-four fighter-bombers from the carriers *Ticonderoga* and *Constellation* hit four naval bases and an oil depot in North Vietnam on 5 August. Twenty-five North Vietnamese PT boats were destroyed and an estimated ninety per cent of the oil storage facilities at Vinh went up in flames. At the same time, the president asked congress for a resolution "expressing the support of the Congress for all necessary action to protect our Armed Forces and to assist nations covered by the SEATO Treaty".[5] It amounted to carte blanche for the use of American military forces in Vietnam. Johnson was asking for it on the basis of a presumed attack which had caused no damage to either American persons or property, which Johnson himself decided later had probably never actually happened in the first place and to which he had already responded with a wholly unreasonable use of force. He nonetheless got carte blanche. He also received general support from the allies. Paul Hasluck declared that the United States "could do no less than take the necessary military measures to protect its naval vessels from attack in international waters", and approved Johnson's own description of the air attacks as "limited and fitting". British Ambassador to the United Nations Roger Jackley said more circumspectly that it was "the right of every nation whose ships are subjected to acts of aggression on the high seas to take appropriate measures in accordance with the right of self defence". This was apparently considered too moderate in London, because British Foreign Secretary R.A. Butler then issued a statement to the press affirming that Her Majesty's Government had "made their position clear in the Security Council when they supported the action taken by the United States Government in accordance with the inherent right of self-defence recognized by Article 51 of the UN Charter", a right which the North Vietnamese could probably have claimed to have been exercizing themselves. Prime Minister Sir Keith Holyoake of New Zealand said that the retaliatory action had been justified under the circumstances; the Malaysian government gave its full support; and Lester Pearson said that the United States was entitled to defend itself against unprovoked attacks, without debating the issue of whether the attacks were really unprovoked or not.[6]

Rusk could well feel gratified at the general response. He hastened to tell Butler "how much we have appreciated the splendid support you gave us in the Gulf of Tonkin affair. Your Government's prompt and forthright statements to the press and the position you have taken in the Security Council have been of great help to us and we very much appreciate it."[7] United States Ambassador David Bruce commented later that the British response might not have been so forthright if it had not been so prompt, as HMG were not really fully informed about the circumstances of the Tonkin Gulf affair at the time when Jackley and Butler expressed their support for the United States action.[8] Nor indeed was congress, when it declared its approval of Johnson's resolve "to take all necessary measures to repel any armed attack against the forces of the United States and ... to take all necessary steps including the use of armed force to assist any member or protocol state" of SEATO.[9] It is however probable that even the fullest briefing on the circumstances of the case would not have altered Paul Hasluck's judgment that there was "no current alternative to using force as necessary to check the southward thrust of militant Asian Communism".[10]

Nevertheless, this welcome verbal support did not presage any increase in allied assistance to South Vietnam itself. Rusk recorded wearily on 14 August that "there has been no great progress since last status report", despite Khanh's appeals to the thirty-four Free World heads of government. The Australians might be offering more medical aid and some scholarships. The Mexicans were thinking about sending military advisers, although nobody knew what kind of military advice the Mexicans had to offer. The Tunisians had agreed in principle to provide symbolic aid, but had not yet decided on the nature of their symbolism. Sweden, the Netherlands, Norway, and Turkey could be counted out as potential providers of anything. The rest were exhibiting "no change".[11] What was even more discouraging, as Undersecretary Hughes pointed out, was that the contributions that had been received were for the most part:

> small-scale grants of economic and technical assistance and represent in most cases a continuation or increase in programs that have been in existence for some time. Most countries have been reluctant to provide military assistance, and where it has been given it has been of a largely token character, such as the training missions from Australia and Great Britain. There has been little evidence of enthusiasm for a more direct involvement, particularly in the form of military aid, and willingness to provide additional assistance has come largely as a response to US urging. Only Nationalist China and, to a lesser extent, South Korea have shown an interest in developing on their own a greater degree of military cooperation with Saigon, including indications of a possible willingness to make available ground forces for use in South Vietnam.

All this, Hughes commented, did not "reflect reaction to the most recent government changes in Saigon", which could only be expected to be wholly negative. Strangely, Hughes did not mention that the department had been concerned actively to discourage any possible military arrangements among South Vietnam, South Korea or Taiwan. But there was no doubt that more desirable indications of regional solidarity were seriously lacking. There was no possibility, Hughes thought, that Burma would extend any assistance. Cambodia's Prince Sihanouk was, in his present frame of mind, "more likely to support North Vietnam than Saigon". Even vehemently pro-Western President Ayub of Pakistan had ruled out any prospect of either military or economic aid. It was highly unlikely that the Japanese would do anything in the military line. Laos was in no position to do anything, even if it were so disposed. Even the Chinese Nationalists preferred "to commit their forces directly against the Chinese Communists", rather than against Vietnamese communists. All sectors of opinion in the Philippines opposed military involvement even to the extent of military advisers, although some thirty-four Philippines Army officers, doctors, nurses, and civic action teams had arrived in South Vietnam. The Thais would not be sending any troops to Vietnam. The Koreans were indeed still talking about sending an expeditionary force of two or more divisions, but they had no contingency plans, lacked skilled cadres and would be dependent on large scale United States assistance. Once again, the only encouraging sign in the whole region was the response of the Australians, who might be giving only token assistance but had at least been immediate and helpful in their response and paid their own bills.[12]

They were also considering doing more. The Australian Chiefs of Staff had already submitted a report to cabinet on "extra aid that could be provided if situation deteriorates further in South Vietnam". They suggested in particular that Australia could send more *Hercules* and *Caribou* transports.[13] Nor was there any doubt that the situation was deteriorating. ARVN losses had amounted to 5,016 killed and 3,663 missing in the first seven months of 1964, nearly double the figure for the whole of 1963. Khanh dismissed his Head of State Duong Van Minh on 16 August, declaring himself president with dictatorial powers. He withdrew his own constitution eleven days later. Nguyen Xuan Oanh was appointed acting premier on 29 August to lead a caretaker government for two months. His first act was to announce that Khanh had suffered a physical and mental breakdown. Khanh responded by firing Oanh on 3 September and bringing Minh back as head of state.

This looked very like the last stages of military and political collapse. Ambassador Taylor nonetheless told a White House press conference that "General Khanh had the backing of the principal elements of the society", and United States MAC Commander General William C. Westmoreland affirmed that there was "a general upward trend" in the military situation, despite the fact that all the indicators were showing a general downward one.[14] Paul Hasluck immediately cabled all Australian representatives overseas that Australian national interests consisted in helping a government in Saigon that would continue to fight the Viet Cong, retaining an active US presence in South Vietnam, and preventing a failure in South Vietnam that would lead to a collapse of will in other countries.[15] The CIA suspected that such a failure might have occurred already, reporting that at present "the odds are against the emergence of a stable government capable of effectively prosecuting the war in South Vietnam". The most they were prepared to concede was that the situation might not be quite hopeless yet;[16] but there was no reason to doubt that it soon would be. Forces loyal to General Lam Van Phat staged a bloodless coup against Khanh on 13 September. They were ousted the same afternoon by forces loyal to Khanh. Then Montagnard tribesmen in the Central Highlands announced their desire to secede, executed seventy ARVN troops, and disarmed their US military advisers most of whom deeply sympathized with the desire of the Montagnards to cut loose from the circus of despair in Saigon. It was a street without joy and a prospect without pleasure.

There were two logical options available to the United States. One suggested by the Joint Chiefs of Staff was to do something sufficiently outrageous to provoke the North Vietnamese into a response severe enough to serve as a pretext for a US bombing offensive of graduated intensity. Undersecretary Ball had a different solution. He told Secretary Rusk that there now seemed little likelihood of establishing in Saigon "a government that can (a) provide a solid center around which the broad support of the Vietnamese people can coalesce or (b) conduct military operations with sufficient effectiveness to clean up the emergency". Moreover, Ball considered, most of the European allies of the United States "would . . . applaud a move on our part to cut our losses and bring about a political solution". Opinion in virtually all European countries would be against "any escalation of the war that might conceivably lead to the involvement of European combat forces on the Asian mainland". NATO Secretary General Brosio, for example, had expressed the view that Italian public opinion "was not sympathetic with the American efforts in Vietnam". Ball had personally observed in Germany a willingness to accept present US policies in Southeast Asia "as a matter of correctness", but Germans in general "would certainly feel deep concern if they ever thought we were becoming involved on the Asian land mass to the point where we might begin to reduce our defense efforts in Europe". Nor could he believe that "any British Government — particularly a Labor Government — would be happy if our air offensive should continue for any length of time against a small Asian country". The French were "already busily promoting rumours that the United States is so involved in Southeast Asia that it can no longer be depended upon to concern itself with Europe". McNamara's argument that South Vietnam was regarded in certain key areas threatened by communism as a test of United States firmness was thus absolutely wrong — at least in Europe, the most significant key area of all. Nothing could reassure Europeans so much as an American disengagement from Vietnam. It also seemed that a majority of Asians would not be unhappy about such a development either.

Ball, however, was not concerned only about reassuring the Europeans. He had become convinced that the situation in Vietnam was intrinsically hopeless. The United States, he argued, could not "substitute its own presence for an effective South Vietnamese Government and maintain a free South Viet-nam over a sustained period of time". The problem was that there was "no effective South Vietnamese Government that can adequately direct the affairs of the country", and "almost every substantive cable from Saigon underlines this point". Moreover, intelligence information disclosed "substantial war-weariness among the South Vietnamese people. This is backed up by a rising curve of desertions and the Government's increasing difficulty in filling the rolls through enlistment." His personal solution was "a localized negotiation between a neutralist South Viet-Nam Government and the National Liberation Front ... The result," he conceded, "might well be an uneasy coalition in which the Communists would presumably be the most aggressive and dominant component. But the full effect of a Communist takeover would be diffused and postponed for a substantial period of time."[17]

Ball's analysis could not have been faulted, as far as it went. It would also be justified by the course of events. But any chance that it might have had of tipping the balance of opinion in Washington was swiftly discounted by a direct challenge to American power by the Viet Cong. Guerillas attacked the US air base at Bien Hoa on the eve of the presidential elections in the United States. Five Americans were killed and six B-57 bombers destroyed. It may or may not have been a response to the American air strikes against North Vietnam in August, but it was the kind of "severe" communist action for which the Joint Chiefs had been hoping. It also demonstrated convincingly that the United States would have to be prepared to commit ground troops if it were not going to disengage, as the ARVN could not be relied upon even to guard US bases. More of the same was no longer a practical option. The Americans had to escalate or escape.

It was not a political option for Johnson, either. He had been returned to the presidency with a spectacular majority of sixty-one per cent of the popular vote, the greatest mandate in the history of the United States. But this resounding endorsement did not reflect general approval of the way in which Johnson had been dealing with Vietnam. Pollster Louis Harris estimated that only forty-two per cent of the American public gave Johnson high marks on that score. Johnson had been given a mandate for change, in one direction or the other. The United States was looking to the White House for clear executive leadership on Vietnam. Johnson was expected either to get out or go in and finish the job.

His military advisers lost no time in making clear what they thought he ought to do. Arguments such as those of Ball, the Joint Chiefs thundered, overlooked the basic reality that "Cambodia, Thailand, possibly Burma and Malaysia would fall almost automatically to Communist domination if South Vietnam goes ... We do not share the views ... as to the potential value of 'reassurances' to others if we lose SVN. There would be no words left that won't have been shown to be hollow, and there would be few deeds left, short of general war, that will be within our capacities." This was not indeed what Ball and others had gathered from the general reactions of allied governments, but the Joint Chiefs saw no reason to be concerned about the reactions of allied governments because they had nothing of significance to contribute. "We had *no* significant support in Korea, other than verbal," they informed the president. "Except for the South Koreans themselves, the U.S. did essentially all the fighting, took all the casualties, and paid all the bills."[18]

This was not strictly accurate, but neither was it really misleading. The United States had actually provided roughly ninety per cent of the total United Nations forces in Korea, and almost exactly ninety per cent of their total combat casualties. Assistance from Turkey and certain Commonwealth countries had been militarily useful and diplomatically highly convenient at the time. It might nonetheless be assumed that the United States would have intervened unilaterally in that particular situation if no third country support had been forthcoming. Korea was not Vietnam, however, and the Joint Chiefs did seem to have overlooked that vital point. Third country support in this instance was significant to the point of being absolutely essential. It was therefore immensely encouraging to the Johnson administration that one at least of the allies was making a real effort to ensure that it would be able to make a significant contribution to US involvement. Australian Prime Minister Menzies introduced a programme on 10 November 1964 providing for a dramatic escalation in defence spending over the next four years. Original plans brought down only two years previously had provided for an outlay on defence spending of $440 million annually up to 1965–66. This had been increased on 23 May 1963 to $539.2 million for 1965–66, $554 million for 1966–67 and $539 million for 1967–68. In 1964 Menzies proposed increasing this again to $740 million in 1965–66, $843.4 million in 1966–67 and $852.2 million in 1967–68. It amounted to raising the level of defence spending from a perfunctory 2.6 per cent of GNP to a very respectable 4.6 per cent. Most of the money would be outlayed on re-equipping Australia's decrepit defence forces. The carrier *Melbourne* would be refitted yet again and furnished with fourteen S2E *Tracker* anti-submarine aircraft. The RAAF was to get twelve C130E *Hercules* transports, as well as ten P3B *Orion* maritime surveillance aircraft. The Australian army would be expanded from 22,750 to 37,500 by the introduction of selective military service. This last measure came as something of a surprise, as Army Minister Alexander J. Forbes had told the Congress of the Returned Sailors', Soldiers' and Airmen's Imperial League of Australia (later known as the Returned Services League) as recently as 26 October that compulsory military training was wasteful and would aggravate the deficiencies rather than alleviate them. But it would help to convince the Americans that Australia would have the capability to make a significant troop commitment overseas if it were required to do so in the future. Menzies made a point in his speech introducing this legislation of stressing that "in the Southwest Pacific, Australia and New Zealand had allies, including Great Britain and the United States, who are rich in power and goodwill. Without them, Australia's task in defending so vast a territory with so few people would be a fearful one."[19] As Noela McKinnon put it, "it was a result of these quite substantial expansions of the Australian armed forces which gave the Australian Government the confidence to propose a more substantial commitment in Vietnam. This concrete fulfilment of Australia's 'alliance' obligations was hoped would ensure continued U.S. presence in the area."[20]

Ambassador Waller lost no time in advising Rusk of the Australian military build-up. He explained to the Secretary that the introduction of selective service would mean that Australia "would have one combat-ready division and two divisions on call. He added that legislation had already been secured which permits sending voluntary forces overseas, and he did not think this proposal would run into any great trouble in Parliament." Rusk "expressed his pleasure, and inquired when it would be debated. He was particularly pleased about the combat-ready forces and asked the Ambassador to point out to his government that Australia has an ally in ANZUS and SEATO which maintains conscripted forces in peace and war and keeps 200,000 troops west of Honolulu where they are taking casualties every week in Vietnam ... The Secretary promised to forward the budget message to the President."[21]

A very satisfactory understanding seemed to have been reached between Washington and Canberra. It became even closer over the next few days. Hasluck and Howson arrived in Washington on 24 November to deliver in person the news that Federal Parliament had approved legislation two days before providing for two years' selective military training for twenty-year-olds. There could be no clearer assurance of the intention of the Australian government to commit ground troops to Vietnam if the United States were to take that step. This was in itself the strongest encouragement that the hawks in Washington could have received; but the Australians were prepared to do more than that. Howson raised with US Air Force General Curtis LeMay "the subject of greater defensive action in South Vietnam, with possible further operations against the North Vietnamese". He "found a ready ear" in LeMay, who gave the Australian party to understand that "anything we can do to help push the hard line at the present time will be well received, certainly by the USAF". Air Force Secretary Eugene M. Zuckert similarly asked Howson at lunch "to open up the question of Vietnam, to again push the hard line".[22] The Australians were equal to the task. No harder line could ever have been pushed than that deployed by Hasluck in a press conference on 25 November. "The rising power of China," he argued, was "the most significant factor in the long-term problem of world peace." Vietnam represented "an active struggle against the southward spread of Communist dominance in Asia. Here," he proclaimed, "is an immediate need to maintain the independence of new nations." Australia was "closely concerned in what steps are to be taken next to ensure success and what will be expected of us." Australia's new defence programme "provides further proof to our neighbors of South-East Asia of our deep, unswerving commitment to the fight for peace in the area".[23]

These Australian démarches might not have been decisive but they were undeniably perfectly timed. Opinion had been strengthening in Washington in favour of the hard line ever since the election. Ambassador Taylor confessed later that in fact it had never "occurred to me to recommend withdrawal. There were too many good reasons for not thinking about retreat. In the first place, we had not exhausted our alternatives or made inroads into our vast resources. We could still try a number of things which might supply the new ingredient we were seeking to reverse the adverse trend."[24] His views in this regard were shared by the Joint Chiefs, by Defense Secretary McNamara, by Rusk, and most importantly by Johnson himself. It was, however, only the Joint Chiefs who seemed to have no inhibitions about significantly escalating the level of military involvement unilaterally. Johnson himself had emphasized to Kennedy the absolute necessity of securing the participation of appropriate regional countries in such an operation. Unilateral commitment of United States ground forces in a conflict not manifestly involving American security would be the most desperate political decision a US administration could very well make, short of actually initiating nuclear war. The Australians had ensured that such a decision would not have to be made. The regional country whose active support was most welcome on every ground was not only advocating escalation by the United States in the most forthright terms, but was evidently preparing itself to contribute actively to such escalation. It was the most positive encouragement at the most critical time from the most welcome source. Australia's credentials as a partner in war in Vietnam were outstanding. It was diplomatically expedient to keep the Taiwanese out, troublesome complications could be envisaged with the Koreans, nobody could be certain what the Philippines might actually do, and the Thais had a venerable tradition of cautious diplomacy which ensured that they would not be first in the line for any potentially hazardous enterprise. Anyway, they would all be expecting to be paid for whatever they did. There were no problems with the Australians and there would be no expenses. They were a free country and they would be paying their own way. Nobody could ask for more.

Planning in Washington proceeded at an accelerated pace in the wake of the visit by Hasluck and Howson. Any inhibitions resulting from misgivings about unilateral intervention no longer applied. William P. Bundy produced a draft discussion paper on 27 November outlining a programme of flexible response in Vietnam. Phase 1 would involve reprisals against North Vietnam for "spectacular" Viet Cong operations in South Vietnam as well as strikes against "infiltration-associated" targets in Laos. Phase 2 would come into operation thirty days or so later, and would involve low-level reconnaissance in southern North Vietnam and strikes against "infiltration-associated" targets in North Vietnam in a programme of graduated military pressure, starting south of the nineteenth parallel and working north. It could encompass measures such as air strikes on all military related targets in North Vietnam, aerial mining of North Vietnamese ports and a naval blockade of the country.[25] Details were to be released to the outside world on a highly selective basis. Thailand should be "asked to support our program fully, to intensify its own efforts in the north and northeast and to give further support to operations in Laos, such as additional pilots and possibly artillery teams". There would be immediate and full consultation with the United Kingdom, Australia, New Zealand, and the Philippines, which were designated as "key allies". Johnson was to explain in particular the concept and proposed actions fully to British Prime Minister Harold Wilson, "seeking full British support, but without asking for any additional British contribution in view of the British role in Malaysia". Australia and New Zealand would, however, be "pressed, through their Ambassadors, not only for support but for additional contributions". The Philippines would be "particularly pressed for additional contributions along the lines of the program for approximately 1800 men already submitted to President Macapagal". By contrast, Washington would merely convey "our grave concern to key interested governments such as Canada, India and France but avoid spelling out the concept fully".[26] There was a very clear and thoroughly pragmatic distinction being made as to how much should be told to what governments and what measures of support could be hoped for from whom. Australia, and secondarily New Zealand, were in the highest category of those to whom most would be told and from whom most would be expected.

Defense Secretary McNamara informed Hasluck immediately that "if it was necessary to apply increased pressure on North Vietnam by way of air attacks, for example, it would be very helpful for the United States to have Australian aircraft either participating in these attacks or standing by to protect Thailand, Laos and South Vietnam against expected counter attacks ... it might be very helpful to have Australian *Sabres* available". Rusk spoke in similar terms, although he stressed that "the United States would be looking chiefly for a public demonstration of Australian support".[27] William P. Bundy depicted the situation comprehensively to Ambassador Waller, New Zealand Ambassador George Laking and British Labour Foreign Secretary Michael Stewart on 3 December. He told them that Washington was "deeply concerned about fragility internal GVN situation ... situation is still slowly deteriorating on the military side although little likelihood really major VC military successes at least in next two months or so". He suggested that any further dramatic increase in VC activity might be opposed by air strikes and the stationing of surface-to-air missile launchers guarded by a division-sized deployment of US Marines near the border with North Vietnam. Such a force, he added, "would be much more effective if it included at least small units from GOA and GNZ [Government of New Zealand]. In the meantime, Bundy suggested that "UK increase numbers of police advisers. Australia consider 200-man augmentation combat advisers, and GNZ likewise seek to increase its contribution markedly. Indicated President had deep personal concern this aspect, would discuss this with Wilson, and would send personal messages to Menzies and Holyoake early next week."[28]

Johnson and his advisers were not counting on getting anything very substantial from the British. They had in fact been considering just the previous day the prospect of having to increase United States assistance to enable the United Kingdom to cope with its own international commitments. Prime Minister Wilson told his cabinet colleagues after his return from Washington that "it was quite untrue that a pistol had been put to his head on Vietnam", although he admitted that Johnson had actually "asked him outright for a military commitment". As Wilson himself told the story for public consumption some years later, Johnson had "raised the question, without excessive enthusiasm, of our cooperating with him in South Vietnam, even if only on a limited — even a token — basis. I made it clear that we could not enter into any such commitments. We were co-chairman of the Geneva Conference, under the Agreements of 1954 and 1962, and would have a role to play in seeking a way to peace. But I stressed the fact also, which seemed new to him, that we had as many as 54,000 troops in Malaysia." Johnson, according to Wilson, was so impressed by this figure that he "virtually promised us all aid short of war" in Malaysia. He also told the British Prime Minister how much he appreciated "the help which we had given him in the election and all that Harold Wilson's speeches had meant for him". One of Harold Wilson's cabinet colleagues "found this extremely funny", but feared that "the humour was entirely unconscious".

Wilson may indeed have missed a number of the more subtle elements in the situation. His figures of British involvement in Malaysia, for example, did not really come as a surprise to Johnson, because the CIA had provided the president with full details on this aspect the day before; and the Americans had never asked seriously for British troops in Vietnam because they knew that Wilson "couldn't possibly have done it". On the other hand, the British Prime Minister had offered Johnson "our jungle training team in Malaya and also our teams for anti-subversive activities", despite the constraints of the Geneva Accords.[29] McGeorge Bundy, who did indeed find the British Prime Minister unconsciously quite amusing at times, noted that Wilson seemed concerned "to suggest a trifle more agreement than there actually was" in his exchanges with the president, but thought that on the whole it was "better for him to err in this direction, and there is no real harm in it".[30]

It was well worth humouring Harold Wilson to keep even the most miniscule British presence in Vietnam. Rusk summed up the achievements of the more flags campaign to date. Fifteen countries were providing aid in some form or another and ten more had promised to. There was a total of 584 Free World personnel in Vietnam, not counting the Americans or for that matter the French, who had 482 people mainly engaged in education and medicine. Chief contributors among those counted were the Australians, who had supplied 80 combat advisers, 6 aircraft with their attendant crews, an 8-man agricultural team and 3 agricultural experts — amounting to 167 in all.

Two Australian combat advisers had been killed already, and another wounded, to give added significance to their contribution. Moreover, there were good hopes, the Secretary considered, that "Australia can be persuaded to make a significant increase in her contribution to Viet-Nam". Next in size as contributors came the Koreans, with a mobile army surgical hospital and 10 taekwando instructors — amounting to 140 in all. The Koreans were also "not only willing to send military help to Viet-Nam, but are even anxious to do so, provided we pay the bill". The problem as Rusk saw it at the time was, remarkably, "finding useful things for them to do. The language difficulty makes them virtually useless as combat advisers ... There is also the problem of Asian 'face'. The Vietnamese have not responded well to advice or direction from other Asians."

It was the Vietnamese themselves, however, who had been making approaches to the Koreans, the Taiwanese, the Filipinos, and the Malaysians over the past ten years. They might not have responded well to advice or direction from other Asians but they had no problems about asking for it. In fact, no problems of face had arisen with the Taiwanese, who had provided the third largest contingent after the United States and Australia, comprising eighty-five experts in the fields of agriculture, electricity power supply and psychological warfare. They would, according to White House Specialist on Vietnam Michael V. Forrestal, "undoubtedly be prepared to do more, including the sending of combat advisers". But Forrestal could see very practical reasons for limiting the scope of Taiwanese involvement. It would be undesirable, he told President Johnson, to "introduce into the struggle in Viet-Nam any element of the Chinese Civil War. Neither did we wish to encourage Chiang K'ai-shek's propensity for engaging us further in his efforts to hit at the Mainland. There is also the political fact that the Chinese are not popular in South Vietnam, and except in the case of Father Hoa's efforts in the Ca Mau Peninsula, our people in Saigon do not believe they would be useful as combat advisers." It was however proposed to ask Taiwan to send more noncombatant assistance.

None of these objections seemed to apply to help from the Philippines, who had unfortunately been as reluctant to deliver as they had been enthusiastic to offer. They had only sent thirty-four people, principally engaged in medicine and psychological warfare. Forrestal reflected that both Macapagal and the opposition "talk big about aid to Viet-Nam", but "boggle when it comes down to actually sending military forces abroad for the first time since the Korean War". Manila would however be pressed for the early dispatch of an eighteen hundred-man task force, "which will include fighting security forces as well as engineers and a military medical unit". This unit, Forrestal advised, "has been developed as a result of conversations between a U.S. team from Saigon and the Philippines military. It will be a real help if we can get it." As to the chances of actually getting it, he thought that if "we not only pay for all Philippine contributions, but also increase our MAP [Military Assistance Program] grant assistance, the best guess is that we should be able to get the task force out, but not rapidly".

Among the rest, the New Zealanders, it was noted, had been distinctly less forthcoming than the Australians, presumably because New Zealand was "also involved in Malaysia, and has a rather small military establishment (7,000) ... We believe," Forrestal concluded, "it will be difficult to get additional help from New Zealand, but some can be expected." Similarly, "a strong approach to the British ... might produce a relatively small amount of additional economic non-military assistance, but the chances of getting much more are not good". Equally, there was virtually no possibility of getting anything at all from the Canadians, who had only one person in Vietnam and were talking about "withdrawing from the ICC and from their involvement in Southeast Asia altogether. In short, they are in a sour mood. The chances of getting much more help are slim, and we do not propose to him them again." The Europeans in general remained strongly convinced that "the war in South Vietnam does not involve them", and they did not want "to be associated with what they regard as a losing game". It might have been possible to obtain "politically significant but essentially token assistance" from some of the Latin Americans, the best bets being Brazil and Argentina. Japan could be counted on to continue economic assistance but would not contribute military help. India had sent nothing and nobody and was being increasingly intransigent and obstructive in the ICC, but Forrestal nonetheless intended "to probe again to see if some feasible form of token assistance could be provided, basing our argument upon India's current concern with the Chinese expansion". The best hope, he thought incorrectly, lay with those countries "to whom we have given heavy military assistance, and who have, as a result, developed substantial standing armies with particularly useful units such as combat engineering and construction battalions and medical units. Such countries include Turkey, Iran, Greece, as well as the Philippines, Taiwan and Korea. There is no doubt that much more can and will be accomplished."

Forrestal did not know what to make of the Thais. They had up to the end of 1964 contributed only seventeen personnel, mainly associated with aviation. However, they had also made a covert contribution "of great significance" of over three hundred combat troops to assist United States efforts in Laos and were also providing jet transitional training for VNAF fliers. He nonetheless did not "anticipate another approach to Thailand at this time".[31] Indeed, it would have been unlikely to be successful. The Thais were making their own assessments of the situation. These were not in favour of increasing their involvement in Vietnam. Secretary General of SEATO, Konthi Suphamongkhon, told Howson that he was convinced that Thailand could be held with American, Australian and British help, even if Vietnam were to go. Australian Ambassador Alan Loomes gathered that the Thais did "not expect the situation to deteriorate a great deal further in Vietnam, and therefore they are not prepared to make any further preparations for greater defence by foreign services in Thailand itself". They were, he thought, "a proud people who do not like to seem to be begging for aid", although Suphamongkhon had certainly given Howson the impression that they both expected aid and would welcome it. They also seemed to be developing an interest in multilateral aid to Vietnam, contrary to previous indications. Foreign Minister Thanat Khoman suggested in the United Nations on 9 December that a combined force of regional nations should be created to assist the United States in Vietnam. South Vietnamese Foreign Minister Kam Dang Lang immediately asked Howson for an indication of Australia's attitude toward such a proposition. Howson thought that "if the aid was brought into Vietnam in the same way that we were bringing in aid — that was, in an advisory capacity — then well and good, but if it was in the nature of a third force of its own, then we had some reservations". Such a proposition would indeed have been contrary to every perceived Australian interest. Australia was only in Vietnam incidentally to support South Vietnam. It was there to earn credit in Washington by its support of the United States. This meant that the unavoidably minute Australian contribution had to be kept identifiable and distinct. Its whole desired impact would be lost if it were to become merged in a general regional effort.

Howson was finding the whole issue of requests for Australian aid rather confusing. Vietnamese Prime Minister Tran Van Huong asked in December 1964 for "an increase in direct Australian aid by the army and by the air force", adding that "the Americans . . . felt lonely and hesitant in their present position and needed stiffening by the support of nations like Australia". This seemed very probable, and Australian Ambassador Anderson suggested to Howson that Huong's request had been inspired by the United States in the first place. However, the US embassy in Saigon hastened to assure Anderson that "without excluding possibility situation could in future develop so that Australian forces would be required in defense of SEA, we did not now foresee the need for combat forces in South Vietnam for counterinsurgency purposes nor were we thinking in terms of unified command in Korean pattern. However, additional third country aid was in fact much needed and there were many opportunities in both military and economic fields." They emphasized in this connection the desirability of "Australian [sic] taking over full responsibility for some major projects in economic field". Taylor's own comment to Rusk on the episode was that "although to a degree undoubtedly reflecting some of his own attitudes, Huong's remarks on combat forces and USG [United States Government] attitudes should not be taken too seriously at this time. In making a strong pitch on additional Third Country aid accordance our previous conversation with him, he was obviously pulling out all the stops."[32]

It was about all that Huong could have done under the circumstances. It was impossible to be specific or even coherent about soliciting foreign aid as long as Washington continued to behave as if military action by air and sea was not combat, but military action on the ground would be. It might be a convenient fiction from a political viewpoint but it was not helpful to clear thinking and planning. For example, a decision was taken in Washington on 11 December "on highest authority . . . to exert all feasible pressures for increased third country representation in Vietnam", presaging "early formulation of third country assistance including military forces tailored to provide help in non-combat role". A staff meeting was held on 14 December to discuss the employment of Philippines forces in this way. Confusion understandably arose immediately. President Macapagal insisted that he wanted to send only genuine combat forces. Opposition leader Ferdinand Marcos insisted that he did not want to send any forces at all. It was finally agreed that a task force of 2,480 should be deployed, comprising a reinforced infantry battalion, a reinforced engineer battalion, civic action personnel, a navy contingent, and an air force contingent.³³

One could hardly agree to send units of all armed services into a civil war situation unless one were prepared to accept the possibility that they might have to do some fighting, if only to defend themselves. Similar problems were arising with other regional countries. An approach had been made at the same time to the Koreans for military forces in a non-combat role. President Park responded immediately that he was ready to provide two combat divisions any time that the United States was prepared to pay for them. The American ambassador in Seoul was instructed to tell him that combat troops were not needed. However, the Vietnamese then leaked reports to the press that Ambassador Taylor had called on Foreign Minister Lang to request the Koreans to send combat engineering troops to Vietnam. "The cat," US Ambassador to Taiwan Jerauld Wright reflected, "was really out of the bag."³⁴ It was not merely that this was the first press reference to the current campaign to solicit Free World military participation in Vietnam. What was even more troublesome, according to US Ambassador in Korea Winthrop G. Brown, was "the implication that it is the U.S. and not the GVN which is requesting the help".³⁵

This would of course be a continuing problem. Its prime cause was the continuing failure of the South Vietnamese to determine what kind of aid they actually wanted, let alone who they wanted to get it from. But it was not only the Vietnamese who did not seem to be tackling the aid issue with the appropriate professionalism. President Johnson asked Prime Minister Menzies directly to supply two hundred additional combat advisers, minesweepers, tank landing craft, salvage and repair ships, and hospital ships. Menzies had to reply that Australia had no landing ships, repair ships or hospital ships; that its six available minesweepers were already on duty in Malaysian waters; and that its combat instructors were all required at home to train the new draftees being inducted under the National Service legislation that the Americans were so pleased about.

It was disturbing enough that policymakers and advisers at the highest level in Washington did not seem to know what the ally of the United States making the largest and most enthusiastic contribution in Vietnam actually had to offer. What was even more worrying was the implication that the Americans had not clearly thought through what they and their allies were supposed to do next. Menzies accordingly suggested to Johnson that he send representatives "to discuss the possible positioning of United States, Australian and New Zealand troops in the northern parts of South Vietnam". Hasluck meanwhile assured Ambassador Waller that the inability of the Menzies government to respond positively to Johnson's appeal did not mean that Australia was in any way qualifying its support for the American effort in South Vietnam, but that it was "important to know how far the United States were prepared to go and what would be the outcome of escalation and/or negotiation".[36]

Decision, direction and coordination were manifestly highly desirable in the circumstances existing at the end of 1964; but it was the Vietnamese themselves, both North and South, who finally brought things to what Menzies called the point of action. Khanh had abruptly dismissed the High National Council on 20 December, arresting a number of politicians who had failed to endorse his programme to defeat corruption and abuse of privilege by firing all generals who had served more than twenty years. Ambassador Taylor suggested in exasperation that maybe Khanh himself should be included among those who had outlived their usefulness. Khanh responded to Taylor's lack of support with an Order of the Day on 22 December rejecting in advance any more aid that the United States might be inclined to supply. It was better, he proclaimed, to live poor but proud as free citizens of an independent country rather than in ease and shame as slaves of the foreigners or the communists. Taylor's own conduct, he declared, "was beyond imagining as far as an Ambassador is concerned"; but Taylor was prepared to go further still in the exercise of what he saw as his responsibilities. He furiously confronted Nguyen Cao Ky, Nguyen Van Thieu, Nguyen Chanh Thi, and Admiral Cang on 24 December. "I told you all clearly at General Westmoreland's dinner," he reminded them, after asking if they could understand English as they did not seem to have comprehended his French, "we Americans were tired of coups . . . I made it clear that all the military plans which I know you would like to carry out are dependent on government stability. Now you have made a real mess. We cannot carry you forever if you do things like this . . . this is a military coup that has destroyed the government-making process that, to the admiration of the whole world, was set up last fall through the statesman-like acts of the Armed Forces . . . I have real troubles on the U.S. side," he warned. "I don't know whether we will continue to support you after this. Why don't you tell your friends before you act? . . . You people have broken a lot of dishes," he concluded, taking what he described as a friendly leave, "and now we have to see how we can straighten out this mess."[37]

Ambassador Taylor's concern was thoroughly justified. It was also beside the point. What the South Vietnamese might or might not do would never be the deciding factor. The ARVN generals and the Saigon politicians could always be counted on to provide excellent reasons for the United States to wind down its involvement as quickly as possible. The Viet Cong and the North Vietnamese could equally be counted on to provide even more compelling reasons to build it up. A bomb blast outside Brink's Hotel in the capital killed 2 Americans and injured another 52, as well as 13 Vietnamese. It was the signal for a devastating offensive by the VC that shattered any remaining illusions of ARVN defensive capability. The VC seized Binh Gia on the coast, 67 miles west of Saigon, and held it until 1 January 1965. They then withdrew at leisure, after ambushing and crushing repeated ARVN counterattacks, killing 177 South Vietnamese and 6 US advisers at a trifling cost to themselves. It meant, General Westmoreland reported, "The beginning of an intensive military challenge which the Vietnamese government could not meet within its own resources". "All the reserve — the strategic reserve — was fixed:" US Marine Brigadier Carl Youngsdale assessed the situation, "the airborne and the four Marine battalions had all been committed. There was absolutely no strategic reserve left."[38] Washington could no longer evade the choice between disengagement and massive intervention. It was the strategic moment for Australia to help push the hard line.

5

We Must Pursue the Tough Line (1965)

Hasluck was relaxing at his home in Perth when he received the news of Binh Gia. He immediately telexed Acting Permanent Head of External Affairs Sir Patrick Shaw to tell him that both he and Defence Minister Shane Paltridge were "gravely concerned at outlook and the necessity of taking whatever steps we can to advance Austrlaia's vital interest in securing success in South Vietnam and not merely hanging on until the eventually steady erosion brings disaster".[1] Renouf had acted already, however. He had gone at once to see William P. Bundy, who confided to him that "the situation in Vietnam is now likely to come apart more rapidly than we had anticipated in November", and that the introduction of limited US ground forces into the northern area of South Vietnam accordingly "still has great appeal to many of us". Renouf "clearly indicated . . . that [Australia] might be disposed to participate in such an operation. The New Zealanders," however, were "more negative and a proposal for Philippine participation would be an interesting test."[2]

It was by no means clear that even the attack on Binh Gia and Renouf's indication of Australia's readiness to join with the United States in sending in ground troops would be enough to enable the hawks to carry the day in Washington. The major problem was still Johnson himself. Air Vice Marshal Sir Valston Hancock complained to Howson that the president was "probably moving slower than both Pentagon and State Department would wish". There was some indication "that USA will step up activity in North Vietnam, but . . . this will be done in slow stages and could take some months to build up".[3] Waller for his part was in despair over American reluctance to take decisive action. He was convinced that the situation in South Vietnam now "left you with a position in which unless direct military assistance was made available, the whole thing might collapse".[4] United States policy, however, "was once again in the doldrums, nor was it expected that mounting military pressure upon North Vietnam would be decided upon even after the American elections. Apparently the President preferred that the United States should 'muddle along' in South Vietnam trying to do better with policies which had not succeeded in the past."[5]

Johnson and his advisers had in fact been moving closer to a decision for direct military intervention since Renouf's conversation with William P. Bundy. But even the most resolute of United States hawks recognized an inherent problem in South Vietnam itself which never deterred the Australians. Ambassador Taylor recommended that the United States "look for an occasion to begin air operations", but only after "we have satisfactorily compromised the current political situation in Saigon . . . The rock-bottom criterion," he considered, was "for a government to exist and to have the strength of voice able to ask for U.S. help."[6] Washington could not sensibly intervene in support of anarchy. There had to be a minimal factor of credibility in Saigon. The problem was that no credible government was likely to emerge in Saigon unless the United States were to intervene to create the conditions in which it could emerge. One could also ask if any Vietnamese regime could have credibility if it could emerge only in conditions created by foreign intervention.

These complications do not seem to have concerned the Menzies government and its advisers. It is no doubt true that, as Carolyn O'Brien commented, "due to its regional perspective, Australia constantly overlooked America's global objectives and commitments".[7] It is also true that the Australian government was simply not concerned with Vietnamese domestic problems, any more than with United States domestic problems. What it was concerned with was committing the United States to the Asian mainland north of the Australian continent. Vietnam was the obvious place for such an American commitment and it was highly disturbing that the Americans should continue to dither on the brink while South Vietnam became ever less viable as a defensive position. Australian military advisers warned cabinet on 13 January 1965 that "the prospects of victory had become remote. They were convinced that without strong and stable leadership or without the introduction of a new factor such as counteraction by the United States or other nations the situation would deteriorate further." Cabinet decided on 15 January that Australia should be "forthcoming with the Americans" and should "encourage the United States to plan for Phase 2 ... Australia's willingness to take part in military talks was once more expressed".[8]

Australia had never been less than forthcoming with the Americans as far as verbal support was concerned, but Australia's physical inability to provide tangible assistance of the kind that the Americans actually wanted continued to prove an embarrassment. United States Ambassador in Saigon U. Alexis Johnson told Anderson that "highest priority need as for up to 200 additional Australian combat advisers who could be employed at sub-sector level advising combat units of regional and popular forces". Anderson was however compelled to remind Johnson that "recent passage of peacetime conscription legislation meant that almost all available Australian officers and experienced non-coms would be needed for training Australians. He agreed, however, to transmit the requirement and see what he could get." What this might be was perhaps indicated by the fact that Anderson then started talking about projects for water supply, hospitals and even "development of port complexes for major cities" as "symbol of Australian commitment to and confidence in outcome in Vietnam".[9]

This was not what the Americans really meant by showing a flag in Vietnam; and it was certainly not what the Australians hoped the Americans would be doing there. Menzies and Hasluck decided to increase verbal encouragement for American involvement in the absence of a more practical Australian effort. They resolved on 17 January to promise "full public and diplomatic support for the United States if that country decided upon increased military activity". Renouf, however, was concerned that the Americans might not decide on increased military activity. They were, he reported, "worried over Saigon's political stability". Military staff talks with Australia "would be relevant if the situation improved". Hasluck thought that they might be even more relevant if the situation did not improve. He warned Waller urgently on 19 January of "Australia's grave concern at the outlook and instructed that he should take advantage of any opportunity to bring certainty to American policy and planning". "Certainty" in this context meant a resolve to escalate the conflict to a level sufficient to avert a communist victory. Waller was of course "to be tactful because of the disproportion in power between Australia and the United States, but he was to suggest that Australia would give full public and diplomatic support if the United States were to initiate air strikes against North Vietnam's system. He was informed that the Government did not belive that the Viet Cong threat was negotiable."[10]

Canberra was hardly in a position to comment on whether the issue was negotiable or not. It would certainly be in Australia's interest if it were not negotiable, as this would more likely ensure an American military presence indefinitely to the north. Waller in any case was careful to assure Assistant Secretary of State Leonard Unger on 19 January that "he and his government did not of course mean to be suggesting what the United States should be doing, knowing that we bore the full burden of the problem". Unger nonetheless asked Waller exactly what the Australian government did think Washington ought to be doing in Vietnam, seeing that it apparently did not think it was doing enough. He pointed out that there could be no possibility of a follow-up on any of the programmes adopted "without some stability in Saigon and some knowledge that there would be at least a minimum of cooperation among the important groups involved". That, he explained, was why the United States had felt compelled to delay taking decisive action. Waller asked if Washington was going to insist upon a civilian government in Saigon. Unger told him that it was not the form of the government that mattered but rather that "the Vietnamese themselves must arrive at some formula which assures at least that the country is governed and that there is someone with whom we can work and follow through on decisions". Waller then enquired if there would be consideration of proceeding with Phase 2 once Washington was satisfied with the form of government in Saigon. He also wondered about the use of ground forces. Unger said that he was "unable to talk about decisions in this field". They concluded with "a further exchange on the question of what makes the Vietnamese behave as they do".[11]

It had not been a very satisfactory exchange from Waller's point of view. His meeting with William P. Bundy was even less so. Bundy had just received Ambassador Johnson's account of his own unsatisfactory exchange with Australian Ambassador Anderson over the issue of more Australian combat advisers for Vietnam. Bundy cut short Waller's enquiries of the possibilities of more effective American action by asking why Australia could not provide even another thirty instructors if it was so concerned about what was happening in

Vietnam. He ended the conversation by telling Waller flatly that there could be no escalation in Vietnam without political stability.

Waller could only cable back to Hasluck that "Australia must keep up the pressure" on the Americans to take action which they seemed still to find compelling reasons for not taking. Any idea of waiting for political stability to emerge in Saigon, however, became less promising when five thousand students sacked the United States Information Service library in Hue on 23 January, demanding the recall of Ambassador Taylor and denouncing Premier Huong as Taylor's lackey. Khanh threw out Huong's government on 27 January, declaring that it had proved itself "unable to cope with the present critical situation". Khanh himself was naturally appointed to cope with it. Confronted with yet another coup, McGeorge Bundy told Johnson that he and McNamara were "pretty well convinced that our current policy can lead only to disastrous defeat . . . The Vietnamese know just as we do that the Viet Cong are gaining in the countryside. Meanwhile, they see the enormous power of the United States being withheld, and they get little sense of firm and active U.S. policy. They feel that we are unwilling to take serious risks. In one sense, all of this is outrageous, in the light of all that we have done and all that we are ready to do if they will only pull up their socks. But it is a fact." They considered that the only alternatives were either to "use our military power in the Far East and to force a change of Communist policy" or to "deploy all our resources along a track of negotiation, aimed at salvaging what little can be preserved with no major addition to our present military risk". They favoured the first course. However, they warned the president that both alternatives should be examined very carefully and admitted that Secretary Rusk did not like either of them on the grounds that "the consequences of both escalation and withdrawal are so bad that we simply must find a way of making our present policy work. This would be good if it were possible. Bob and I do not think it is."[12]

Australia was meanwhile doing what it could to keep up the pressure, as Waller had suggested. Hasluck cabled Menzies, who was in London at the tiem, as he often tended to be, that Australia "should be concerned to sustain the Americans in their commitment to Vietnam while Australia was doing its share in Malaysia".[13] Defence Minister Paltridge announced in Saigon that a further seventeen Australian combat advisers would be sent, raising the total in Vietnam to one hundred.[14] Hasluck then received another cable from Waller, urging "that we make clear to the Americans our willingness to consider committing combat troops to South Vietnam should they deem it desirable and should circumstances permit it", as it was necessary for Australia to do all in its power to strengthen an American resolve to follow a firm line based on a credible deterrent against North Vietnam.[15] The minister did not hesitate. White House Specialist on Vietnam Michael V. Forrestal was visiting Canberra. Hasluck told him that it would be possible for Australia to send a combat battalion and an SAS (Special Air Service) squadron to Vietnam, if the Americans were planning to commit ground troops themselves. His offer could not have been better timed.

In the first place, the Koreans had finally managed to assemble exactly the kind of force with non-combat functions but combat capacity that the Americans had been vainly seeking from their Asian partners. It comprised an army engineer company, an army transport company, an LST (Landing Ship [Tank]) with crew, a security battalion, a service unit, a liaison group, and a mobile hospital, numbering a massive 2,416 in all, or about 15 times the total number of Australians presently in Vietnam. Australian capacity to influence United States policy had hitherto been supported by the fact that Australia had not only been first in the field, but had also maintained the largest "Free World" contingent in Vietnam, apart from the Americans, and of course the French whom Washington excluded from its calculations. Canberra would have to increase the numbers or effectiveness of its contribution massively if it were to maintain its high profile with the Americans in the face of this challenge from Seoul. It could do this only if the United States were to pursue the option of committing combat troops. This option was virtually guaranteed when Ambassador Taylor withdrew what had been his major reservation about escalation. He told President Johnson on 2 February that "we would probably never have in the foreseeable months a stable government [in Saigon] as we use the term in the U.S. and Europe".[16] One could only hope for a government which had the support of the armed forces; and that they had already. There was nothing more to hope for, so there was nothing left to wait for.

This did not mean that the president and his advisers were ready to send in ground troops. McGeorge Bundy set to work drafting a memorandum advocating "the development and execution of a policy of sustained reprisal against North Vietnam — a policy in which air and naval action against the North is justified by and related to the whole Viet Cong campaign of violence and terror in the South". Bundy was not claiming that this would be enough. He insisted that he could not "estimate the odds of success with any accuracy — they may be somewhere between 25% and 75%".[17] The hawks in Washington, however, did not have only the Australians to count on for support. There was always the Viet Cong, who frequently seemed miraculously astray in either their sense of timing or their comprehension of American psychology. Nine United States personnel were killed and another seventy-six wounded in a major VC attack on the American advisory compound and airstrip near Pleiku on the same day. Johnson's response was gratifyingly uncomplicated. "I want three things," he told his advisers. "I want a joint attack. I want it to be prompt. I want it to be appropriate."

Appropriateness in such matters is necessarily a matter of opinion. Joint and prompt the American response undeniably was. Twenty-nine navy bombers from the carriers *Ranger*, *Hancock* and *Coral Sea* were strafing VC training and concentration areas around Dong Hoi within twelve hours of the attack on Pleiku. The following day, VNAF aircraft raided Vinh and Chap Le, led by Air Vice Marshal Ky in black jumpsuit, with violet scarf and white helmet streaked with orange. Paul Hasluck declared that the method of the response was "fitting and the targets were appropriate ... The aggressor," he explained, "holds the answer. He either has to stop or be stopped."[18] British Labour Foreign Secretary Michael Stewart also justified the attacks in the House of Commons on the grounds that the situation in Vietnam had been dangerous for some time and that the American response had not made it any more so. This view was contested by the government of India which observed that "in Viet Nam one thing has led to another", and that therefore "as a first step there should be an immediate suspension of all provocative action ... by all sides involved in the Vietnam situation", so as to assist in "the creation of the necessary atmosphere which would enable a Geneva-type conference to be held with the least possible delay".[19]

Canberra naturally had different views. Defence Minister Paltridge assured Governor Averill Harriman on 9 February that his government was still ready to participate in any staff talks on the implementation of Phase 2. He also suggested to William P. Bundy the possibility of mounting a SEATO operation in Vietnam, but Bundy never seemed responsive to Australian suggestions. He told Paltridge that a SEATO operation could be mounted only if Saigon were to ask for it, and that it would not be a very good idea anyway, in view of the likely reactions of some of the treaty partners. Waller was nonetheless delighted with "the new spirit of urgency and robustness in the United States Administration and believed the beginning of Phase II was close".[20] So it was, and it was the VC who were acting infallibly to bring it closer.

An ARVN battalion was ambushed and massacred by the VC north of Qui Nhon on 10 February. It was the greatest single ARVN defeat of the war so far. Some three hundred were killed and a similar number wounded. A supporting troop of armoured infantry escaped, which is not the normal role of supporting armour but helps to explain why the VC were able to gain victories of this kind over a technologically superior enemy. They then launched an attack on a United States enlisted men's hostel in Qui Nhon itself, killing twenty-one American noncombatants, by far the biggest loss of life that the Americans had taken in a single day. Howson concluded that this meant that "USA have decided to implement phase 2 of the Vietnam struggle and to start bombing targets in North Vietnam. It looks as if the whole issue in Vietnam will come to the boil within the next few weeks."[21]

Some other governments hoped that this would not happen. French Prime Minister Pompidou and Foreign Minister Couve de Murville declared that these latest developments "only confirm France's position on this serious question. The French Government considers that the problems of South-East Asia cannot be settled by armed force. Only an international agreement excluding all foreign intervention ... can open the way to internal and external peace in this unfortunate region."[22] British Labour Prime Minister Harold Wilson was terrified that Johnson's forbearance, such as it was, "might falter and that he would give way to the hawks in the Administration and, above all, in the Services", who were expressing a desire to "blast the hell out of" the people responsible for the attack on Qui Nhon. He accordingly rang Johnson on the hot line at 10.30 p.m. Washington time, 3.30 a.m. London time, to suggest that he might fly over and talk about it. Johnson did not think that this would be helpful. He told the British Prime Minister that he had already asked everybody to share the problem of Vietnam with the United States and that they "were willing to share advice but not responsibility ... I won't tell you how to run Malaya," he continued, "and you don't tell us how to run Vietnam ... If you want to help some in Vietnam send us some men and send us some folks to deal with these guerillas. And announce to the press that you are going to help us. Now if you don't feel like doing that, go on with your Malaysian problem." He concluded by suggesting that it would not be a good idea if Wilson were to jump across the Atlantic with his shirt-tails flying every time there was a critical situation.[23]

Wilson's account is consistent with Ambassador Bruce's recollection that Johnson had for some time been expressing the view that "it would be useful if some British troops were engaged in the war in South Viet Nam, and . . . if some British troops were killed it would be helpful to the overall picture because it would possibly induce other members of the . . . Southeast Asia Organization to extend themselves further than they had done".[24] Not even the Americans really thought that Wilson would go that far, but a substantial faction of his own Labour Party were horrified at just how far he apparently was prepared to go in support of United States policy. Education Minister Richard Crossman decided after a cabinet meeting the following day that the rapport between London and Washington was such as to "put us temporarily completely in the hands of the Americans . . . Harold had shown a solid determination to recreate the Anglo-American axis, the special relationship between Britain and America, very much along Bevinite lines . . . Britain is not taking the mediating role in Vietnam which we always demanded in Opposition. Once again we are taking the subsidiary role, the pro-American line."[25]

Wilson was put under much graver pressure by the magnitude of the American military response. More than one hundred navy aircraft stormed over Chanh Hoa on 12 February while USAF and VNAF planes battered Chap Le again. Johnson affirmed that the United States had "no choice now but to clear the decks and make absolutely clear our continued determination to back South Vietnam and its fight to maintain its independence".[26] United Nations Secretary General U Thant protested about "the dangerous possibilities of escalation, because such a situation, if it should once get out of control, would obviously pose the gravest threat to the peace of the world". Military methods, he argued, "have failed to find a solution of the Southeast Asian problem for the last ten years and I do not believe the same methods will bring about a peaceful settlement of the problem . . . only political and diplomatic methods of negotiation and discussion", he considered, "may find a peaceful solution".[27] His views were echoed by the majority opinion of a Special Report from the International Control Commission. The Indian and Polish representatives condemned military action taken by the United States since 7 February, although not similar action taken by the VC, and requested the co-Chairmen "to consider the desirability of issuing an immediate appeal to all concerned with a view to reducing tension and preserving peace in Viet Nam". Canadian representative Blair Seaborn argued ingeniously that the developments since 7 February did not "stem from any essentially new factors in the situation in Viet Nam ... rather they are dramatic manifestations of a continuing instability which has, as its most important cause, the deliberate and persistent policy of aggressive and largely covert policies by North Viet Nam directed against South Viet Nam". He quoted the conclusions of the ICC's Legal Committee in support of this contention. The Poles and Indians united in dismissing these conclusions and Seaborn's own arguments.[28]

U Thant's intervention and that of the ICC made the issue of multilateral support more critical than ever. There was no hope that intervention in Vietnam could have the sanction of the United Nations, as had been the case in Korea. Nor would it be supported by even a majority of the signatories of the Geneva Accords, William P. Bundy set himself once again to tally up what flags might hopefully be shown in Vietnam if the conflict were to escalate. It was a depressingly familiar pattern. Ambassador Bruce had just met with Harold Wilson, who had reiterated that he "would solidly support our policy, but he also expressed deep concern over the statement that 'we do not expect to touch upon readiness for talks or negotiations at this time'. He said that he thought continuance of air action without the prospect of parallel talks or negotiations would have disturbing repercussions in Britain and in many other countries." Bundy accordingly decided that the United Kingdom would have to be listed with India and Canada as countries which were "with us, but wobbly on negotiations". Presumably the impression foremost in the Assistant Secretary's mind was that of wobbliness, as there is no evidence that India had ever been "with" the United States on any issue and least of all on Vietnam. There had been, he reported, "officially, strong public support to date" from the British Labour Government, but this had been accompanied by "private pressures to get a negotiating track started. Press and public generally accept our actions to this point (except for the Left Wing)," but the British had "always put us on notice that substantial military action would create great public opinion pressures on them to take a negotiating initiative. They are also concerned over their relations with the Soviets. We think they would continue to stand firm in public, but we would need extremely close consultation at all stages," even though, "despite some back-bench pressure, we do not believe Wilson would take any negotiating initiative that he had not fully discussed and cleared with us."

Canada was in virtually the same position. Lester Pearson had "supported us to date, indeed quite strongly, but he has privately stated his great interest in proposals for early negotiation ... The Canadian press has been generally favorable, but there is clear concern that the conflict may widen. Past experience with Pearson would suggest that he will be very active in trying to find a diplomatic answer, and not easy to control. He is plainly anxious to have Canada in on negotiations, and he is well aware that he won the Nobel Prize for Suez mediation."

"With us tepidly", according to Bundy, were Japan, Malaysia, Latin America, and the other NATO allies, but their attitudes were hardly to be distinguished from those of the British and Canadians. Prime Minister Sato of Japan had "gone along at least with our actions to date and has expressed understanding of them". However, he too had "expressed himself against taking the war to the North". The Japanese doubted that air strikes would resolve the problem in any event and would also "particularly be concerned about possible Chinese Communist reactions and about the effect of our actions on the Sino-Soviet split". Their concerns on this aspect were, moreover, likely to increase. Among the NATO allies, German Chancellor Erhardt and Italian Prime Minister Aldo Moro had given strong expressions of support, but both the German and the Italian press had indicated doubts as to where United States actions might be tending. The French of course had "made it abundantly clear that they are not with us on this one". Even some of the previously hardline regional countries were apparently having second thoughts. Official reaction had been unreservedly favourable in South Korea, but there was now "an overtone of concern that in an escalating situation Korea itself might be threatened", and there was "always the possibility that some adverse event might shake them". Similarly in Thailand there was "fear that the Communists may now spread the war and there has been one suggestion of diplomatic approaches between the US and the USSR". Prospects of getting a substantial contingent from the Philippines were now "hung up on financial questions, but also because of political uncertainty", since Defence Minister Perlta had "brought negotiations over the proposed 2,300-man Philippine contingent to South Vietnam to a standstill by insisting that the United States provide per diem payments equal to those paid US personnel".

This added up to there being literally only one country in the world that unequivocally supported the United States position, relentlessly pushed the hard line on escalation, dismissed any prospect of negotiation, and was fully prepared to bear itself the human, diplomatic and financial costs of participation. In Australia alone, Bundy recorded with relief and perhaps with wonder, "official reaction has been wholly favorable, and the Australians have been urging us to take stronger action for at least two weeks prior. They are also most anxious to engage in joint planning for the contigency of possible ground force needs in northern South Vietnam ... Press and public reaction have echoed the government reaction. We believe the future reactions will continue to be favorable." This was more than could be assumed in the United States itself. Even New Zealand, where the official reaction, both public and private, was "wholly favorable", was, Bundy considered, "somewhat less firm than Australia as to negotiating possibilities".[29]

Bundy's confidence in Australian support was fully justified. Hasluck assured Secretary Rusk the very next day that "in the immediate situation the only determinant of American action would be the effect such action would have in checking aggression and strengthening morale in Saigon".[30] Howson, noting apprehensively that the United Kingdom might be "getting soft on supporting the USA in Vietnam", concluded that "while there is a crisis to our north we have the protection of UK and USA. But if the crisis is solved, then we could find ourselves defensively naked until our new preparations are complete in 1968–69".[31] It was a new concept of regional defence that saw Australian security as residing in instability to the north, rather than stability. It was a very convincing argument for seeking to dissuade Washington from following the path of negotiation — at least for the next few years — but instability brought its own problems for those anxious that the Americans escalate their involvement. Phase 2 had been planned to commence on 20 February, but Khanh was ousted by a bloodless military coup on 18 February, two days after he had appointed Phan Huy Quat as premier. Khanh regained control on 21 February after another bloodless coup. The Armed Forces Council then demanded that he resign, as it did not seem possible to get rid of him any other way. Khanh obligingly left the country to take up his new duties as Ambassador at Large to the United States and Europe. Quat was then promoted to president in his stead. It was becoming very hard to tell whether anybody ruled in Saigon any more.

A state of complete anarchy in South Vietnam could well make foreign intervention impossible as well as unrewarding. Hasluck consulted urgently with United States Counsellor in Canberra Jack W. Lydman. The minister "expressed some misgivings about internal political situation in Saigon", as indeed he might, although he emphasized that "this did not in any way detract from GOA support for contemplated joint action in Vietnam".[32] The only question was whether the opportunity for joint action might not have passed. There was certainly no time to be lost. The Australian government accordingly agreed officially on 24 February to participate in staff talks on the use of ground forces. It was, however, considered necessary to stress that "this was not an agreement to contribute ground forces, and that further information as to the planned use of forces was required".[33]

Meanwhile the Koreans were on the move. Six hundred men of the incongruously named Dove Unit arrived in Vietnam on 25 February. They were supposed to operate in a noncombatant role but were authorized to fight back if attacked, as long as they did not pursue the enemy outside their designated operational zone.[34] It could be a delicate tactic to operate in practice and the Koreans were not noted for delicate tactics, but the time for equivocations and half-measures was just about over. "Order the Marines to start landing!" the Joint Chiefs directed on 6 March. It was indeed not quite as simple as that. "Do you suppose in Washington they know what time it is in Da Nang?" Marine Brigadier General Frederick J. Karch wondered. "This means a night landing at this point."[35] He got the order delayed until the following morning. USMC (United States Marine Corps) Battalion Landing Team 3/9 splashed ashore on 8 March. Beautiful Vietnamese college girls waited to greet them with flowers. Less beautiful US Army combat advisers who had been taking casualties in Vietnam for five years or more waited opposite the girls to greet them with a banner inscribed "Welcome to the gallant Marines".[36] Some of the leathernecks themselves were wondering exactly what they were supposed to be doing there. "Shee-it," one reflected, "this is a grunt battalion, not a bunch a gate guards."

There would be plenty of work for grunts to do over the next incredible seven years. Their arrival was already sending shock waves around the world. Affluent young Australians on the grand tour demonstrated outside Australia House in London against the latest escalation of a policy their government had done more than any other in the world to encourage. Members of the Young Against Conscription Committee picketed the offices of the Department of Labour and National Service in Melbourne to protest against the drawing of the first ballot for selective military service. Forty-five British Labour MPs signed a motion insiting that Prime Minister Wilson make a far more decisive effort to stop the war in Vietnam.

Wilson was not prepared to go that far yet, although he complained privately that the Americans "were just as obdurate as the Soviets in refusing even to consider the idea of negotiations".[37] Canadian Minister for External Affairs Paul Martin similarly defended with impressive dignity the role of Blair Seaborn in the ICC, and denounced the "determined and longstanding attempt of the Hanoi regime to bring South Viet Nam under its control through the pursuit of aggressive policies", but stressed that the Canadian government intended "to continue using all means at its disposal to see if the prerequisites for negotiation exist, and where possible to help create these requisite conditions".[38] By contrast, Alan Renouf was seeking to inspire the Americans to undertake yet stronger and more hazardous action. Time, he warned White House Assistant for Asian Affairs Chester L. Cooper, "was getting short in Vietnam". Renouf "agreed entirely with our attacks on the North, and with our attitude towards negotiation", namely, that there should not be any. "He felt that our negotiating position had been strengthened during the last several weeks, and that we now had 'many more things to sell': our strikes against the North, our air attacks against the VC in the South, the Marines at Da Nang and, of course, the very substantial U.S. presence through Vietnam". He was also "pleased with the arrival of the South Koreans, and indicated 'the more of this sort of thing the better". He favored a shipping block [sic] of North Vietnam", which Nixon did not dare to impose until 1972, and "could not overemphasize the extent to which Australia supported U.S. policy in this area". He was, moreover, "annoyed with Holyoake of New Zealand", because Holyoake had wanted to have the next ANZUS Meeting in Washington so that he could drop in on the way back from the Commonwealth Prime Ministers' Meeting in London, whereas "Renouf felt that it would be a good thing for Australia if key American officials used the ANZUS session to visit Australia".[39]

There was no real need for Renouf to fear that the New Zealanders might somehow distract American attention from what Australia was doing for the common effort in Vietnam. The CIA reported with gratification that the Australian commitment had now been augmented to 100 combat advisers, a 73-man RAAF unit with 6 *Caribou* transports flying daily missions in support of the Vietnamese, an 8-man surgical team and some civilians. The agency considered this effort "most significant", especially in view of Australia's "heavy military commitments to Malaysia and the pressing need for training cadres for the newly instituted draftee program in Australia". The Koreans now had a "top notch 130-man Mobile Army Surgical Team (MASH)" and 10 military instructors in Taekwando in Vietnam, as well as the first 600 engineers and guards out of a 2,000-man task force. The Philippines had two military medical teams, a 4-man civilian medical team, and a military psychological warfare detachment. Negotiations were still in train for an additional 34-man medical civic action team and a task force of 2,200. The New Zealanders had provided a 25-man army engineer detachment and a 6-man surgical team, as well as training 62 Vietnamese. Thailand had a 17-man military air detachment actually flying operational missions in Vietnam and was also training VNAF jet pilots. Paradoxically, the most valuable aid in strictly military terms may have been that provided by the Malaysians, who had trained some 2,000 Vietnamese officers in counterinsurgency and jungle warfare since 1962 and were conducting month-long courses in police training for groups of 30 to 60 Vietnamese, based on their experience of the Emergency.

Equally paradoxical was the fact that the people who were making by far the most substantial effort in the civic action field were the French, who had some 500 men and women engaged in education and medical services and had expended $111 million in aid so far. However, State Department pointed out that "it must be recognized that French assistance to Viet-Nam is by no means a result of our requests nor our policy goals in Viet-Nam". This meant of course that it was almost the only foreign assistance that was responding to the actual needs of the South Vietnamese themselves, rather than the diplomatic convenience of the United States. Nobody else was indeed doing much in the humanitarian field at all, except the Japanese, who had sent a 6-man medical team and had provided over $55 million of economic assistance. Germany had sent 26 medical personnel with another 9 to come, and had provied $18 million in credits and development loans. The United Kingdom had sent a 7-man mission and provided $2.5 million in aid. They had also been requested to supply "additional assistance primarily in the field of combat advisers", and "now have the matter under serious consideration". Canada had also provided $2.5 million and was training 125 South Vietnamese. Italy had sent a 9-man surgical team, as might the Dutch. That completed the catalogue of the major donors. That of the minor ones might have seemed comical, if anybody in Washington had felt like laughing. Austria had agreed to provide medical supplies, blankets and tents. Ireland had contributed $1,000 through the Red Cross; so had Sweden. Spain was sending some medical supplies. Switzerland was sending microscopes. Pakistan had contributed 35,000 rupees. Brazil would be sending medical supplies. Belgium would be sending an ambassador. India had offered equipment for a sugar refinery and a blood bank. Greece might be sending an army officer but was as yet unsure.

Then there were the complete failures. Argentina had indeed sent two military observers to Vietnam but would not be making any contribution because, as United States Ambassador Martin reported, "the Argentine Foreign Minister is in an uncooperative mood because of our position on the oil issue". Bolivia would not send any aid unless it received additional military assistance which the State Department was resolved it should not receive. Columbia, Ecuador and Peru pleaded internal difficulties. Chile would not do anything unless Ecuador and Peru were to change their minds and decide to do something. Mexico and Panama had flatly refused. Nothing was likely to be forthcoming from Paraguay, Uruguay or Venezuela. Iceland was giving nothing. Neither was Luxembourg. Norway did not want to get involved. Portugal had provided nothing and it was considered that "the possibility of obtaining any participation by Portugal is not likely". Finally, nothing could be expected from any of the African countries except for South Africa, which was not going to be asked.[40]

What this disheartening chronicle did at least show beyond any question was that the "Free World" was still free as far as involvement in Vietnam was concerned at least. Nobody was getting involved there who did not want to get involved for their own reasons. There was no question of leverage. Washington was putting the question and in virtually every case it was not getting the answer it hoped for.

Menzies may have had a point when he spoke of Australia's responsibility to defend the frontiers of those countries characterized by the freedom of the spirit. They were nearly all demonstrating the freedom of their spirit by refusing to get involved in Vietnam.

There could of course hardly be any serious question of the United States applying leverage when the Americans were increasingly losing confidence in the utility or legitimacy of intervention themselves. Even Ambassador Taylor warned Rusk in 1965 that the introduction of a United States Army division into Vietnam not only "obviously increases U.S. involvement in the counterinsurgency, exposes greater forces and invites greater losses", but also would "raise sensitive command questions with our GVN allies and may encourage them to an attitude of 'let the United States do it'. It will increase our vulnerability to Communist propaganda and Third Country criticism as we appear to assume the old French role of alien colonizer and conqueror. Finally, there is considerable doubt that the number of GVN forces which our action would relieve would have any great significance in reducing the manpower gap."[41] Such arguments were clearly pertinent in their own right. They were particularly impressive considering whom they were coming from. However, Taylor's cautions were followed immediately by a proposal by the Joint Chiefs that two US divisions and a Korean division should be sent to Vietnam "for active operations against the VC".[42]

One of the strongest arguments in favour of having a war is that it normally encourages solidarity within one's own ranks, but the Vietnam issue was already creating more and wider divisions within the Western system and within the United States itself. Black civil rights spokesman Martin Luther King, Jr., told demonstrators in Washington that "I don't know if I can approve of black boys being drafted and sent to a war 10,000 miles away, in the interests of the white man's world".[43] British Foreign Secretary Michael Stewart flew across the Atlantic for urgent consultations with Secretary Rusk; but Australian representatives vigorously affirmed at Honolulu Canberra's readiness to increase the size of its operational force in Vietnam. Admiral Sharp expressed his delight to Air Chief Marshal Scherger, assuring him that the Australian task force would be "a welcome addition to Free World forces . . . General Westmoreland is looking forward with pleasure to discussion of planning details with the joint service Australian team".[44] The Australians themselves had been looking forward to a discussion of planning details for some time. One point that needed to be resolved without further delay was the exact nature of the legal obligation under which Australia was so anxious to act in support of the United States. It was recognized that Article IV of the SEATO treaty would have provided a "useful umbrella" for Australian intervention. However, Saigon had never invoked SEATO in respect of the Australian forces because of their hitherto noncombatant role and of "the very small response they represented". State Department was in any case strongly opposed to involving SEATO formally in the Vietnam issue because many of the major signatories were very clearly opposed to intervention in any form. It was accordingly agreed at Honolulu that the British should be given to understand that discussions between Australia and the United States on joint planning were merely "informal talks arising out of ANZUS affairs. No suggestion was made that these crucial talks as a result of which Australian combat troops were committed to Vietnam, were in any way part of a SEATO operation."[45]

Nobody could have believed that they were part of an ANZUS operation, either. United States and Australian armed forces, public vessels or aircraft were not under attack in the Pacific area. In fact, ANZUS was never invoked by anybody. There was no legal obligation for Australia to become involved; and the implications of involvement was becoming more alarming daily. Ambassador Taylor told the media on 22 March that "no limit existed to the potential escalation" of the war in Vietnam.[46] No better reason for disengagement could have been imagined. Then in a miracle of bad timing the United States Defense Department admitted that Washington was using a non-lethal irritant gas in Vietnam. It was in fact a variety widely used for crowd control in domestic riot situations and therefore incomparably more humane than shooting people or blowing them up, but gas has a capacity to inspire moral outrage surpassed only by nuclear weapons. Prime Minister Wilson immediately cabled the Foreign Secretary, directing him not to make any public statement until the following morning, for fear that "Foreign Office pressure would be exerted on Stewart to express support" for the use of gas by the Americans in Vietnam.[47] Stewart saw President Johnson privately to work out a suitable form of words. What he finally told the National Press Club at lunchtime on 23 March was that in the choice of measures "everyone responsible should consider not only what is militarily appropriate for the job in hand but the effect on people around the world. What I am, in fact, asking the United States to display is what your Declaration of Independence called 'a decent respect for the opinions of mankind'."[48]

It was a most appropriate and felicitous warning that the British government was experiencing increasingly grave misgivings about the way the Vietnamese situation was developing. Paul Hasluck was meanwhile explaining why Australia had no misgivings whatsoever. The real enemy, he explained to the House, was not communist insurgency in Vietnam but communist Chinese expansionism. What was happening south of the seventeenth parallel was not a local rebellion occasioned by internal discontent but "the application of the methods and doctrines of Communist guerilla warfare first evolved in China and then successfully used in Vietnam". The response of the Americans to this situation reflected "the recognition and acceptance of the great responsibilities which their own greatness has laid upon them . . . If the United States did withdraw," he warned, "the same conflict would be renewed somewhere else. Within a brief period, the struggle now taking place in Vietnam would be shifted to Thailand. If there were abandonment of Thailand, it would shift to Malaysia — to Indonesia, to Burma, to India and further." For Australia in such a situation "neutralism is not a choice . . . We stand firmly with Britain and the United States of America."[49] It was the falling domino principle expressed in the most uncompromising form.

Hasluck's timing might have seemed peculiar. Eisenhower had originally contemplated the decline of the dominoes when it had still seemed reasonable to assume a monolithic unity of purpose identifying Beijing with Moscow. China and Russia in alliance might constitute a potential threat against which no precautions could be deemed excessive; but they were very clearly no longer in alliance. Bitter ideological conflict within the Communist world has been evident for the past four or five months at least. Even as Hasluck spoke, the *People's Daily* in China was denouncing the present Soviet leadership as "illegal" and "schismatic", was calling upon them in true ecclesiastical style to recant their "errors", and was even accusing the Russians of the well-nigh unforgivable sin of being engaged in "a futile attempt to extinguish the revolutionary struggle of the South Vietnamese people". If this were really the case, then the Chinese would dare to become heavily involved in Vietnam themselves only if they were seeking to provoke a clash with the Soviets, which was presumably what Western hawks like Paul Hasluck desired most. Beijing embroiled with Moscow had never looked less like a threat to anybody than when Hasluck was envisaging it as embarking upon a programme of world conquest.

Howson nonetheless thought that the minister had made a good speech. "It is obvious," he reflected, "that we are fully committed to helping the USA in North Vietnam to get a satisfactory negotiated peace. Therefore we must pursue the tough line at whatever cost to us." But he did not think the cost would be very high. "I believe," he noted, "we could even get to the conference table within twelve months."[50] It took three years, in fact. It was another five years before peace came to Vietnam, and it came as the result of a communist victory.

Secretary Rusk spoke to CINCPAC and Mission Chiefs along similar lines the following day. "US conduct in the Viet-Nam conflict is not only crucial in itself," he told them, "but is regarded as a touchstone of the US commitment in the rest of the area. Initiation of air action against North Viet-Nam has been generally regarded as demonstrating a previously questionable US determination. Many countries believe, however, that the pace of US actions must be further stepped up and our goals further spelled out if our policy is to be clearly understood by both our enemies and our friends." He added that it was important for Washington "to continue to further the increasingly responsible policy" of Australia and New Zealand towards the area as a whole, "stressing particularly our growing defense relationships".[51]

A real identity of Australian and US thinking seemed to have been achieved. Rusk was certainly responding to what he had been hearing from Waller, Renouf and Hasluck for the past three years and what he had heard again from Hasluck during the past twenty-four hours. Views of the kind which the Secretary had described as being "generally" held by "many countries" in "the rest of the area" had actually been expressed, privately or publicly, only by the Australians, the South Koreans and the Taiwanese. The Americans had consistently discounted the statements of the South Koreans and the Taiwanese as reflecting the special interests of those regimes in getting the United States involved in a war with China, which was not part of the policy of any administration in Washington. The fact of the matter was that most other countries in the region had shown by their determination not to become involved that the last thing they wanted was for United States actions to be further stepped up. Global opinion, generally, earnestly hoped that they might be stepped down.

Australian encouragement continued unabated. Waller told the State Department on 29 March that the firm support of the Australian government for current US action was based on the belief that it would "check aggression, restore confidence in South Vietnam and lead toward an acceptable settlement".[52] Michael Stewart was at the same time delivering in the House of Commons a more qualified defence of the US position, with a significantly different nuance. He was at pains to stress the difficulty facing Washington in determining the basis for a ceasefire "so long as there is no indication from the other side of its preparedness to consider a settlement on any terms. If and when there is a clear indication to that effect," he emphasized, "when the other side communicates in any form that it desires a cessation of hostilities or considers that there is room for negotiation, then the door would be open and there would be something which could be regarded as a basis for negotiation." In the meantime, he assured the House, the British government was "in earnest agreement" with the express aim of non-aligned nations of "Reaching a peaceful solution for the serious situation in Viet Nam", and Minister for Foreign Affairs Patrick Gordon Walker would be visiting capitals in the Far East, in an attempt "to secure not merely a military but a satisfactory political settlement of this vexed and agonising and threatening question".[53]

While Stewart was speaking in Westminster, Lester Pearson was delivering an equally refined commentary in Philadelphia, the "City of Brotherly Love", where he had gone to receive the Temple University World Peace Award. The motives of the United States in intervening in Vietnam, he insisted, were "honorable; neither mean nor imperialistic". Nor could the situation be expected to improve until North Vietnam "becomes convinced that aggression, in whatever guise, for whatever reason, is inadmissible and will not succeed". However, he also stressed that "there does appear to be at least a possibility that a suspension of . . . air strikes against North Vietnam, at the right time, might provide the Hanoi authorities with an opportunity, if they wish to take it, to inject some flexibility into their policy without appearing to do so as the direct result of military pressure". But they were not going to get the opportunity. President Johnson had just decided to increase the intensity of military pressure against North Vietnam. It did not make him happy to have to listen to people telling him to do exactly the opposite.

Pearson had barely finished his speech when he was informed by telephone that President Johnson wanted him to come and have lunch. The Canadian thought it would be a good idea to accept. Lunch itself was not very rewarding, as the President spent almost the entire time on the telephone discussing the latest developments in Vietnam with his advisers. Then he got to work on Pearson, haranguing him for more than an hour on what had been wrong with his Temple University speech. The president explained that he was "getting tired of receiving advice (and nothing else) from foreign visitors: Wilson, Stewart . . . (whom he particularly resented), Couve de Murville, etc. None of these people really knew anything about the situation; they had no policy or solution of their own but that didn't prevent them from criticising his . . . The President," Pearson reflected afterwards, "seemed to feel a little forlorn at not being understood better by friends." More seriously, Pearson suspected that there was "no doubt that the President is tired, under great and continuous pressure and that he is beginning to show it. He is more worried about US policy in Vietnam than he is willing to show. His irritation at any indication of lack of full support for his policy; his impatience of criticism and his insistence that everything is working out in accord with a well-conceived plan; all these really indicate a feeling of insecurity about the situation, rather than the reverse. As the President said: 'It's hard to sleep these days.' 'I'm beginning to feel like a martyr; misunderstood, misjudged by friends at home and abroad.' " Vietnam was going to be a great test for the president. Pearson was not sure that he would be able to meet it.[54]

Pearson did not know the real reason why the president was so worried about United States policy in Vietnam. Johnson had just agreed to "overtures to GOA, GNZ and to ROK, seeking combat support from them", meaning specifically "an Australian Army battalion to Vung Tay to close by 21 May".[55] The decision had been taken. The United States was getting into a ground war on the Asian mainland again and it was getting in because it would not be getting in alone. Australia would be there too.

Johnson indeed needed all the support he could get. Two thousand and five hundred Protestant ministers, Roman Catholic priests, and rabbis ran a full-page advertisement in the *New York Times* on 4 April exhorting the president, "In the name of God, STOP IT!" Fifteen thousand students marched on the White House in the first great anti-war demonstration. By contrast, the Australian government decided it was evident that the United States in 1965 really "wished to have a contribution of Australian forces in Vietnam", and that Australia "should offer a battalion to the defence of such a strategically important area". It was assumed that if Australia were to agree to a request from the United States, "a request from the South Vietnamese Government would follow".[56]

Renouf had acted already, even before Canberra had officially advised its position. He told Assistant Secretary Leonard Unger on 7 April that Australia would not yet be able to accept any further responsibility for training regional forces because it "would have trouble finding enough personnel in view of expanded demands of conscription", but that "if infantry battalion were sent to SVN, some trainers — perhaps 100 — might be attached to it". New Zealand Ambassador George Laking was much less forthcoming. Secretary Rusk told him that "Australians had given strong indication GOA would be willing send infantry battalion to SVN if we and GVN request". However, Laking insisted that "in case of GNZ matter not so clear-cut"; asked "if we envisaged international force"; and "said his government would need rather detailed explanation of our concept of force in which NZ would participate and role their element would play. Said he would transmit our request in principle to Wellington, but could not say with certainty what the response would be." Rusk accordingly told Taylor that he "should not pursue further with GVN question of a NZ force contribution to SVN until you receive further instructions; those will depend upon our receiving favorable response from GNZ".[57] Australia, to judge from Renouf's comments, apparently had no reservations about participating in military action in Vietnam. New Zealand, like every other democracy in the world, apparently had.

There were technical difficulties, too, even with Australian participation. Rusk advised Taylor on 8 April to suggest to the South Vietnamese government that they formally request Canberra to provide an infantry battalion for use in South Vietnam. Taylor decided to wait for a "propitious moment to raise the matter".[58] Hasluck was getting anxious, however. Fears were developing in Canberra that "the United States was again considering the possibility of negotiation, in which case the offer of a battalion would have been inappropriate". Hasluck accordingly directed Waller on 9 April to repeat to Johnson that the Australian government had decided to send a battalion in the belief that it "would be important in itself and of great importance in present and future Australian defence relationships".[59] No approach had yet been made by or to the Vietnamese. However, Ambassador Anderson then cabled that the fragility of the political situation in Saigon was such that there would be considerable merit in having prior discussions with the Vietnamese, rather than just advising them of a decision arrived at independently by Washington and Canberra. He repeated this message the following day and went to Ambassador Taylor, suggesting that it might be a good idea to talk to Quat. Taylor agreed but said that he had to wait for a directive from Rusk. But Rusk was waiting on advice from Waller, who told him on 12 April that he intended to notify the Secretary formally on 13 April of "GOA readiness send battalion to SVN subject to consultation on timing, mission and location". What was causing the delay was that "for some reason [Waller] set store by more formal and high-level USG request, and this we expect to make tomorrow. He also indicated that prior to exploration with GVN to elicit GVN request GOA would like to inform UK and GNZ." Taylor was accordingly instructed not to proceed with the issue of a Vietnamese request for an Australian battalion but to await further instructions.[60]

It was evident that the Australians were trying to extract the maximum fanfare from the situation to emphasize the fact that they were acting as a good and indeed almost the only ally of the United States in Vietnam. There should be an official request by Washington and an official response by Canberra. Anderson's problem was that it was the Vietnamese who were supposed to have made the request and nobody had actually asked them to do so yet. Time was dragging on. Waller informed Rusk officially on 13 April that the Australian government "was prepared in principle to supply a battalion for use in Viet-Nam". Rusk replied officially that the president himself "would probably wish to communicate directly with the Prime Minister on this. He expressed his gratification for the Australian decision and said that the battalion would be worth many times its numbers both on the ground and in terms of its effect on public opinion in the world and in the United States." It was agreed in further discussion that the Australians should "proceed at once to inform the British and the New Zealanders . . . Ambassador Taylor would then approach Quat to indicate that the GOA would respond favourably to a GVN request. Both Ambassadors in Saigon would then consult closely with a view to Quat — if he approved — conveying the GVN request to the Australian Ambassador and working out the operational factors." There would not be very much for Quat to work out, however. Rusk and Waller had agreed already that the Australian battalion should join the US force in the Da Nang area. "The present mission of that force," the Secretary explained, "is to hold the perimeter, but . . . it was envisaged that the mission would be expanded to take in actions against the VC when VC forces had been fixed and located by GVN forces."[61] In other words, the Australians, like the Americans, would be there to do the actual fighting.

They had to get there first, however. Taylor cabled Rusk on 17 April that he still had heard nothing after being told on 12 April to await further instructions before approaching Quat about a request to Canberra. He tried to expedite matters by suggesting to the Secretary "the kind of instructions . . . which it would be most helpful to receive for use in presenting to GVN what I take to be a new policy of third-country participation in ground combat". These could be along the lines that, " 'We are prepared to bring in addition U.S. ground forces provided we can get a reasonable degree of participation from other third countries. If the GVN will make urgent representations to them, we believe it entirely possible to obtain the following contributions: Korea, one regimental combat team; Australia, one infantry battalion; New Zealand, one battery and one company of tanks; PI [Philippines] one battalion.' "[62] He then waited for the order to see Quat to tell him how to ask Canberra for what Washington had decided he was getting.

The Australians were meanwhile preparing the maximum diplomatic exposure for their intervention. A round-robin directive was sent to all West European posts, "emphasizing Australia's concern at the failure of the Europeans to realize the sinister nature of events in Vietnam and China's 'aggressive' intentions in the area. Our diplomats were instructed to convey this concern to the foreign ministries of the respective countries to which they were posted. They were told to tell the Europeans that we Australians, by virtue of our closer association with Asia, were better able to make an objective analysis of what was happening in Indo-China. I doubt if any government would impose such embarrassment on its diplomats," an embarrassed Australian diplomat reflected, "unless it was firmly convinced of what it was saying."[63] The Australian embassy in Paris would certainly have had an interesting time explaining to the French how it was that Australian perceptions about Indochinese affairs were right and theirs were not.

Europeans were probably not favourably impressed. Washington was. Ambassador Henry Cabot Lodge assured Australian ministers that " 'USA were prepared to stay in Vietnam for a generation' ".[64]

This should have been long enough to complete the necessary preparations for a self-reliant defence policy, if there had ever been any intention of undertaking such preparations in the first place. But there was a sense in which time was running out for Australia very quickly indeed. Combat troops could hardly be sent to Vietnam unless the Vietnamese government were to make some kind of request for them, but it was still showing no signs of making such a request. Taylor finally saw Quat on 24 April. Anderson had tried to see him then as well, but was not granted an audience until the following day. Nor was that exchange very helpful. The Australian ambassador told Hasluck in alarm that "Quat had not yet given his agreement", and that "no one knew when he would do so".[65] Saigon seemed unenthusiastic to the point of discourtesy about the prospect of Australian military support. Meanwhile, political pressures in Canberra were reaching bursting point. Hasluck told Waller to tell Rusk that "if announcement of Australian deployment of battalion to SVN is not done by Thursday April 29, will have to be put off until following Tuesday. They regard this as undesirable because of threatened leaks." Rusk agreed that "politically best sequence would be if GVN first announced its request and then PriMin Menzies followed with his statement".[66] Quat eventually told Anderson on 27 April that he welcomed the Australian government's offer of a battalion. However, he still said nothing about actually asking them to send it.

Matters became desperate when Sydney journalist Allan Reid received a leak from cabinet on 28 April that Menzies planned to announce the following day that an Australian battalion would be deployed in Vietnam. Reid printed the story in the *Daily Telegraph*. Another *Telegraph* journalist lifted Reid's story for United Press International, which reported it in the United States. This, Rusk noted, was going to "make it extremely difficult for GOA not to proceed with statement" on 29 April whether it received a formal request from Quat before then or not. Anderson frantically sought an audience with Quat on 28 April and was at last able to report that he had had "an entirely satisfactory conversation" with the Vietnamese prime minister, and that it had been agreed that "a joint GVN-Australian communique will be issued at the end of today announcing the request of GVN for this military assistance".[67] Anderson then gave Quat a formal letter confirming the Australian offer, Quat's acceptance of it and his request for the dispatch of the battalion. Quat thereupon issued a statement on 29 April that "upon the request of the Government of the Republic of Vietnam the Government of Australia today approved the dispatch to Vietnam of an infantry battalion".

This was not exactly what the Australians had been seeking. Canberra had wanted a request from Saigon for Australian military assistance. What it had got was not a request but a statement that a request had been made. The distinction might not have been significant in practical terms but it had the potential to be politically embarrassing. Menzies nonetheless informed parliament on the evening of 29 April that he was "now in receipt of a request from the Government of South Vietnam for further military assistance", which was not in fact the case. It was yet another example of the difficulty Australian politicians seemed to encounter when it was a question of telling the truth about Vietnam. Menzies was nevertheless quite clear as to the reason why Australian troops were being sent to Vietnam, even if he was obscure about the circumstances of their being sent there. His government had responded positively to the request, he explained, because a communist takeover of South Vietnam "would be a direct military threat to Australia and to all the countries of South and Southeast Asia. It must be seen as part of a thrust by Communist China between the Indian and Pacific Oceans."[68] Nothing could be clearer. No further rationale was needed. Australia was not concerned simply to prevent a communist takeover of Vietnam. It was concerned to prevent a takeover by the proxies of Chinese aggression, of which Australia would be the ultimate target or at least the ultimate victim. There were a couple of difficulties here. One was that neither Menzies nor anybody else ever produced any evidence confirming that the Vietnamese communists were in fact proxies of China or anybody else and that China was indeed committed to a programme of Pacific hegemony. Another was that a single infantry battalion was a strangely small commitment to make to a struggle in which nothing less than the future of Australia itself was apparently at stake. Most Australians seemed prepared to accept Menzies's judgment, however. Howson thought that intervention would probably divide the nation politically, but this would not matter very much because "more than 70 percent support the government's decision". There were indeed "a few thoughts that we should hold a snap election on this issue". He also noted that "the official reaction to the news from the UK is lukewarm".[69] This was not surprising. Menzies had committed Australia to a proxy war in Vietnam just when Harold Wilson was discussing with the Pope the power of the Commonwealth to contribute to world peace.

6
A Mark of Appreciation of a Good Ally (1965–1966)

Harold Wilson's audience with Pope Paul VI was apparently an uplifting experience, even for an agnostic. His Holiness told him that the advent of the British Labour Government to office "held out a new and real hope for peace, partly because of our links with the non-aligned world and our influence in the Commonwealth, particularly Africa". He also questioned Wilson about "my views and my judgments about the U.S. President's real willingness to take the steps necessary for peace. He told me with deep sincerity that he prayed about Vietnam every night." Wilson for his part promised that he would keep in touch with the Pope on Vietnam, "and from that time forward we had a continuing, almost regular exchange of views and analyses, through H.M. Minister to the Vatican".[1]

Wilson might perhaps have given the Pope the impression of being in a position to exert more control over events than was actually the case. London's influence even in Africa would soon be shown to be extremely limited. Australia was very clearly out of its control. Johnson and his advisers were indeed hoping that Australia might by contrast be able to exert some influence over British policy, with a view to bringing it more into accord with the perceptions of Washington and Canberra. A meeting of the SEATO Council was about to be held in London. And SEATO, the NSC considered, was still "a useful security instrument for the U.S.", and it was desirable to "have SEATO take whatever action is necessary in Viet-Nam or elsewhere in Southeast Asia". SEATO was in fact "the only treaty commitment of the U.S. relating to Viet-Nam, although it has not been specifically invoked". This was of course due to the fact that

France and Pakistan in particular were "not in sympathy with the course being followed by other SEATO members on the conflict in Vietnam". Even the United Kingdom was not as firm in its support of United States policy as were Australia and New Zealand. However, the NSC proposed to take advantage of "a provision in the ANZUS Treaty authorizing the ANZUS Council to engage in consultation with other states. Potential members of an enlarged ANZUS might include Thailand, the Philippines, Malaysia, Viet-Nam and the United Kingdom."[2] Ambassador Bruce was accordingly given directions by Rusk.

> Endeavour work out with UK Ambassador Rumbold and Australian and New Zealand representatives agreed approach to Council treatment Viet-Nam issue. Our objective is to ensure that . . . SEATO appear more closely identified with an involved in Viet-Nam crisis than previously. If we fail to achieve this, we are going to have very serious problems to deal with at home with respect to both SEATO and our role in Viet-Nam . . . UK officials may boggle slightly at your initiating consultations with Australia and New Zealand representatives, but we believe it useful for you to proceed to do so promptly. Our estimate is Australia will be with us but New Zealand may be more difficult to bring aboard.

There would not be any real problem in obtaining Thai and Filipino support, after the usual protracted exchanges. Where there could be a real problem was of course with the Vietnamese, who were showing no more disposition to request assistance from SEATO than they had been to request assistance from Australia. "At some point," Rusk decided, "we shall have to approach GVN about request to Council for action by Council members under Treaty since we consider new request by GVN clearly desirable. We may therefore want to try to reach agreement with UK, Australia and New Zealand in time for our Embassy in Saigon contact GVN and have GVN instruct observer to make request to Council."[3]

It was obviously going to be difficult to represent military assistance to South Vietnam as being provided in any way under the terms of SEATO. There was no way that it could be represented as being provided under the terms even of an enlarged ANZUS. Australia, New Zealand and the United States were not under attack in the Pacific area from North Vietnam or the Viet Cong. This absence of any discernible *casus belli* was helping to make the precise role of the Australians in Vietnam a little obscure. Ambassador Anderson assured General Westmoreland that "with luck, the [Australian] battalion should arrive during the first week in June", and that the Australian government had agreed "to put the battalion under U.S. Command and to authorize the use of the troops for the defense of base areas, for patrolling in the vicinity of these bases, and for deployment as a mobile reserve". They were, however, prohibited from "participation in pacification operations. We shall have to find out just what the Ambassador understands by pacification", Taylor told Rusk. Nor, he noted, did Anderson's instructions cover the use of the battalion "as part of an international mobile security task force involving third countries such as Koreans and Filipinos", which seemed to the Americans to be about the most practical way of utilizing the rather marginal contributions of their allies.[4] Anderson's instructions had not covered that aspect because the Australian government had never contemplated the use of the battalion in such a role. Merging what was intended to be a very small Australian contingent into a heterogeneous regional force would have dissipated fatally the public relations impact of their commitment — and the Australian commitment to Vietnam was nothing if not an exercise in public relations diplomacy. Military considerations such as the most combat-effective employment of the troops once there were irrelevant to the real purpose of the exercise.

Nothing very positive was achieved in London after all. The communique which emerged from the SEATO Council Meeting on 5 May "welcomed and expressed warm support for the policy of the United States to provide assistance to South Vietnam to defend its independence," and affirmed that "until the Communist aggression is brought to an end, resolute defensive action must be continued". However, the French had refused to attend the meeting at all; none of those present other than the Americans and the Australians had actually indicated any intention of contributing to such resolute defensive action; and the British were concerned primarily with launching the Commonwealth Peace Mission which Wilson had canvassed with Pope Paul, even though British Foreign Secretary Michael Stewart was at pains to assure the House of Commons that one of the Labour Government's main reasons for undertaking the Mission was that "we ought, against all difficulties, to put it beyond doubt that it is not our side that is refusing negotiations".[5]

That was about all that could be reasonably hoped for from the British. More tangible, if hardly substantial, support for Washington came from its junior ANZUS partner, New Zealand. Prime Minister

Sir Keith Holyoake announced in parliament in Wellington on 27 May that he had received a message from Vietnamese Premier Quat on 10 May asking that "New Zealand should send combatant troops to assist in the struggle against Communist aggression". The New Zealand government, Holyoake explained, had "heard, and indeed encouraged, the expression of views from all sections of the community", and he believed that the great majority of the nation would support the decision of the government that "a New Zealand combatant unit should take its place alongside the forces of South Vietnam, the United States and a growing number of countries pledged to assist in the defense of South Vietnam". Holyoake might well have seemed to be on far surer political ground in this regard than Menzies, who had never actually received a request from Quat and had certainly never encouraged public debate on the issue of involvement in Vietnam. Holyoake had nonetheless no intention of testing the resolve of the New Zealand public too severely. The unit he proposed to send would in fact consist merely of a single battery of artillery and would be replacing the army engineer detachment which the New Zealand government had already sent to Vietnam.

They would, however, unquestionably be combatant troops who, as Holyoake explained, "would be able to take their place with the Australian forces, alongside whom New Zealanders have stood before in the tradition of ANZAC in resisting aggression".[6] 1st Battalion Royal Australian Regiment was sailing for Vietnam on board HMAS *Sydney* while Holyoake was evoking the tradition of ANZAC in Wellington. It was sailing towards an increasingly ominous military situation. A major VC offensive opened on 28 May in Darlac, Pleiku and Phu Son provinces. Saigon lost over one thousand of its best troops within a week. Even more alarming was the manner in which they were lost. United States observers commented bitterly that "ARVN commanders on the scene had displayed tactical stupidity and cowardice".[7] Even the indefatigably optimistic Westmoreland admitted on 7 June that "ARVN forces are experiencing difficulty in coping with ... increased VC capability", and that it would therefore be necessary to deploy allied forces actively in support of the South Vietnamese "when ... the general military situation requires it".[8] This envisaged far more serious fighting than the Australian and New Zealand governments had imagined. Menzies, Hasluck, Waller, Renouf, and presumably Holyoake had been thinking about making gestures. Westmoreland was thinking about making war, on an increasingly intense scale, against an increasingly capable enemy, in support of an apparently increasingly incapable ally.

All concerned would find out later what they had let themselves in for. At least the gesture had been made and the Australian combat forces were in place. On 3 June 222 Australians joined 173d Division, US Army at Vung Tau. Another 470 were due to land on 8 June. Hasluck accordingly thought it appropriate to suggest to Counsellor Lydman that he might "transmit a 'nudge' " to the State Department over its failure to replace Ambassador William C. Battle, who had left Canberra nearly ten months before. Hasluck "feared that if post should remain vacant much longer, Australians might begin to harbour notion that we considered them unworthy in some way".[9] It would indeed have been difficult not to harbour the notion that even the decision to send troops to Vietnam had done little to raise Australia's rating on State Department's order of priorities. This would not auger well for the success of Australian efforts to develop the sense of habitual closeness between Canberra and Washington which Renouf had hoped to achieve.

Prime Minister Menzies himself was probably untroubled by intimations of irrelevance. The most mobile of Australian politicians was in the United States at the time, assuring his audiences of the moral imperative of intervention in Vietnam. He deployed before the Australian-American Association in Washington a horrific picture of communist China "coming down over the whole of the Southeast Asian peninsula, pointing first at Malaysia, then at Indonesia with all the strange things that go on in that country, and then across a strip of water to my own land". He also promised the Americans that they would "in the long run, perhaps not in the very long run . . . feel that you are the actors and the spokesman for an almost unanimous world opinion".[10] It was perhaps Menzies's unluckiest prophecy since he forecast that the United States would come to endorse the British assault on Egypt in 1956.

Nor were Menzies's perceptions of Chinese communist plans for conquest shared by Johnson's own advisers. Uri Ra'anan commented that "the signals from Peking as early as the spring of 1965, esoteric at first, and somewhat less esoteric later on, were perfectly clear — namely, that the people who were winning the struggle for power in Peking were people who were not prepared to make major sacrifices for the North Vietnamese, with the exception of some extreme contingencies which later on were outlined fairly clearly and, I think, understood fairly clearly ... China was not going to interfere at any price, provided that the war stayed in the South."¹¹ Top US advisers were clear at least that the last thing that the North Vietnamese wanted was Chinese intervention. JCS Chairman General Earle G. Wheeler told Johnson on 21 July 1965 that "the one thing all North Vietnam fears is the Chinese. For them to invite Chinese volunteers is to invite China taking over North Vietnam."¹² Ambassador Taylor similarly "doubted that either Hanoi or the Vietcong would ever request or accept Chinese combat forces in their country. For centuries the Chinese had been regarded as hated, foreign oppressors by all Vietnamese, North and South, and that historical attitude was not likely to change."¹³ On this basis, the most effective way to safeguard against Chinese southward expansion would have been to facilitate a North Vietnamese takeover of the South, assuming of course that the Chinese had any plans for southward expansion. The Australians had a perception of Chinese intentions in this regard shared by nobody else in the world, except obviously by the North Vietnamese themselves. There might seem to be a certain paradox here; but there was at least no element of subservience. Australia was not seeing the world through anybody else's eyes. Canberra was applying its own policy in its own way, based on its own assessment of the situation, which unfortunately happened to be wrong.

Another independent Australian perception sadly wide of the mark was Menzies's conviction that world opinion would eventually rally in support of United States policy. Harold Wilson on the contrary was absolutely certain that a majority of the delegates to the forthcoming Commonwealth Heads of Government Meeting in London, "including almost all the Asian, African and Caribbean delegates, would take a strong anti-American line". This was the more serious in that the commonwealth countries would "represent more than a sixth of the total UN membership of 117 countries, and almost exactly a quarter of the world's population". It would clearly be preferable from a British point of view not to have them united in condemnation of American and consequently of Australian and New Zealand intervention in Vietnam. Wilson accordingly suggested to Michael Stewart that he should "put to the Conference at its opening session a proposal to set up, with the authority of the whole Commonwealth, a mission of four prime ministers — or five, if this became necessary to secure balance — representing every point of view on the Vietnam issue", to visit Moscow, Washington and Beijing, as well as Hanoi and Saigon, in an attempt to discover a formula for peace in Vietnam. The two Labour leaders agreed that it was "vital to get Sir Robert Menzies' reactions at the outset; fortunately," Wilson recorded, "I was to dine with him at the Australian High Commission that evening, 14 June."[14]

This might have seemed a daunting prospect, given the total commitment of the Australian government to intervention in Vietnam; but it appeared that Menzies could never resist an approach from London, even when made by a British Labour Prime Minister. He welcomed Wilson's proposal enthusiastically and even agreed to support it in representations to the Americans. Waller and British Ambassador Dean went together to see Rusk the following day. Dean explained that the aim of their two governments was "to be helpful to the U.S. It was hoped that by floating this proposal on the first day of the Commonwealth Prime Ministers' Conference, the Conference discussion of Vietnam could be turned into constructive channels." Waller for his part assured the Secretary that Menzies and Hasluck "fully endorsed the initiative", adding that the Australian government "also wished to make clear that its support for the Commonwealth initiative did not detract in any way from Australian support for what the U.S. was doing in Vietnam".[15]

Meanwhile, back home Wilson and Stewart were acting like the accomplished political operators they were. The prime minister informed cabinet dramatically on 15 June that "a big initiative was now on the way", thereby, as Richard Crossman recognized, "pre-empting any serious discussion of the Vietnam issue in Cabinet". Michael Stewart, whom Crossman regarded as being "100 per cent Anglo-American in a highly prim and proper way", scored a masterly debating success on familiar territory at the Oxford Union, after a disastrous performance by Henry Cabot Lodge, who apparently had not been told that he might expect some criticism of United States policies in such a forum. Stewart, serenely at home in the milieu, explained that what his government wanted was "a conference that will be accompanied with a cessation of the fighting and which will bring about a solution whereby the people of Vietnam will have a genuine freedom to determine the course of their own affairs". President Johnson, he insisted, "was prepared to enter into discussions without conditions", whereas "North Vietnam and China in their present policies and frame of mind are not". Stewart had achieved, Crossman conceded, "a brilliant television success and put the American case more competently than any American has ever put it".[16]

Wilson formed his Peace Mission on 17 June. It consisted of himself, plus the heads of government of Nigeria, Ghana and Trinidad. It was, he admitted, unfortunate that there could not have been an Asian representative, but it would have been "difficult to appoint India or Pakistan without offending the other or, for that matter, Malaysia, and we therefore asked the Prime Minister of Ceylon; but, mainly on grounds of health, he felt unable to accept". Even Harold Wilson had his problems in dealing with the inherent anomalies of the commonwealth. But he could feel that he had done all that could be done in the circumstances. Menzies clapped the British prime minister on the back. " 'I give this trip to you, old boy. Really, it was your idea. Full marks.' " If it failed, then " 'we will have tried — and it is better to have loved and lost than never to have loved at all.' "[17] There was an authentic Menzies quality about both the philosophy and the manner of its expression.

The mood in Canberra was less exuberant, however. Ambassador Anderson had finally been assured by Canberra that there would be "no restriction on the flexibility of employment of the Australian battalion in a strike reaction role".[18] But a growing number of Australians were exhibiting their objections to the use of the nation's military forces in Vietnam in any role at all. The Youth Campaign Against Conscription published an advertisement in the national daily the *Australian*, on 19 June, declaring that for young men to be sent to fight in Vietnam "would be a moral wrong and an unjust call upon our lives by the Government of our country. We share a fundamental belief that to safeguard the future of our nation, Australia's role in these perilous times is to seek an end to South East Asian disputes, through negotiations for peaceful settlements — not to pursue the murderous path to world conflict through prolonging the slaughter in Vietnam."[19] Howson himself was increasingly beset with misgivings. RAAF attache in Saigon, Wing Commander K.G. Brinsley, had told him that he felt that Warlord of the Air, Marshal Nguyen Cao Ky, who had succeeded Quat as Premier on 12 June, was "unlikely to last longer than his predecessors". Howson agreed that "the government of South Vietnam was not the most ideal to pick as the best horse to support in a trial of strength in SE Asia. But militarily it is the best for our sort of strength — in air and naval power. Anyway," he reflected helplessly, "the time for second thoughts on that subject is long past — the die is cast, and we must realize that we just have to win this trial of strength. The alternative is 'Fortress Australia'."[20]

Fatalistically accepting the situation in Vietnam was undoubtedly more appealing than thinking of ways to change it. Ky's regime established a new record in irrationality by breaking off diplomatic relations with France on 24 June, accusing the government which had made a larger contribution than anybody except the American themselves to public welfare in South Vietnam of "having helped the enemy directly or indirectly and created confusion among the armed forces and people of Vietnam". Nor were the communists being any more amenable. The Commonwealth Peace Mission had made its first approach to Soviet Premier Kosygin, who told the ambassadors that nobody had authorized the Soviet Union to undertake talks on a settlement and that it was not going to. Wilson nonetheless presevered with a communique declaring that the objectives of the mission were "(a) a suspension of all United States air attacks on North Vietnam; (b) a North Vietnamese undertaking to prevent the movement of any military forces or assistance or material to South Viet Nam; (c) a total cease-fire on all sides to enable a conference to be convened to seek a peaceful solution".[21] Beijing immediately claimed that in all its actions the British government was "siding with the US aggressors against the Vietnamese people", and was now "rendering yet another service to the US aggressors", by "actually appropriating the name of the Commonwealth to launch a new 'peace talks' plot . . . In view of the above, the Chinese Government cannot but sternly reject a visit to Peking by the Mission described in the British Note."[22] Hanoi delivered the final rejection on 1 July. The way of the peacemakers in Vietnam was singularly discouraging.

Undersecretary Ball was still convinced that a way to peaceful negotiation had to be found, if only because there was no rational alternative. "The South Vietnamese," he warned President Johnson, "are losing the war to the Viet Cong. No one can assure you that we can beat the Viet Cong or even force them to the conference table on our terms, no matter how many hundred thousand *white, foreign* (U.S.) troops we deploy." He accordingly proposed that the United States should "(1) Complete all deployments already announced — battalions — but decide not to go beyond a total of 72,000 men represented by this figure. (2) Restrict the combat role of the American forces to the June 19 announcement, making it clear to General Westmoreland that this announcement is to be strictly construed. (3) Continue bombing in the North but avoid the Hanoi-Haiphong area and any targets nearer to the Chinese border than those already being struck." Approaches for a peace conference should be made along essentially the same lines as those proposed by the Commonwealth Peace Mission, namely, that "(a) The U.S. will stand down its bombing of the North (b) The South Vietnamese will initiate no offensive operations in the South, and (c) The DRV [Democratic Republic of Vietnam (North Vietnam)] will stop terrorism and other aggressive action against the South". Ball then addressed the problem of possible allied responses to such a démarche. "The Republic of China and Thailand," he considered, "are staunch allies whose preference for extreme U.S. actions including a risk of war with Communist China sets them apart from all other Asian nations." However, they were not actually doing any of the fighting in Vietnam, so they could hardly object strongly to any moves leading to a cessation of the fighting. The Republic of Korea and the Philippines were "equally staunch allies whose support for strong U.S. action short of war with Communist China would make post-settlement reassurance a pressing U.S. need". But the Filipinos were not doing any fighting either and the United States "might be able to cushion Korean reactions to a compromise in South Vietnam by the provision of greater military and economic assistance". This left Australia and New Zealand. These were, Ball thought, "special cases since they feel lonely in the far reaches of the Pacific. Yet even their concern is far greater with Malaysia than with South Vietnam and the degree of their anxiety would be conditioned largely by expressions of our support for Malaysia."[23]

The Australians had perhaps never felt less lonely. Everything in Hasluck's eyes was going very well indeed. "Wilson, Healey and Stewart are a good trio in UK," he assured cabinet, "and adopting a good line with USA and ourselves . . . Position at ANZUS meeting in Washington very good indeed. Our stocks have never been higher."[24] This did not of course mean that they were all that high. The Americans were contemplating a massive military build-up in Vietnam, but they were not counting particularly on Australian support. Assistant Secretary of State for International Security Affairs John T. McNaughton indeed suggested to General Goodpaster that "for the purposes of the study it might save us time if we assumed that we would get no meaningful forces from anyone other than the ROKs during the relevant time frame. (If the Australians decide to send another battalion or two, this should not alter the conclusions of the study significantly.)" Korean support was another matter. General

Westmoreland, McNaughton wrote, had "equated the 9 ROK battalions with 9 US battalions, saying that, if he did not get the former, he must have the latter".[25] What was really wanted, Defense Secretary McNamara told the president, was much more of both. The situation in South Vietnam, he argued, noting the same circumstances as Ball but drawing the opposite conclusions from them, was:

> worse than a year ago (when it was worse than a year before that) ... The VC main and local forces, reinforced by militia and guerillas, have the initiative and, with large attacks (some in regimental strength) are hurting ARVN force badly ... Since June 1, the GVN has been forced to abandon six district capitals; only one has been retaken ... the Government is able to provide security to fewer and fewer people in less and less territory as terrorism increases ... The economy is deteriorating ... The odds are less than even that the Ky government will last out the year ... Rural reconstruction (pacification) even in the Hop Tac area around Saigon is making little progress.

This had seemed to Ball the best possible reason for disengaging from an intrinsically hopeless situation. McNamara's solution was, however, to "expand promptly and substantially the US military pressure against the North Vietnamese in the North". To this end he recommended an increase in total US personnel in Vietnam from 75,000 to 175,000 with the understanding that "the deployment of more men (perhaps 100,000) may be necessary in early 1966, and that the development of additional forces thereafter is possible but will depend on developments".[26]

What this amounted to was exactly the opposite of what the Commonwealth Peace Mission had sought to achieve. Conflict in Vietnam was to be expanded significantly in terms of both intensity and extent. The United States, Menzies was informed, would begin making "limited attacks upon two newly installed surface-to-air missiles sites forty miles north-west of Hanoi". American forces would be increased to forty-four battalions and a search and destroy strategy applied. This would, it was hoped, send "a clear signal to the world — and perhaps especially to Hanoi — of the solidarity of international support for resistance to aggression in Vietnam and for a peaceful settlement in Vietnam". Rusk also explained that he fully appreciated the difficulties involved in augmenting the Australian commitment but "hoped that, when the full scope of United States decisions became known, the Australian Government might also take additional build-up measures that would permit an earlier contribution that present military plans would allow".²⁷ Two days later, President Johnson told the White House press corps that he had ordered to Vietnam the Air Mobile Division "and certain other forces which will raise our fighting strength from 75,000 to 125,000 almost immediately. Additional forces will be needed later and they will be sent as requested." He did not, he added, "find it easy to send the flower of our youth, our finest young men, into battle . . . This is the most agonizing and the most painful duty of your President."²⁸ Some of the flower of America's youth also seemed to find their duty painful and agonizing. Private Winstead R. Bolton of the 1st Cavalry responded to his president's orders by going on a hunger strike to protest against United States involvement in Vietnam.

Menzies and his advisers did not, by contrast, seem to have experienced any emotional distress about sending 1st Battalion RAR to serve in Vietnam. Nor do they seem to have been impressed by Rusk's appeal for a more substantial Australian contribution, despite the fact that a vastly greater effort by somebody was obviously going to be necessary to avert total collapse in South Vietnam. However, such an effort could only be made by the United States. Nothing that Australia was in a position to do could make any significant difference, so there was no particular urgency, practically speaking, for Australia to do any more than it had done already. Menzies duly consulted with External Affairs about the possibility of responding positively to Rusk's appeal for an increased Australian commitment. He was assured that the government could "only look for marginal extra contributions in the immediate future", of which "the most attractive in political terms is the idea of building up the battalion to a battle group". External Affairs was moreover convinced that the government should not plan for a two battalion effort in Vietnam early in 1966, and should in any case not tell the Americans even if it were to plan for such an effort. There was no point in encouraging inconveniently high expectations of what Australia could or would do. Nor should any decision be made without "a careful examination in the light of continuing United States and British policies in South East Asia", which interestingly had not been done, because nobody had asked for it to be done.

Departmental and Service advisers reported to cabinet in mid-August. Their recommendations were based on the three criteria of "what was necessary for the military effort in Vietnam, what was necessary to continue to attract American support in the area, and what would satisfy Australian public opinion". It seemed that these criteria could be satisfied with very little extra effort indeed. Cabinet agreed that the battalion should be augmented to a Battalion Group by the addition of ancillary and supporting units; that the Americans should be told that Australia could not make a more substantial contribution, and why; and that the National Service intake should be retained at the existing level of 8,400 annually. No planning or preparation whatever was to be made on the assumption that "an additional battalion or any other additional forces would be committed to Vietnam". Waller was directed to present the decision to augment the battalion "in a way that will make the greatest favourable impact on the Americans", which was certainly going to tax his admirable diplomatic skills. There was of course no consultation with the Vietnamese. They were simply told that the battalion would be augmented "in context of a step in pursuance of their earlier request", which they had not actually made.[29]

Chairman of the National Leadership Committee, Major General Nguyen Van Thieu, duly expressed his pleasure at the news on 18 August that an additional 350 Australian troops would be sent, and even asked "what the possibilities were if, at some time in the future, the Vietnamese Government were to make a request for additional forces".[30] The only truthful answer would have been that nothing that the Australian government had done or ever would do in this regard would be in response to any request from Saigon. Whatever might happen in South Vietnam was not the issue, except as an occasion for encouraging the United States to interpose its military power between Australia and China. Howson put the Australian position exactly when he noted that "even if we lose the war in Vietnam, the justification of our present Defence Policy is: 1. We honour our obligations in ANZUS and SEATO and therefore can expect our allies to help us if the Australian mainland is attacked. 2. We gain *valuable time* to re-arm in 1964–68."[31] ANZUS and SEATO were not really the issue either, as neither had ever been invoked with respect to the defence of South Vietnam. Nor was there any ally other than the United States which could really be expected to come to the help of Australia if its mainland were attacked.

It was a highly pragmatic policy, but its success depended upon the willingness of the Australian people to continue doing whatever was required to encourage the Americans to stay in Vietnam, and the willingness of the Americans to respond to such encouragement.

The United States Secretary of State, Mr Rusk, and the Prime Minister, Mr Menzies, in Canberra during the meeting of the ANZUS Council. (Reprinted courtesy of the Department of External Affairs, *Current Notes on International Affairs* 33:5 [May 1962]:27.)

The New Zealand Prime Minister, Mr Holyoake, the Australian Prime Minister, Mr Menzies, and the Australian Minister for External Affairs, Sir Garfield Barwick, in Canberra during the meeting of the ANZUS Council. (Reprinted courtesy of the Department of External Affairs, *Current Notes on International Affairs* 33:5 [May 1962]:28.)

The Australian Ambassador to the United States, Mr J. K. Waller, talking with President Lyndon B. Johnson on 18 September 1964, after presenting his credentials to the President in Washington. (Reprinted courtesy of the Department of External Affairs, *Current Notes on International Affairs* 35:10 [October 1964]:20.)

The late Prime Minister of Australia, The Rt Hon. Harold Holt, C.H., M.P. (Reprinted courtesy of the Department of External Affairs, *Current Notes on International Affairs* 38:12 [December 1967]:534.)

The Vice-President of the United States, Mr Hubert H. Humphrey (left), with the Australian Prime Minister, Mr Harold E. Holt, and the Leader of the Opposition, Mr A. A. Calwell, at Parliament House, Canberra. (Reprinted courtesy of the Department of External Affairs, *Current Notes on International Affairs* 37:2 [February 1966]:56.)

President Johnson puts a friendly arm around Harold Holt during his visit to Australia in October 1966. (Reprinted by permission of the *Age*.)

Presidents Lyndon B. Johnson (United States), Park Chung Hee (Korea), Ferdinand E. Marcos and Mrs Marcos (Philippines), and Nguyen van Thieu (Republic of Vietnam) at the Memorial Service for the late Mr Holt at St Paul's Cathedral, Melbourne on 22 December 1967. (Reprinted courtesy of the Department of External Affairs, *Current Notes on International Affairs* 38:12 [December 1967]:537.)

The British Prime Minister, Mr Harold Wilson (left) with the Australian Prime Minister, Mr John McEwen (right) and the Minister for External Affairs, Mr Paul Hasluck, after his arrival in Australia to attend the Memorial Service for the late Mr Holt at St Paul's Cathedral, Melbourne on 22 December 1967. (Reprinted courtesy of the Department of External Affairs, *Current Notes on International Affairs* 38:12 [December 1967]:537.)

The Minister for External Affairs, Mr Paul Hasluck, addressing the United Nations General Assembly on 27 September 1966. (Reprinted courtesy of the Department of External Affairs, *Current Notes on International Affairs* 37:9 [September 1966]:532.)

Doubts about official American regard for Australia were allayed finally by the arrival of distinguished Texan lawyer Ed Clark to take up his responsibilities as US Ambassador in Canberra on 23 August 1965, one week short of a year since Battle had left. Waller thought Clark's appointment "an excellent choice", as "the person who would help Australia most . . . would be a man who was a personal friend of the President's", and if he were also a Texan, "so much the better, because there's a great physical similarity between Texas and large parts of Australia".[32]

Signs of unofficial disapproval were mounting ominously in both countries, however. The National Co-ordinating Committee to End the War in Vietnam sponsored a series of nation-wide demonstrations in the United States. Sympathy rallies followed in Australia. On 18 October David J. Miller, a volunteer worker with a relief programme run by the *Catholic Worker*, was arrested by the FBI in Hookset, New Hampshire, for burning his selective service card. Norman R. Morrison, a Quaker of Baltimore, Maryland, poured a gallon jug of kerosene over himself and burned himself to death in front of the Pentagon to express his concern over the loss of life and suffering in Vietnam. A week later, *Catholic Worker* member Roger A. La Porte burned himself to death in front of the United Nations headquarters in New York as a protest against the war. Then 35,000 marchers converged on the White House on 27 November. Australian policymakers might have done well to reflect on these portents. They were not going to retain much credit in Washington by encouraging the US administration to pursue a policy which the American people themselves were increasingly tending to reject.

There was another fundamental problem of credibility. Fear of China was the only serious justification that the Australian government had ever presented for its support of United States intervention in Vietnam; but China's own international position was looking more fearful by the month. The People's Republic seemed to be in the truly desperate situation of confronting irreconcilably both superpowers at the same time. China and the United States had been in an apparently total adversary relationship since the expulsion of Chiang K'ai-shek from the mainland in 1949. Relations with the Soviet Union had become sensitive in June 1959 when the Russians formally abrogated whatever agreement might have existed with respect to supplying China with technical assistance to achieve nuclear capability. Soviet technicians were withdrawn in August 1960, along with all the blueprints for joint projects not yet completed. The twenty-second CPSU Party Congress in October 1961 openly acknowledged the existence of a schism within the communist bloc, despite the presence in Moscow of Zhou Enlai. Their quarrel became public in January 1963. Relations were deteriorating at an accelerating rate through 1965. The Beijing press ran a series of articles denouncing the anti-Chinese attitude of the Soviet Union. Chinese Ambassador to Russia Pan Tzu-li protested in March 1965 against the excessive violence used by the Moscow militia towards Chinese students demonstrating outside the United States Embassy, of all places. The *People's Daily* then denounced the Soviet leadership for seeking to "extinguish the revolution struggle of the South Vietnamese people against U.S. imperialism and its lackeys", and accused them of entering into a "love feast" with the United States. Soviet Premier Kosygin counter-charged on 7 May that some people contended that "only a new world war can bring about the unity and solidarity of the international communist movement", and insisted that there was "no more important task than to prevent a new world conflagration". The Chinese press responded by accusing Kosygin of not departing from "the essence of Khrushchev's policies", including "Soviet-American cooperation for the domination of the world".

Circumstantial support for the proposition that the Russians had become converted to the way of peace while the Chinese were still committed to the way of war was provided by a lengthy analysis released by Chinese Defence Minister Lin Biao on 2 September. It encouraged "the waging of peoples' wars by the revolutionary peoples of Asia, Africa and Latin America", as the means by which the "colossus of U.S. imperialism could be split up and defeated". It also denounced the "general line of the Khruschchev revisionists" as being "nothing other than the demand that all the oppressed peoples and nations and all the countries that have won independence should lay down their arms and place themselves at the mercy of the U.S. imperialists and their lackeys". However, there was no implication that the People's Republic itself was going to get militarily involved in any of these peoples' wars. It was rather a rallying call for the oppressed peoples of the world outside to do for themselves what the Chinese people had done, and presumably to do it by themselves, as the Chinese people had. One needed a clear eye for the fine print and a good ear for the nuances of language to be able to interpret Chinese official statements with any degree of accuracy. A sense of humour helped too, especially when dealing with the statements of Zhou Enlai.

It was not merely the case that there was a vast gulf between what the Chinese were saying and what they were actually doing. There was also a vast gulf between what they appeared to be saying and what they were really saying. One could conclude at the time that the PRC, racked by internal economic and ideological tensions and bitterly at odds with both Washington and Moscow, was in no position to undertake any aggressive foreign adventures whatever.[33] Nor had the past record of the PRC indicated any such intentions on the part of its leaders. They had indeed conducted their power plays since 1949 with a sense of restraint which could only be termed artistic. They had moved massively into Korea in order to forestall an attempt by General MacArthur to overrun the communist north totally, but they had settled for a ceasefire which effectly restored the status quo of June 1950. They had engaged in a delicate game of bluff over the Offshore Islands with the ultimate poker player, Dwight D. Eisenhower, on two occasions, withdrawing from the game both times with minimal loss of face and, in 1958 at least, with great urbanity and good humour. They had conducted a totally successful military operation in October 1962 to repel Indian troops intruding into the disputed zone between the two countries, and had then withdrawn unilaterally, having made their point. These were not the actions of desperate people, ready to win or lose all on a throw of the military dice, however desperate the position of their country might seem to the world outside. Even those governments most concerned to portray the leadership in Beijing as the greatest living menace to human survival had no qualms about doing business with it. The Australian What Board signed an enormous contract on 8 November to sell 500,000 tons from its coming harvest to the People's Republic. The Russians had never stopped signing agreements for the expansion of trade, cultural cooperation and the mutual supply of supplementary goods. They were signing more than ever as ideological tensions mounted between Moscow and Beijing.

The abiding Australian fear of a Beijing-Jakarta axis was dissipated when an attempted coup, in which the Indonesian Communist Party was involved, was crushed by Right Wing Army forces in October 1965, with a consequent loss of life estimated at close to one million. Pressure for a more convincing Australian demonstration of support for United States intervention in Vietnam was rising, however, just as the chief motivation for such support was losing all conviction. McNamara had visited Saigon for another first-hand look at an ever more disheartening situation. He reported back to President Johnson that "the presently contemplated Phase I forces will not be enough (approx. 220,000 Americans, almost all in place by end of 1965) . . . Nor will the originally contemplated Phase II addition of 28 more US battalions (112,000 men) be enough." What would be required was "up to 74 battalions by end-66: total to approx. 400,000 by end-66. And it should be understood that further deployments (perhaps exceeding 200,000) may be needed in 1967." Air action should moreover be escalated over the next six months "until . . . it includes 'controlled' reconnaissance of lines of communication throughout the area, bombing of petroleum storage facilities and power plants, and mining of the harbors. (Left unstruck would be population targets, industrial plants, locks and dams.)"[34] McNamara suggested to Ambassador Anderson that Washington would welcome an enlarged Australian effort in sympathy with the vastly augmented American commitment. Even allowing for the population disparity, 1,557 Australians hardly compared with the proposed deployment of around 600,000 Americans. The Secretary moderately raised "the possibility of another combat battalion by October 1966. The Ambassador said that the Australians would certainly consider the request very seriously. The implication was that they will provide such a battalion as fast as their growing training base would permit."[35] United States embassy staff in Canberra were told, however, that "although the matter of additional GOA troops for Vietnam now under consideration at Cabinet level, problem had become somewhat complicated by UK approach concerning possible Australian assistance in Zambia".[36]

This was a little hard to take seriously. Menzies was indeed responsive, more perhaps than any other Australian politician before or since, to the calls of Empire or even of the Commonwealth. He had after all been proposing in 1950 to send Australian troops to Malaya, where they were not needed and had not been asked for, instead of Korea, where they were and had been. But there was little intrinsically less likely than Menzies sending Australian troops overseas at the request of a British Labour government to defend a black African dictatorship against incursions by white Rhodesians, whom Menzies himself was supporting in every way possible.[37] It was only an excuse. Menzies was in the last stages of winding up the most successful political career in Australian history. He was hardly going to risk spoiling his last hurrah by sending any more Australian troops anywhere. That could be left to a new leader for whom nostalgia for the Empire was meaningless and the Commonwealth only an irrelevant distraction from the real issues of Australian national interest. Cabinet decided in the last weeks of Menzies's reign that it "saw no need to rush into a decision" on augmenting the Australian commitment to Vietnam. If an extra battalion were committed, "it could not be done before March or April 1966; the defence group did not favour further piecemeal contributions; and a decision should await the outcome of ministerial discussions with the United Kingdom in the latter part of January 1966".[38] Opposition leader Arthur A. Calwell asked Menzies on 10 December if there were any truth in the current rumours that the government intended to send another battalion to Vietnam and would be sending conscripts in March. The truth was that the Americans had said that another Australian battalion would be appreciated and appropriate, that they had been given reason to expect that another battalion would in fact be sent, that cabinet had considered the possibility, and that it had been decided to delay actually doing anything about it until the new Liberal leadership had been installed. What Menzies told Calwell was that the government "has made no decision of any kind and can accept no responsibility for such such rumours as existed".[39] His reply was true as far as it went, like most official statements made about Vietnam in Canberra and Washington. It was, however, deliberately contrived to mislead the questioner on the actual point about which information was being sought.

This was almost Sir Robert Menzies's last contribution to the saga of Australian involvement in Vietnam. His very last contribution was to announce on 17 December that "approval had been given for the award to troops serving in the area of a special (South) Vietnam's clasp".[40] Then he prepared himself to step down from the position of supreme power which he had exercised in Canberra on and off for some nineteen years, preparatory to undertaking the responsibilities of Lord Warden of the Cinque Ports. No more appropriate choice could possibly have been made.

More than medals would be needed, however, to improve matters in Vietnam from those governments still making any kind of effort in that direction. Harold Wilson met with President Johnson on 15 December. His purpose was to warn the president that the limits on

British support were contracting. He had just received a cable signed by sixty-eight British Labour parliamentarians demanding that the United States cease air attacks on North Vietnam. Wilson appealed to Johnson "at least to suspend the bombing to test the sincerity of North Vietnamese hints that there might be a response on their side, possibly leading to negotiations". He also warned Johnson that "if US aircraft were to bomb Hanoi or Haiphong we should be forced publicly to dissociate from that action". Johnson's response was surprisingly subdued. He "referred to Britain's position as Geneva co-chairman and said that he wanted his people to know he regarded our task as that of trying to get the parties to the conference table. He would support any initiative we proposed to that end. It was a far cry from the hot-line explosion ten months earlier."[41] Wilson chose to interpret this display of resignation on Johnson's part as "an absolute promise from the President that he would be allowed to work for peace and not send British troops to Vietnam".[42] It was in fact rather a further manifestation of the sense of exhaustion and despair gradually overwhelming the Johnson administration. Lester Pearson had doubted eight months earlier whether Johnson would be able to meet the test of Vietnam; and the test was getting tougher all the time.

Efforts being expended were showing no signs of achieving the desired results. The administration's only solution was to increase the efforts, which necessarily implied increased demands on the allies, as well as on the United States itself. Secretary Rusk instructed the US embassy in Seoul on 8 January 1966 to begin prompt negotiations to obtain a Korean regiment for Vietnam by April and a full division by July. His sense of urgency was strengthened by a despairing report from Assistant Secretary of Defense McNaughton that "we are in an escalating military stalemate". Even an increase in the US commitment to 400,000 troops by the end of 1966, as recommended by McNamara, would not, he considered, guarantee success.[43]

Canberra was immune from such forebodings. Howson welcomed the New Year with the anticipation that "in twelve months' time I expect that we should at least be well on the way to a reasonable solution — the eventual establishment of a pro-Western, anti-Chinese form of Government in Saigon".[44] It was a sense of complacency amounting to euphoria which was wholly characteristic of a new and poignantly brief era in Australian politics. Federal Treasurer Harold E. Holt's accession to the prime ministership on 31 January was like a new dawn, which would never have a noon. The outgoing and incoming prime ministers symbolized perfectly the transition from the dream of an imperial past to the vision of an American future. Menzies had ensured that he would always be identified as the "Queen's Man" by those who never knew of his bitter altercations with Winston Churchill in the early years of World War Two. Holt by contrast might have emerged from a Hollywood casting office as the stereotype of a forward-looking executive, silverhaired and silvertailed, a George Raft endowed with muscles and charm, faultlessly photogenic, indefatigably articulate, impressively physical on the beach in a spearfisher's outfit with his three beautiful daughters-in-law draped about him like scarves, and ideally supported by a wife chic, witty, sociable, and exotically named Zara. He seemed a leader as theatrically appropriate for Australia's future as Menzies had been for its past. A few intimates knew that Holt believed his own future would be an early death.

Cartoonists were delighted to discover a certain miniskirt-and-bikini quality about the new leadership, wholly congenial to the spirit of the times. But Holt also had a vision of a new role for his nation as the regional partner of the United States in the Pacific, assuming the responsibilities about to be vacated by the United Kingdom. It would be the realization of what John Curtin and Herbert Vere Evatt had sought after Pearl Harbor and what Alfred Deakin had dreamed of in the early years of federation. It depended absolutely on the willingness of the Americans to remain committed militarily to the defence of Southeast Asia. Holt soon had an opportunity to proclaim Australian solidarity with that commitment. On the day that he became prime minister, twenty United States senators appealed to President Johnson to prolong the pause in the bombing of North Vietnam proclaimed on 24 December. United Nations Secretary General U Thant considered that "the situation during the cessation of bombing is more congenial for fruitful discussions than a few weeks ago when the bombings were taking place". He hoped that the pause would be protracted so that the situation could continue to improve. Canadian Prime Minister Lester B. Pearson similarly expressed the hope that "those who are more directly concerned than we are and who are bearing the burden of this issue will be able to maintain the patience and wisdom they have been showing in recent weeks".[45]

It was a forlorn hope. General Westmoreland reported on 28 January 1966 that he was going to need 459,000 troops in Vietnam by the end of the year — up 59,000 from McNamara and McNaughton's forebodings. He also insisted that the communists were merely employing the bombing pause to regroup and consolidate. Bombing resumed on 31 January. Lester Pearson warned United States Ambassador J. Walton Butterworth that the decision to recommence the air strikes was to be regretted because he "did not think that any military solution was possible", and because President Johnson would "find it difficult to secure an international 'consensus' supporting indefinite and 'escalated' military intervention".[46] Surprisingly, the British Foreign Office announced that "H.M. Government had hoped that the North Vietnamese would take advantage of the suspension of the bombing to respond to repeated American offers to negotiate. H.M. Government regret that the North Vietnamese still refuse all offers of this nature. Consequently, H.M. Government understand and support the decision of the U.S. Government to resume the bombing which they had suspended in the hope of reaching a peaceful settlement."[47] This was not what HM Government really felt about the situation. Ninety-six British Labour and Liberal Members of Parliament immediately sent a cable to US Senator J. William Fulbright, Chairman of the Senate Foreign Relations Committee, calling on him to continue to oppose the extension of the "cruel and dangerous war". Wilson for his part was furious that the Foreign Office, "falling over itself to get into line", should have "issued a press statement supporting the President's reaction. By an error, this was not submitted to me for approval." He assured the House of Commons that he "would not have agreed to a statement in those terms", and that he had "pressed in Washington for the Christmas truce, both in ground fighting and bombing to be extended". However, he also commented that it was necessary to understand President Johnson's position and that he would "have liked to have seen the peace lobby outside the Chinese Embassy demanding that the Chinese Government should use their influence ... on Hanoi ... to make peace".[48] The French naturally expressed their "regret and disapproval".

There was nothing regretful or equivocal about Harold Holt's opinion as expressed on 1 February. "North Vietnam," he declared, "cannot be allowed to mount operations against the South Vietnamese, American, Australian, New Zealand and Korean troops taking part in the defence of the territory."[49] A meeting two days later with British Defence Secretary Denis Healey reinforced Holt's convictions about the general desirability of fostering the Pacific connection with the United States in every way possible. "I believe," Howson recorded after the talks, "that most people realize that the UK will move from Singapore, if not in 1970, then within five years from then, and so 'Fortress Australia' must then come into focus."[50] Holt himself told a press conference in less alarmist terms that he was "hopeful of an indefinite continuance" of the British presence at Singapore, but that it made "sense to us to examine together what practical arrangements would need to be made in the event of the British presence there becoming untenable at some point of time". This of course fitted into "the current concept of interdependence, of SEATO planning and this sort of thing. What we do in Viet Nam," he added, however, "is perhaps more directly between ourselves and the United States than between ourselves and a lot of other people, but at least on the basis of what has been conveyed to us, we can say, well, it looks as though this is the sort of thing that would be expected of us by the British . . . Now, knowing what the picture looks like there, we turn and see what we can do or ought to be doing in other directions, including Viet Nam."[51]

There could be no doubt that this was what would be expected by the Americans. Defense Secretary McNamara had already expressed the hope in testimony to the Senate Foreign Relations Committee on 21 January that the allies would be making some additional contribution in support of the vastly increased United States efforts. President Johnson announced that he was going to Honolulu for personal discussions with South Vietnamese leaders and United States military and diplomatic advisers. A Joint Communique issued on 8 February committed Washington and Saigon to "a policy of growing military effectiveness". It was also announced that Vice President Hubert H. Humphrey would be visiting Saigon and other Asian capitals, presumably to encourage demonstrations of solidarity with the Honolulu Communique.

Humphrey arrived in Canberra on 19 February. There was no question of any intention to exert pressure on the Australians. It was, Ambassador Waller considered, simply "a mark of appreciation of a good ally . . . so far as Vice President Humphrey was concerned".[52] Defence Minister Sir Allen Fairhall had been engaged on a submission to cabinet on extra aid to Vietnam for at least a fortnight prior to Humphrey's visit. All that was necessary for the Vice President was to encourage the Australians to continue along the path on which they were already embarked, for their own reasons. He did this appropriately with a "stirring speech lasting about three quarters of an hour chiefly on the determination of the USA to support Vietnam both militarily and economically ... Certainly," Howson continued, "it committed the USA to continue their efforts in Vietnam for a long time to come."[53] As such, it was exactly the kind of reassurance the Australians most wanted to hear. Humphrey himself insisted at a joint press conference with Prime Minister Holt that he had "not made any request to the Government of Australia for additional forces in Viet Nam". Holt however interposed to clarify the situation.

> We are in almost daily, certainly close and continuous discussion and consultation at some level or other with the United States of America. What the Vice President has said about our talks today I confirm completely of course ... I can say with entire sincerity and frankness that at no time has any pressure been put upon this country of an improper or irregular character by the Government of the United States or any representative of it. But we are grown people, we can think and speak in realistic terms about these things. And what a remarkable world it would be if at no point in discussions in either service quarters or administrative or government quarters that the question hadn't been raised as to whether Australia could do a little more here or a little more there.[54]

It was the authentic tone of the new Australian leadership, assured, sophisticated, cool. Holt could be assured, because he was telling the simple truth. There could be no question of Australia's being pressed to do more, because Australia was already doing far more than any of the other "Free World" countries which Washington had besought to show their flags in Vietnam. Only New Zealand also had combat troops (119) openly serving in Vietnam. Australia with 1,557 was not in the position of a delinquent client being squeezed to keep up its payments. It was a good friend which had already helped its great partner out a little and would be prepared to help it out a little more, on the clear assumption that it would indeed be only a little more.

Canberra and Washington seemed to have achieved an ideal rapport. George S. Moore, president of the First National City Bank, New York, who had been accompanying Humphrey in Manila and Canberra, wrote to Presidential Aide Jack J. Valenti that Holt had told him he "felt extremely comfortable that President Johnson had such a highly competent back-up man considering the dependency of the whole free world on our Presidency. Apparently the things the Vice President said pleased them and the whole reaction was favorable. I found Australia's attitudes toward the U.S. even more friendly than I had expected. I think," he told Valenti, "they are going to give us some added support in Viet-Nam."⁵⁵

There were indeed. A new and compelling reason had suddenly emerged for another convincing display of solidarity on Australia's part. Canberra would not be able to count on picking up credit as the only ally of the United States in the field in Vietnam for much longer. The Philippines seemed less credible on the military side than ever. Humphrey had been greeted in Manila by massed demonstrators protesting against the idea of sending even a noncombatant engineer battalion to Vietnam. Bangkok, however, had activated the Royal Thai Military Assistance Group, Vietnam, on 17 February 1966; and South Korean President Park Chung Hee announced on 20 February that he would be sending a full division and a regiment of combat troops to Vietnam. Howson gathered from Thai Field Marshal Kittikachorn that the "Thais now think the USA will eventually win in Vietnam, so they are starting to climb onto our side of the fence". There was accordingly an urgent need for Australia to act to maintain its high profile with the Americans in the face of what looked like considerably more substantial Asian participation. In the meantime, Canberra sought to pursue its own particular concern by endeavouring "to get Thais and other Asian nations to declare their policy and to support the need for tough line against China".⁵⁶

This might well have seemed equally unpromising and untimely. Pursuing a tough line against China was a course of action not likely to appeal to countries actually sharing a frontier with the People's Republic. Nor had the need for such a course of action ever seemed less evident. Beijing was just then engaged in denouncing the Soviet leadership for "supporting U.S. efforts to achieve the military encirclement of China".⁵⁷ The Russians counter-charged that Beijing was seeking to bring about war between the United States and the Soviet Union. It was not clear what Australia could hope to gain by contributing to the mood of paranoia that appeared to be developing among the Chinese leadership. It might have seemed more promising to have tried sending a few reassuring signals before the Chinese felt driven to do something really desperate, which they were indeed about to do. The Cultural Revolution was only a couple of months away.

Holt had more immediate problems on his mind, however. He had already decided to replace the augmented Australian battalion with a self-contained task force of some 4,500 men under Australian command. This next commitment to Vietnam was going to be the last one. He explained to Johnson that "the provision of a force of this size represented the upper limit of Army capacity . . . short of a major emergency it would not be practicable to enlarge it . . . The Government had believed that the task force would be the most cost effective contribution Australia could make to the allied effort in South Vietnam and it judged that it should go so far at that time, in consequence of the high importance of the issues at stake in South Vietnam and to make a clear demonstration of Australia's support for the massive efforts of the United States."[58] There remained of course the formality of organizing a South Vietnamese request for the assistance that Holt had told Johnson he would be sending. Ambassador Anderson and External Affairs officers in Canberra had urged that any announcement of an increased Australian commitment "should be preceded by adequate prior consultation with the Vietnamese, in order that it would appear that the Australian decision was taken in response to a Vietnamese rather than an American request". Premier Ky, Anderson warned, was indeed "reported to have said previously that existing arrangements would not cover any further military forces that Australia might wish to send to Vietnam: 'there would have to be a specific request from the Government of Vietnam' ".[59] Anderson was told on 4 March that Canberra had decided to increase its commitment, and that he was to advise Ky accordingly and work out the terms of a request. This hardly amounted to adequate prior consultation with the Vietnamese, but perhaps Ky felt that he was not in a position to raise difficulties about any assistance he might receive, however it might be presented to him. He sent a formal request to Holt on 7 March in which he referred to "the discussions which took place in Saigon last December, during the visit of the Australian Minister of Foreign Affairs . . . Following the consultations which have been taking place between our two governments . . . the Government of the Republic of Vietnam wishes to request the Australian Government for any increased military contribution which it might be able to make in the present situation."[60]

This misrepresented the situation in the manner desired. Holt announced the following day that the Australian commitment would be tripled in size, amounting to a headquarters unit, two infantry battalions, a Special Air Services Squadron, combat and logistic support units and a flight of eight RAAF *Iroquois* helicopters. Moreover, the two army battalions would include, the prime minister told parliament, "a proportion of fully trained and integrated national servicemen as will all future substantial Australian Army units deployed overseas in any theatre". Arthur Calwell's suspicions had been well founded.

Holt's justification for the increased Australian commitment to Vietnam was of course Chinese imperialism. What was happening in Vietnam, he explained, was "the principal present manifestation of the expansionist activities of Communist China", at that moment turned obsessively inward in a rhapsody of self-mutilation. "All of the countries of Southeast Asia," he asserted, "are facing the threat of Communist China's expansion in one form or another."[61] This hardly applied to Indonesia, where communists and Chinese were being massacred impartially, where a military and implacably anticommunist government had been installed which had broken off diplomatic relations with Beijing. Defence Minister Allen Fairhall was even more uncompromising. He thought that there was "not the slightest doubt that the North Vietnamese are puppets of the Chinese", and that what was happening in South Vietnam was "perhaps only the first round of an attack by the Chinese Communists to dominate the world".[62] Nothing was of course inherently less likely than that Vietnamese of any description would ever consent to be puppets of the Chinese, and one could only feel that if the Chinese themselves were in fact planning to conquer the world, they were going a strange way about it.

What was really happening in Vietnam was not the point. What mattered was that the United States was increasing its involvement and Australia was seen to be actively encouraging it to do so. Howson thought that things were working out very satisfactorily. It was obvious, he considered, that "defence problems in SE Asia are crystallizing. We can rely on UK at least for next ten years either in Singapore or on the Australian mainland. Vietnam will take many months, but there is now every indication that we won't lose and will probably achieve a fairly honorable settlement."[63] All South Vietnam had to do was last that long.

It might well have seemed that any help coming to South Vietnam would be too little, too late or the wrong kind. Things were falling apart again. Ky dismissed Lieutenant General Nguyen Chan Thi as District Commander in Hue on 10 March on charges of having acted independently of the government. General strikes followed in Hue and Da Nan g, calling on the United States to get out of Vietnam and appealing for support against Ky. Buddhist demonstrations followed in Saigon itself, demanding a return to civilian rule. Ky's response was to declare that he would make no concessions of any kind. More general strikes and demonstrations followed. He then announced that he would be making some concessions after all, and appointed a committee to draft a new constitution.

Nor was it only in Vietnam that ominous signs of discontent were manifesting themselves. Howson had discovered that even in Australia the government was beginning to meet "much opposition in the electorates", and that it would be necessary to "plan for a bigger public relations campaign 'to sell the government policy' ".[64] The US embassy in Canberra thought so too. It reported that "while the GOA is not yet in serious trouble over its decision to send conscripts to Viet-Nam, the situation is clearly becoming a major one. The initiative seems to have passed from the government to opposition forces. The Embassy stresses that this shift is not in public opinion on the issue, which they are not yet able to assess. Heavy weather is forecast, with substantial attacks not only on the GOA, but also US policies." Reports from almost everywhere else in the world were no more encouraging. In the Philippines Marcos was "being subjected to increasing press criticism for spending too much congressional time on Viet-Nam". The Danish Foreign Minister had informed parliament that "the war was not Denmark's war ... Denmark had at no time endorsed US policies nor had it been asked to do so, but ... the Government had not tried to conceal its disagreement on certain issues with American policy". Public protests continued in Germany, even though these were expected to arouse "minimal public interest". The Swedes endorsed US peace efforts but condemned US military efforts and associated their position with that of the United Nations. The Indians said remarkably that they had "gone to great lengths to explain and justify the US point of view" and considered now that " 'we have done our best for you' ". Even the Israeli left wing was "being progressively committed, if not to the NVN and VC cause, at least to 'solidarity' with it against US 'intervention' ". There was no point in suggesting even an R & R programme for allied troops in Pakistan, which might have seemed a rather improbable venue for such a programme anyway, because "the GOP [Government of Pakistan] would almost certainly shy away from a scheme which might seem to commit it to public support of the US position in Viet-Nam".[65]

It was the old story. The more flags campaign had not rallied "Free

World" solidarity with United States military intervention in Vietnam. All that it had done was divide the "Free World" conspicuously between the tiny handful who were prepared to get involved and all of the rest who categorically refused to do anything of the kind. It had not encouraged support for US policies. What it had done was to establish the almost universal lack of support for them.

Johnson in such circumstances had to take his comfort where he could find it. The Australians had made a renewed gesture of support, even if they had also made clear that they intended it to be their last one. The South Korean National Assembly decided on 30 March to dispatch to Vietnam the Ninth White Horse Division with support troops numbering 23,865 in all to reinforce the 18,904 men of the Capital Division and the Marine Brigade there already. Harold Wilson was back in office in London. Johnson might very well have preferred to see the Conservatives in power there instead but he was prepared to make the best of what he had got. "Sleep well, my dear friend," he cabled the enigmatic Yorkshireman. "It's mighty comforting to me to know you are still at the helm. I feel better about the future."[66] Johnson always had a credibility problem, even when he was not telling the truth; but credibility problems went with the territory in Vietnam.

7

The PM Has Been Mesmerized (1966–1967)

South Vietnam itself had never looked less credible than why Ky flew to Da Nang at the beginning of April 1966, threatening the use of armed force against Buddhist demonstrators. Undersecretary of State Cyrus R. Vance warned Johnson that the political situation in Vietnam was "confused and chaotic" once more, and that it was "not clear whether Ky will survive". This was a matter for very serious concern indeed, because, as Lester Pearson had pointed out, it would be difficult to convince anybody that the United States was really defending democracy in South Vietnam if there were yet another coup in Saigon. Vance could however still draw reassurance from the fact that "the morale of our troops is magnificent. Even the men in the hospitals," he told the President, "are in good spirits. They have a sense of dedication and display a professional competence which makes one proud to be an American. In addition, the morale and competence of our Korean, Australian and New Zealand allies are outstanding. They are proud to be fighting with us in the common cause."[1]

The doctors were clearly in fine shape. Unfortunately, the patient was dying. George W. Ball reiterated at a White House meeting on 9 April that "there are no really attractive options open to us", and urged again that the United States should halt the deployment of additional forces, reduce the level of its air attacks on the North, and maintain ground activity at the minimum level required to prevent the Viet Cong from substantially improving their position. Assistant Defense Secretary McNaughton noted after talks with another US official just back from Saigon that Vietnam was "in unholy mess. We control next to no territory. Fears economic collapse. Militarily will be same place year from now. Pacification won't get off ground for a year." Even William P. Bundy now feared that "as we look a year or two ahead . . . the war could well become an albatross round the Administration's neck at least equal to what Korea was for President Truman". The Pentagon concluded after a study that the air bombardment had had no measurable effect upon the ability of North Vietnam to mount and support military operations in the South at the current level.[2] Some ripples of the mounting wave of United States disillusionment were at last reaching as far as Canberra. Howson felt that the news "of almost certain civil war between Buddhists and Catholics raises issues that are almost too terrible to contemplate. I am usually fairly optimistic and look on the bright side of life — but I'm damned if I can see any brightness whatsoever in this issue."[3]

Howson and his colleagues might possibly have derived some comfort from the mounting internal and external pressures vexing China. Zhou Enlai took the desperate step of calling on 30 April for a "fierce and protracted struggle to wipe out bourgeois ideology in the academic, educational and journalistic fields, in art, literature and all other fields of culture".[4] It was to have the effect of retarding technological development in China by perhaps two student generations, and would obviously have ruled out any immediate plans that Beijing might have been harbouring for world dominion, if indeed it had ever had any. Even the electoral problems in Australia were proving milder than Howson had anticipated. Public opinion polls hovering between sixty-three and sixty-eight per cent showed support for the increased call-up for military service, and therefore presumably for the war which had required the increased call-up. Harold Holt was back in Canberra on 3 May after a ten-day visit to Southeast Asia, including Vietnam — remarkable for being the first trip ever made by an Australian prime minister to that part of the world, and also for the totally favourable impression Holt had made on everybody he met, including Australian soldiers in the field. Columnist Wallace Brown remembered Holt twenty years later "on the Bien Hoa airstrip in South Vietnam, as he addressed the First Battalion of the Royal Australian Regiment on an Anzac Day parade, with Viet Cong mortar bombs going off 1 km away. It was a moving occasion, and it happened to win him votes. It deserved to."[5]

Holt for his part had been favourably impressed by everything he saw in Vietnam, in contrast with President Johnson's advisers, who tended to be increasingly depressed by everything they saw there. The military situation, he assured cabinet, "will be much improved by the end of the year". The political situation admittedly was "difficult, but should not be exaggerated. The US will stay there whatever happens." His optimism did not abate over the next two weeks. " 'The USA are there to stay,' " he told Howson. " 'We will win there and get protection in the South Pacific for a very small insurance premium.' "[6] It was the reason for Australia being there, after all. Security in the South Pacific was the prize; South Vietnam was merely the battlefield. Australia and the United States might be allies but they were fighting different wars for different concerns. What was most remarkable and most ominous for their association was that even Holt, temperamentally the Australian politician most sympathetic to American concerns, did not seem to recognize as serious circumstances that were rendering the Americans desperate.

South Vietnam and the United States almost went to war in the air over Da Nang only two days after Holt had spoken so reassuringly to Howson. Marine jets scrambled to warn off VNAF planes strafing United States compounds presumably under the impression that they were centres of Buddhist resistance. Ky responded by sending over more VNAF aircraft. The Marines sent up more F-8s. Two hours of perilous aerobatics ensued before the South Vietnamese finally went home. "It was almost a full year since Nguyen Cao Ky had taken the reins of South Vietnam with little concern for either freedom or democracy," the authors of *The Vietnam Experience* commented, "and it would not have been inappropriate to ask if there was any South Vietnamese Government to be saved or worth saving."[7] Matters deteriorated still further when Ky used ARVN units as well as police to break up massive Buddhist demonstrations in Saigon two days later. Buddhist leader Tri Quang began a fast in protest against United States support for Ky on 8 June. ARVN troops then moved into the old capital of Hue, as well as seizing the United Buddhist Church's Secular Affairs Institute, the principal Buddhist stronghold in Saigon. Things did not seem to have changed much since the days of Diem, except that then there had been the option of military rule as a last resort. South Vietnam had tried military rule and it did not seem to be much of an improvement.

The Australians at least had cause for satisfaction. 1st Battalion RAR was coming home. Commanding Officer Lieutenant Colonel Preece summed up the Battalion's achievements at the final ceremonial parade at Tan Son Nhut Airport, Saigon. "Look," he told reporters, "what we have done is show this man can be beaten." They had certainly done that. General Westmoreland was unstinting in his praise. "I have never seen a finer group of men," he told the departing Australians. "I have never fought with a finer group of soldiers." The Australian people were equally unreserved in their enthusiasm over what their soldiers had achieved in Vietnam. The returning veterans were hailed by 300,000 Sydneysiders with a wild ticker-tape reception on 8 June. Their triumph was only enhanced by the intervention of a young woman smeared with red paint who threw herself at Colonel Pearce. Media and public alike applauded Pearce for the manner in which he marched on imperturbably without the slightest deviation, hand at the salute, while police unwrapped the woman from around his neck. National television channels allowed prime time to veterans of former wars to speculate happily about the forms of physical assault best calculated to bring young female demonstrators to a clearer understanding of what life was all about. It was a different world then and it had almost ended.

Traditional values might have seemed secure enough even in mid-1966. But one traditional element of Australian national security was all too obviously about to come to an end. Harold Wilson told the Parliamentary Labour Party Caucus on 15 June that his government intended "to take speedy action in withdrawing from the Far East every unit whose continued presence there ceases to be necessary".[8] It was what Barwick had warned of three years before and what Menzies had taken Australia into Vietnam to guard against. It was clearly time to confirm whatever assurances of United States support he might have gained by that decision. Harold Holt left for Washington on 27 June. He could not have picked a more dramatically appropriate time. US aircraft began a series of air strikes against oil installations in the areas of Hanoi and Haiphong the following day. A pall of smoke hung over the Vietnamese capital. United Nations Secretary General U Thant deplored the American escalation of the war. Indian Prime Minister Gandhi and French President Charles de Gaulle expressed concern and alarm. West Germany was ominously silent. Protestors thronged Grosvenor Square outside the US Embassy in London while Harold Wilson stated gravely that his government "have noted with regret that United States aircraft have attacked North Vietnamese targets touching on the populated areas of Hanoi and Haiphong ... we have made it clear on many occasions that we could not support an extension of the bombing to such areas . . . we feel bound to reaffirm that we must dissociate ourselves from action of this kind".[9] By contrast, Harold Holt, in a mood of post-prandial exuberance following a stag luncheon at the White House, proclaimed in the words of Johnson's own victorious campaign slogan that Australia would "go all the way with LBJ" in support of measures taken in the defence of Vietnam. He was of course referring to verbal support. Australia had so far lost twenty-four men killed in action in Vietnam. The United States had lost over five thousand. With sixteen times Australia's population, the Americans were taking two hundred times its casualties. With about two and a half times Australia's population, the Koreans had nine times as many troops in Vietnam. Holt was certainly not implying that Australia would go all the way down the road of action. It was accordingly incumbent on him to make the best impression that he could with words.

His performance at the stag luncheon was of course very much a *jeu d'esprit*, in distinctly unbuttoned circumstances, but it was by no means inappropriate. There was every reason in the world why the Australian government should give unreservedly enthusiastic support to what the Americans were doing in Vietnam. Australian politicians and diplomats had been seeking for years to get a United States military presence established securely to their north. The black clouds from the burning oil depots around Hanoi and Haiphong were the most convincing symbol possible of Johnson's resolve to maintain and even escalate US military intervention in Vietnam for as long and as far as was necessary. Australia could hardly not go all the way with LBJ when LBJ was going exactly the way that the coalition and its advisers wanted him to go.

Holt put the situation precisely when an incredulous American journalist asked him at the National Press Club in Washington the following day, "Sir, we are not used to having our policies so enthusiastically supported. Isn't there anything wrong with American foreign policy?" "Well," the Australian Prime Minister replied, "frankly, not in our eyes." It was no more than the truth. After a long period of hesitations and heart-burnings, the United States was at last doing everything right, in Australian eyes at least. But not in British eyes. Australian alignment with the United States was very clearly driving a rift between Canberra and London, which made the United States alignment all the more crucial. Wilson had not merely regretted the June air raids and dissociated his government from them. He had also refused to dispatch British troops to Thailand to assist in containing guerillas in the north-east of that country despite urging from both Washington and Canberra, as well as from the Thais, who were "very nervous about subversion in the region". Wilson admitted to Cecil King that his refusal to send troops meant that "relations with the U.S. are not so good, as Johnson does not like criticism".[10] They were also becoming strained with Australia. Hasluck did not conceal his displeasure with British Foreign Secretary Michael Stewart, asking him angrily "what is Britain's policy in S.E. Asia. If she won't help the Thais now, when she has troops to spare after confrontation ends, when would she help." Everything seemed to emphasize that Australia "must not lose sight of the need for an ultimate insurance policy", which had to be the United States, because there was not going to be anybody else.[11] Hasluck's annoyance was of course nothing compared with Johnson's. The president had apparently, according to British Treasury Representative in Washington John Stevens, not particularly resented Wilson's statement dissociating the United Kingdom from the Hanoi bombing. He had even been prepared to live with Wilson's refusal to send troops to Thailand. But Defence Secretary Denis Healey's statement "that we are hoping to sell bombs to the U.S. on condition that they are not used in Vietnam had roused Johnson to fury and to send a message to Wilson that the Americans were not a 'bunch of Pakistanis', this last put through the British Embassy on the Telex machine!"[12]

Holt attempted characteristically to defuse the situation by stressing his grand vision of Australia's emerging role as partner of the United States in succession to the United Kingdom, in areas where the British could no longer make an effective contribution. Holt was also at pains to make the point that this contraction of the traditional British role in the region was not just a matter of diminishing physical resource. "Great Britain and the countries of Western Europe," he told the National Press Club in Canberra, "tend to be inward looking into their own affairs rather than outward looking in a way which would embrace the problems of areas as remote as ours." Australia in consequence found itself "in a position where both the United States and the United Kingdom look to us as a country of influence, a country capable of playing a significant part in the future of the area". On the issue of "American participation, American resolution to see the issue through in South Vietnam, Australia," he affirmed, "is All the Way". But he assured the journalists that "there is no escalation in dimension in contemplation" as far as Australian military intervention was concerned. The premiums had been paid in full. What had been gained was a secure and expanding role in the region in partnership with the greatest power on earth. "The United States," Holt explained, "would, I think, believe that Great Britain will tend to decrease its role in this area of the world. It sees Australia a country ... of increasing population, increasing economic strength, able to play an increasing part in the affairs of the area. And it is understandable that we should be regarded as a partner."[13] It was a vision of the future that would resolve all Australia's besetting problems of identity and security, and Harold Holt looked and sounded in July 1966 just the person to lead his nation into that future. His own future, however, had just another eighteen months to run. His vision died with him.

Holt had been more frank in private with the Americans about the implications for Australia of the decline of British influence in the region. Rusk told Johnson that Holt had informed him that "for the first time in history the Australian papers were openly questioning the value to Australia of the 'fiction' of allegiance to the Queen". The Commonwealth, he and Holt had agreed, "has become little more than a figure of speech; it has meager meaning in a power sense — and not much meaning in a collective sense. The 'new' Commonwealth has no collective significance; at most it is a series of bilateral arrangements that are rapidly wasting away." Nobody should have "any illusions as to the outcome. When the chips are down, — Britain will not put troops into Thailand; — She will maintain Singapore only a few years longer; — She will fall back on Australia and bring her troops home once confrontation is ended." All this however "should not make us too unhappy ... British troops in Germany have an immediate relevance to Britain's participation in Europe. British troops in the Far East are a distraction from the role that Britain should play over the next few years."[14] It was exactly the way Kennedy and his advisers had thought about the Netherlands at the time of the crisis over West New Guinea. Menzies had been far more concerned about the Dutch leaving than Holt was only four years later about the British leaving. Since then Canberra and Washington had acquired a rapport impossible in the days of the anglophile Menzies.

Harold Wilson had no doubt that a new relationship was ripening between Australia and the United States at the expense of those previously existing between both of them and the United Kingdom. He was feeling understandably apprehensive at the prospect of another session with Lyndon Johnson. "Mr Harold Holt," he noted, "had had a hero's welcome" in Washington "as a result of his decision to commit Australian troops in Vietnam. Mr Keith Holyoake of New Zealand had received a similar economium for following suit." Their visits had moreover decided Johnson "to follow up his good fortune by sending a round robin to all his friends asking them to join the bandwagon". Wilson had received "a very urgent and personal message" from the president telling him that Johnson "understood our problems as co-chairman of Geneva; he knew, too, how stretched our forces were, and the heavy commitment we were bearing in NATO. But could we not send even a token force? A platoon of bagpipers would be sufficient; it was the British flag that was wanted. I replied courteously but firmly — there could be no British troops."[15]

For the first time in its history Australia was committed as the ally of a foreign country to a war in which the United Kingdom refused to take part. It was, moreover, a war of which Australian leaders seemed to have formed perceptions significantly different even from those of their great ally's. Paul Hasluck continued to insist in federal parliament that "the military situation in South Vietnam has improved greatly during the year, although it is difficult to see it as being other than a lengthy struggle".[16] Coincidentally, just as Hasluck was speaking, 100 men of 6th Battalion RAR were fighting for their lives in a desperate encounter with about 25 times their number of North Vietnamese and VC at Long Tan. They finally drove the enemy off, losing 16 of their own number dead. Some 245 communist soldiers were left to be buried by the Australians. It was one of the most outstanding feats of arms in the history of the Australian Defence Force (ADF) and it could very easily have resulted in a massacre ending Australian involvement in Vietnam.[17]

Victory at Long Tan had saved the policy of Australian involvement, but such victories were not going to save South Vietnam. As Sir Robert Thompson insisted, "winning ... demands that the Vietnamese Government must steadily regain the countryside, area by area, through a pacification program, and that it must then restore a functioning civil administration to hold it. Progress in these two fields," he commented with perfect truth, as "as yet almost non-existent." Worse still, the bombing offensive was in his mind a fatal "miscalculation which is distracting attention and diverting resources from the development of a winning strategy in the South".[18] Thompson's views on this aspect were endorsed by the Institute for

Defence Analyses in Washington, which reported on 29 August that "U.S. bombing of North Vietnam . . . has had no measurable direct effect on Hanoi's ability to mount and support military operations in the South at the current level . . . The available evidence clearly indicated that Hanoi has been infiltrating military forces and supplies into South Vietnam at an accelerated rate during the present year."[19]

Even McNamara seemed to Cecil King to be approaching the edge of frustration and even despair. He thought that "the hostile Vietnamese, North and South, are losing, in killing and disabled, about 100,000 men per year", but their population was "such that they can keep it up indefinitely". McNamara also seemed wholly unperturbed about the Chinese. Indeed, he considered that "the tremendous build-up of American forces within five hundred miles of the Chinese border must seem to them a most serious threat". King tried McNamara with Ambassador Patrick Dean's theory, which was indeed the rationale of Australian involvement, that "South Vietnam was just an excuse and that the Americans were building up a string of bases for the military containment of China. He said there was nothing in this idea: the Americans wanted to get out of Vietnam as soon as possible . . . the Great American public wouldn't play."[20] Yet only a few weeks later Hasluck was declaiming in the United Nations General Assembly about the way China "overhangs the region with a population of 1,000 million under a regime which, while calling itself communist, represents all that is most illiberal and backward-looking and violent in Communist throught".[21] Canberra and Washington seemed to have seriously different perceptions about the purpose of the war they were both engaged in.

It was clearly expedient to try to establish some general agreement among the allies on the goals to be sought in Vietnam and the efforts to be devoted in seeking them. President Marcos of the Philippines proposed a conference of the troop-contributing nations. White House Special Adviser on Vietnam Walt Whitman Rostow hoped that the exercise might serve "to present a dramatic picture of collective support being given to South Vietnam". He suggested that Johnson should consider making a special visit after the conference to Australia, where he could at least be sure of finding support. "There are no difficult issues outstanding in our relations with Austrlaia," Rostow told the President with perfect accuracy, "and I am sure the whole atmosphere of the visit will be excellent — although there may of course be some demonstrations. All forecasts have Holt winning his election easily, aided by the continued death wish of the Labour [sic] Party."²² In the event, Johnson decided to go to Australia before the conference. He might well have felt that he needed some encouragement. McNamara had apparently descended into total despair since speaking with King. Pacification, he told the beleagured president, "has if anything gone backward ... Nor has the ROLLING THUNDER program of bombing the North either significantly affected infiltration or cracked the morale of Hanoi ... we should," he urged, "consider terminating the bombing in all of North Vietnam ... for an indefinite period in connection with covert moves toward peace." He also proposed, in perhaps the most striking image ever of a strategy at the end of its tether, constructing an electronic infiltration barrier running from the sea and across Laos near the seventeenth parallel, at an estimated cost of $1 billion.²³ It would, as the unimpressed Joint Chiefs pointed out, need to be at least as far beneath the ground as above it, to prevent the VC from tunnelling under it, and would need to be protected by at least 500,000 US troops to prevent them from sabotaging it.

Johnson would hear no such counsels of despair in Australia. "In each of the five Australian cities he visited," his aides summed up, "Canberra, Melbourne, Sydney, Brisbane and Townsville — Australians gave the President a tumultous welcome. There were some anti-war demonstrations and in Melbourne youths hurled plastic bags of paint at the Presidential limousine, but the demonstrators were unable to diminish the warmth of Australian official and public welcomes."²⁴ Defending counsel for the paint-bag throwers actually pleaded that the intention of their clients had been to add to the warmth of the welcome. They explained that they had "meant no distress or anxiety to any person". Nor was their action "inspired by any malevolent feeling towards you or the great Nation you represent, but it was rather the effervesence of youthful gaiety and jocularity excited to fever pitch by your presence and the consequent air of exaltation and triumph". All they were seeking to do was "merely to highlight in a manner typical of students and young people, your successful tour".²⁵ It was the last time that anybody would ever pretend that they were throwing things at a representative of the United States just to make them feel more welcome.

Paradoxically, it was the warmth of a genuine welcome that caused Johnson the only moments of distress that he experienced on his Australian tour. Queensland Premier Frank Nicklin called on the people of Brisbane to give the president of the United States a real Queensland welcome. They turned out in tens of thousands, many in their pyjamas, to do just that, even if they killed Johnson in the process. Queensland police would get plenty of practice over the next five years in dealing with anti-American crowds. They were quite unprepared to cope with this pro-American one. There were a few minutes of terror while Johnson stood pale and silent against his limousine as his Secret Service guards fought with every natural weapon to save him from being crushed to death by his well-wishers in Brisbane. Twenty years later, it is very hard indeed to imagine how a US president could be exposed to that kind of danger in Australia again.

Official discussions in Canberra were less tumultuous but equally cordial. Johnson and Holt agreed in private talks with their senior advisers that "the military position in Vietnam was that North Vietnam could not achieve a military victory, but that it would be necessary to maintain the present allied military effort until a satisfactory settlement could be negotiated".[26] Developing the theme of collective effort, Johnson "spoke of the series of alliances which America had entered into since World War II . . . Once the United States had pledged its word," he assured the Australians, "there would be no faltering — the would-be dictators of Asia should understand that. However, the United States," he pointed out meaningfully, "had been disappointed in the SEATO alliance on the issue of Viet-Nam, in particular with Britain. It was a great disappointment to him that Prime Minister Wilson had dissociated Britain from the United States position in Viet-Nam." Holt and Hasluck would not have disagreed with that. They would also have been gratified with Johnson's assurance that he had "not come to Australia to ask for a man or a dollar or anything else: Australia would continue to reach its own decisions on offering assistance". He also "paid tribute to the job that Australia was doing". Having done so, however, Johnson made it quite obvious why a rather more substantial effort might reasonably be expected from Australia. "He was here," he explained, "and the U.S. had committed forces, because the Communist aggression in Viet-Nam was dangerous for Australia, for America and for freedom everywhere. If the United States were to pull out of Viet-Nam tomorrow, other countries of Southeast Asia would quickly fall. The aggressor would get to Australia long before he got to San Francisco." While Holt and his ministers were pondering this prospect, Johnson concluded that he "wanted Australia and others to stand up with them to show that it was not just an effort of the United States. The seven participants in the Manila meeting might get this across to a hundred other nations."[27]

This perception was of course the ultimate justification for any efforts Australia might make to ensure a continuing United States military presence in Southeast Asia, assuming that there was indeed aggression going on in Vietnam and that it would not stop there. This assumption seemed inherently improbable even to Texan Assistant Counsel to the Democratic Policy Committee Harry McPherson. " 'Together we' " he asked himself, "shall what? Fight Asia's wars . . . What are white men doing out here on this stalagmite of a continent, praying the ancient English prayers and talking about a war between brown men four thousand miles away? Presumably making sure that North Vietnamese or Chinese troops do not someday camp in the New Guinea mountains across the Coral Sea. At the moment, as we stand on the baked, barren ground at Townsville, that seems farfetched."[28] In Canberra it seemed exhilirating, however. Holt told Johnson in the most moving and gracious speech of his life that he saw "our destinies beling linked together for as long as our two countries survive and we see importance in the strength of friendship and the closeness of our alliance".[29] Johnson's own speech, in Howson's view, "cemented the US-Aust. alliance and confirmed a common policy in SE Asia. There can now be no doubt that Australia has an umbrella — or a shield. (Three years ago, this was not nearly such a certainty.) . . . This," he reflected, "should in addition be good for the election."[30]

Holt himself had no doubt that the president's visit would indeed be good for the forthcoming federal elections. "He's the biggest fish I ever speared!" the aquatic prime minister exclaimed joyfully as his ratings in the popularity polls rose in Johnson's wake. But the fact was that neither Australian hospitality, Australian military efforts nor Holt's own warmth and charm had made the most significant impact upon the Americans when they returned to Washington. That had been achieved by dour and unappealing Korean President Park. Two million Koreans cheered the presidential cavalcade all the way from Kimpo Airport to Seoul City Hall. "Looks like they turned out the country!" McPherson commented in amazement. Nor was it just the fanfare. There was also far more important the reality of twenty-two Korean manoeuvre battalions in Vietnam, as against two Australian and absolutely none from any of the other allegedly troop-contributing allies.[31] The contrast could hardly be overlooked. "The

Australians and New Zealanders, the Filipinos, the Thais, Malaysians and Koreans, the Japanese and Indonesians," McPherson reflected, "all are glad to have a counterweight to China in the region. All say, publicly and privately, that resistance to the Communists in Vietnam is terribly important to them. Then why has none of them, except for the Koreans, sent substantial numbers of troops there? Because we have," McPherson answered himself.

> If the strongest, richest, etc. country in the world proclaims that stopping North Vietnam is critical to its own security, surely that makes it unnecessary for lesser countries to contribute much to that fight? Prime Minister Holt is a stalwart friend of America's and LBJ's; he thinks it important to fight in Vietnam and has said so; but he could not survive the deficits and long casualty lists that would follow a deeper commitment — so long as America is there ... Here, President Park is in a stronger position. His country is still on a kind of war footing, against a Communist enemy; and he counts his divisions in Vietnam as insurance that a grateful America will not forget him if another invasion comes."[32]

McPherson was not quite right about the deficits. Australia and New Zealand, alone among the allies, actually sent their own troops at their own expense. The rest were on hire. United States payments for Korean troops in Vietnam provided twenty per cent of Korean earnings of foreign exchange in 1969. The Filipinos, who never actually did any fighting, averaged out at $26,000 per man between 1967 and 1969. The Thais, who did quite a lot of fighting, although relatively far less than anybody else who was actually fighting, cost the United States about $50 million annually.[33] This was not the real issue, however. What became increasingly important with every month that the war dragged on was not the financial cost, but evidence of solidarity. Foreign flags and foreign fighting men were what the Johnson administration wanted in Vietnam. It was preferable that they should be there at their own expense, but what really mattered was that they should be there at all.

An increased Australian commitment was certainly implicit in Holt's surprisingly low-key speech opening the federal election campaign in November 1966. "We have a vital interest in the effective presence and participation of the United States as a major power in the Pacific," he told the Australian people. "We have obligations arising from our treaty relationships, from our role as an ally, and from the fact that our own international interests are directly involved in preserving South-east Asia from aggression and from Communist domination."³⁴ It hardly sounded like an invitation to violence. Violence was however exactly what Holt was to encounter when he delivered his first speech on the hustings in New Farm, Brisbane, where Johnson had almost been crushed to death by wildly hospitable crowds. The anti-conscription groups had been preparing a welcome for their prime minister which it would hardly have been appropriate to turn on for the president. Liberal Party managers guessed what might be in store and took the precaution of packing the first fifteen rows of seats with some six hundred of their own supporters. Police stopped two Communist Party members at the door; but they had no power to exclude about one hundred members of the Save Our Sons movement and other opponents of conscription who occupied seats at the back of the hall, produced twenty banners expressing their views, and subjected Holt to a cyclone of verbal and physical intimidation such as no Australian prime minister had ever experienced before. People scrambled on stage to scream at Holt, in shirtsleeves and dripping with sweat in what had been a sweltering Brisbane summer evening even before the excitement started. A few backhanded swipes were exchanged between Liberal supporters and demonstrators. Two or three couples discussed matters more seriously with their fists outside. Holt for his part presented the remarkable spectacle of a man yelling calmly and politely above the din of the fracas. It was in fact a perfect opportunity for him to display three of his most impressive personal qualities, namely, physical courage; a capacity to go on talking under any conditions; and a face which had no bad camera angles and could therefore present an impression of repose and charm, even in the middle of a riot.

Holt had passed with honour through a baptism of fire beyond the call of duty for a Liberal politician. Rough stuff was all in the day's work for his Country Party deputy, John McEwen, universally respected as Black Jack. McEwen was disposed by nature to put things plainly. He certainly left his hearers in no doubt as to what Australia was doing in Vietnam. "As Australia herself would expect help if in need," he affirmed, "we now demonstrate that we are willing to extend our help to a small, free people under attack. We want so to conduct ourselves that the U.S. will not hesitate to stand between Australia and an aggressor. America is the one country that can do this. Our troops in South Vietnam earn for us the right to the protection of the U.S. and our other treaty allies should Australia be threatened."³⁵ Nobody had ever been thinking seriously about the other treaty allies, but what McEwen was saying about the United States was exactly what the government had been hearing from Beale, Renouf and Waller for the past three years.

On 26 November Holt raced to the greatest electoral success in the history of Australian federal politics. The coalition's share of the popular vote rose from forty-six per cent to fifty per cent. Labor's fell from from forty-five per cent to forty per cent. The government's parliamentary majority swelled from a highly satisfactory nineteen to a superabundant forty-one. Johnson expressed his delight with typical exuberance. "With steadfast devotion," he wrote, "we will stand at your side as long as freedom is being challenged and peace is being threatened. We know that we stand with a man of conviction, integrity and wisdom. We know we stand with a friend. The world has taken note of the great vote of confidence given you by your countrymen yesterday. Your gallant men and ours are gratified for the courageous and far-sighted leadership that you are providing in the Pacific and Asia."[36]

Johnson was soon to receive further proof that he had a friend in Canberra. Holt told Hasluck immediately after the election that he wanted "very early Cabinet consideration of sending an extra battalion to Vietnam, and that he did not want to wait to consider the question in the light of a review of needs and capabilities early in the New Year". Hasluck accordingly asked Waller to report personally on the current position of American thinking on the issue of involvement:

> The Embassy continued to receive hints from contacts in the White House, the State Department and the Pentagon that an additional military contribution from Australia would be greatly appreciated by the Administration . . . The Ambassador referred to Johnson's need to seek Congressional approval for a large increase in his budget the following January and to the conflicting pressures on one side from the liberals to "accept negotiations and dangerous concessions to the Communists" and on the other from those who wanted to escalate the war with a view to getting it over quickly. The Ambassador believed that Australia's ability to influence the President's response to these conflicting pressures would be related to the scale of her military contribution and the readiness with which it was made.[37]

There was no question of pressure from the Americans. It came from the Australian government's own advisers in Washington, who were giving it exactly the same kind of advice that they had always been giving. Holt, too, was as positive in his response as Hasluck had always been. Howson was startled when the Deputy Chief of Air Staff and his assistant called on him on 13 December "to brief me on Defence Committee proposals for additional aid to Vietnam. The main problem ahead of us," he noted in bewilderment, "is to decide why we are considering this matter *now*. The only reason apparently is that the PM has given a secret undertaking to LBJ. If so, the advice to Cabinet should be to send the least expensive with the biggest 'public relations' image. Hence a *Canberra* squadron, HMAS *Hobart* and about 900 troops; in place of a third battalion as envisaged by the PM." Holt, he confirmed later, had in fact "decided this without prior consultation" with anybody except Hasluck. "He rang [Permanent Head of the Department of Defence Sir Edwin] Hicks without telling [Defence Minister] Allen Fairhall. No one knows why this is to be decided *now*," Howson moaned. It took the ministers and their advisers about twenty minutes to convince Holt against sending a third battalion on the grounds of cost.[38] Waller was directed on 16 December to advise the Americans that Australian forces in Vietnam were to be increased overall to 6,300 with the additional numbers coming from all three services. He immediately cabled back that McNamara had "expressed particular gratification". Holt had certainly decided on his own initiative to pay a higher premium, but it was reasonable to expect that it would attract an even more secure insurance.

Nobody had consulted the Vietnamese, who learned of the coming increase some hours after Holt had informed the Australian public. External Affairs had advised that "it did not seem necessary or desirable to seek a specific request from the South Vietnamese on this occasion".[39] Holt had already made his own plans to appease the feelings of Marshal Ky. The South Vietnamese premier had some months previously requested Australian Ambassador Sir Lewis Border to get him officially invited to Australia. Border subsequently explained that "whereas we were able to hold up the first invitation, it had been renewed on at least two further occasions, we had to either ask him to Australia or invite a rebuff in Vietnam".[40] With the election triumphantly behind him, Holt hesitated no longer. Figures of the increase in Australian involvement were released on 22 December. Then on the following day he announced that Premier Ky might be visiting Australia in the near future. The Melbourne *Age* called on federal cabinet to cancel the visit on the grounds that the choice before them was "whether to confirm a blunder made by the Prime Minister or to act with a responsible awareness of public opinion and Australia's best interests".[41]

The Prime Minister had not made a blunder, however, at least as far as public opinion was concerned. Ky arrived on 18 January accompanied by a spectacularly beautiful wife. He struck precisely the right note himself when he explained that he had not come to ask for more Australian troops in Vietnam but to thank Australia for the help it had given already. The highly apprehensive Howson decided after Ky's very first encounter with the media that it was "quite obvious that the press were warming to Ky and realizing that their original forecast was likely to be wrong".[42] Harry Gelber questioned with characteristic and appropriate elegance of phrase whether the Australian media had been impressed by "Marshal Ky's display of courtesy and political professionalism or Madame Ky's elegance and beauty. Certainly at his news conference the premier fielded with charm and courage a variety of questions, not all of which were distinguished by subtlety or skill. Mr Holt may have been accused of poor timing in arranging the visit, but its success was materially helped by Mr Calwell, whose charges at demonstrations outside parliament house that Marshal Ky was a 'fascist' and 'a miserable little butcher' proved entirely counterproductive."[43] There was no doubt that Arthur Calwell's credibility had been the major casualty of the tour. The Labor leader had led protest marches in Canberra, numbering about four hundred to five hundred people, of whom twenty-four were arrested, and rallies of some six thousand each in Melbourne and Sydney. The Victorian state branch of the Australian Labor Party had called on federal and state parliamentarians to march with their leader, but as Colin Hughes noted, "outside that state most found business or pleasure to occupy them far from the demonstrations". He quoted with approval the verdict of the Adelaide *Advertiser* that Calwell had " 'emerged from the drama of the Ky's visit a rather lonely and pathetic figure. It is hard to recall any campaign by the leader of a major political party which attracted so little public support.' On the other hand," Professor Hughes reflected, "Mr Holt had achieved another coup."

It was all the more expedient for him to have done so, as his government did not seem to be equipped with a legislative programme. Mr Holt's prime ministerial style already seemed rather too existential for comfort. He left for a trip to New Zealand on 2 February, closely pursued by John McEwen. He increased his personal staff, seemed to prefer to spend his time in Melbourne rather than Canberra, allowed his beautiful daughters-in-law to travel on VIP aircraft to and from official social occasions, and accused Mike Willesee of political bias on the grounds that his father was a Labor senator. Public opinion polls nonetheless indicated early in March that the government was retaining its electoral support. If the prime minister, Colin Hughes considered, "did indeed set himself two goals for his first year of office, projecting his own personality and focussing Australian attention on Asia and the American alliance, he had succeeded".[44]

Success indeed seemed to be in the air in those early months of 1967, after years of deferred hopes. Howson decided after talking with Ky that the military situation in Vietnam "has now reached the turning point, rather like the situation at the time of Alamein".[45] Things would presumably look up from there on until final victory. Sir Keith Holyoake responded to Holt's visit by announcing on 8 March that he could not "escape the conclusion that a further effort by New Zealand was called for", and that the New Zealand artillery group in Vietnam would accordingly be reinforced by a rifle company of 150 men, thus increasing the New Zealand commitment to 360.[46] Holt flew off on 28 March for another overseas visit to Cambodia, Laos, Taiwan, and Korea, returning on 10 April. No previous Australian prime minister had ever involved himself so intensely in the affairs of the region in which Australia was geographically located. Some critics suggested that the prime minister was in fact usurping the functions of the minister for External Affairs, but nobody could seriously deny that the personal touch was supremely Harold Holt's forte or that it was not Paul Hasluck's. Anyway, the tide of victory was still flowing. Federal Treasurer William McMahon wrote contentedly to President Johnson and the First Lady that in Australia the Vietnam War was "gradually easing out of the Press and even the correspondents are now freely admitting the North Vietnamese origins of the war, control by North Vietnam and the atrocities being committed by the Vietcong ... As yet," he regretted however, "they have not appreciated the extent of your Government's assistance in the reconstruction and rehabilitation of South Vietnam but I think this is now only a question of time. I assure you your own reputation here is higher than ever. I will be coming over with Sonia in September. You know that if there was any way we could get the message across of your wonderful standing here we would do so."[47] Then the tide turned.

Hasluck himself received a disturbing impression in talks with

McNamara, who seemed to think that the United States could no longer lose the war but could experience considerable difficulty in winning it, and who made the convincing point that the Australians could obviously clear Phuoc Tuy province more quickly with three battalions than with the two they had there.[48] Westmoreland similarly explained to Lyndon Johnson on 27 April that without an extra 100,000 troops in Vietnam "we will not be in danger of being defeated but it will be nip and tuck to oppose the reinforcements the enemy is capable of providing". "When we add divisions" the despairing president asked, "can't the enemy add divisions? If so, where does it all end?" Westmoreland had the answer. With a force level "of 565,000 men, the war could well go on for three years. With a second increment of 2½ divisions leading to a total of 665,000 men, it could go on for two years."[49] That was where it would end, if the intervening countries were prepared to go the distance. Their record to date did not encourage confidence. Experts in the Pentagon worked out a formula for equitable allied contributions. The United States, they estimated, had at that stage contributed 2,350 troops per million of population; South Korea, 1,570; Australia, 520; and New Zealand, 180. Increases required to match the United States rate would amount to 22,600 from Korea, 21,400 from Australia and 5,800 from New Zealand. Expectations of this order would hardly be realistic. However, these comparisons could provide the basis for renewed pressure on the allies if Johnson were to increase the American commitment along the lines sought by Westmoreland.[50]

It was not only Johnson, however, who was coming under political pressure at home. Colin Hughes suggested that the "great question of Australian politics by the middle of 1957 must be which of the gods has Mr Holt offended".[51] It was not an easy question to answer. The normal explanation is of course *hubris* or arrogance of spirit. This would seem to fit the case of Gough Whitlam, for example, but arrogance of spirit was not a discernible failing of Harold Holt's. Perhaps he was just fulfilling his destiny. Holt was a romantic, if ever the term could be applied to an Australian politician, and it is the essence of romantics to fail and die more poignantly or at least more spectacularly than other people. Failure had certainly become the characteristic style of the new regime. "Throughout 1967," as Don Aitkin put it, "the Holt government stumbled from one reverse to another."[52] Demand had been mounting for the re-opening of an enquiry into the circumstances of a collision between the aircraft carrier *Melbourne* and the destroyer *Voyager*. Holt declared on 3 May that his government had considered re-opening the enquiry but had decided not to. A revolt of his own massive backbench forced him to reverse this decision a fortnight later. Then the Senate defeated three times a government bill to raise Post and Telegraph charges. A referendum to break the nexus between the size of the Senate and that of the House of Representatives was rejected by the people on 27 May. Holt might well have experienced a considerable sense of relief when he left Australia the next day for a visit to the United States, Canada and the United Kingdom, to return on 22 June.

It was not just a matter of escaping temporarily from a singularly discouraging domestic situation. Personal diplomacy was what Holt did best, and his comments on world affairs revealed a pragmatic spirit contrasting strikingly with that exhibited by his minister for External Affairs. He told a Los Angeles World Affairs Council luncheon on 31 May, for example, that "should the Communists be prepared in good faith to enter into negotiations, there is a substantial case for suspension of bombing". He told the Canadians on 3 June that he thought that the spread of communism in the Asian area could be checked without an eventual clash with the People's Republic, because, he considered, "the Chinese are a pretty realist-minded people; the fact that they have limited their involvement in North Vietnam, despite the very obvious interests which they have in that matter, is, I think, some confirmation of this. They are also," he added, "a very patient people, and they may think that they can secure their ends over a period of time without getting involved in serious military loss."[53] Holt had studied foreign relations under Richard Casey, the great pragmatist of Australian diplomacy. It was a way of looking at things far removed from the doctrinaire rigidity evinced by Hasluck three days later when he harangued the Legal Research Foundation in Auckland about "the apparent success of communist imperialism in establishing its authoritarian rule over an Empire of more than 700 million people", as if the Chinese had been conquered by foreigners or as if they had ever known any other form of rule. He also sought to alarm his audience by reference to the attempt by the People's Republic "to dominate the Asian mainland, the clear intention to become a nuclear power, and the current disregard of and isolation from the rest of the world, including", he added, "the Soviet Union".[54]

Holt had his own convictions too. Chief of these was the compelling importance of the Pacific region, not only for his own country but also for those who inhabited its extreme rim or did not even inhabit it at all. He accordingly sought in his talks with Lester Pearson to lay "a foundation ... for a growing Australian-Canadian co-operation in relation to international questions generally and in particular to the growing interest I think we will be finding in Canada in what occurs around the Pacific basin". He told the Americans that his discussions with British Prime Minister Harold Wilson about "the future that Britain has to maintain East of Suez" would involve him "in some of the most important discussions, I think, that any Australian Prime Minister could expect to hold". In London, he treated Harold Wilson and the British media to the wholly unfamiliar spectacle of an Australian prime minister completely at ease with his own *persona*, bewilderingly neither Anglophile nor ocker, and who never stopped talking. He explained to Wilson that it "was in the interests of Britain, of the Commonwealth and of the security and peace of the area for Britain to maintain its presence East of Suez", and that owing to the uncertainty of world events any British decision about withdrawing "British forces East of Suez must remain flexible and should not be final".[55] He pursued the theme again with Lyndon Johnson at Camp David, where he achieved something of a public relations coup by diving out of his swimming shorts in the presidential pool, and kept up the pressure with a letter to Johnson after his return to Australia, urging more pressure by the United States to compel the British to delay their proposed withdrawal. What he received in reply was a warning of more pressure by the United States on Australia to make a more convincing showing with its own forces in the region.

Johnson began by assuring Holt that it had been "a great lift to my spirits to see you again". On the question of a British military presence east of Suez, he had "weighed in again with Harold Wilson, and Dean Rusk did so in more detail with George Brown ... I believe that we have presented our cases as forcefully and logically as possible, and I trust it will have a real effect on the thinking of the British Cabinet." Then he got to the real point. "As to force requirements [in Vietnam]," he warned Holt, "we may well have to do significantly more, simply to meet the military necessities of what the other side is doing, and I want to say frankly that if the need for additional forces becomes clear, we shall need to talk fairly urgently with you and the other troop-contributing nations on whether a substantial part of the need can be met by others. Even since our meetings, it is plain that key members of our Congress feel very strongly about this, and I am sure you would agree that additional burdens should be shared as equitably as possible."[56] Two days later, Johnson and his advisers examined the specifics of what might be extracted from the other troop-contributing nations. William P. Bundy recorded:

> Australia and New Zealand were seen as being prepared to come in with "more" but it was expected that their contribution would be scant in relation to the need, perhaps 2000 or 3000 from the Australians and a few hundred from the New Zealanders. The Philippines were characterized as a "doubtful starter" . . . In Korea, Park himself seemed to be willing, but . . . it was clear that he intended to get his political situation straightened out before he moved with any additional forces for the United States. At best Korea appeared to be a prospect for action in late fall with perhaps an additional division coming through by the end of the year. Thailand was considered a probability with the thought that it might come through with an additional 3–5000 over the next six months [but it would] "take very careful handling".[57]

Australia's role was obviously going to be critical, at least in the sense that very little of significance could be hoped for from anywhere else if Australia were not to make a worthwhile gesture itself. Difficulties in the way of an increased Australian commitment were magnified in Holt's eyes by the release of the British White Paper on Defence on 17 July, envisaging the total withdrawal of British forces from east of Suez by the mid-1970s. These reductions, Holt stated, went "considerably beyond our earlier expectations". Some aspects, he said frankly, were "disappointing to us . . . we very much regret that the British Government should feel itself impelled to plan now for final withdrawal from Malaysia and Singapore at a date so far ahead, and when it is so difficult to predict how the situation in South-East Asia will move".[58] It had suddenly become very difficult for Australia to act responsibly in the region, if it were indeed still prepared to accept responsibilities there. Australian military weakness was of course the problem. Australia could hardly increase its commitment to Vietnam and at the same time retain a capability to fill the vacuum being left by the British. On the other hand, it could hardly expect the Americans to continue to sustain their own military involvement in Vietnam without significant help from their allies, and it was more important than ever to ensure that the Americans would not abandon the region when it was clear that the British was doing so.

At this point political warning bells began to ring at home. A by-election in the federal electorate of Corio on 22 July was won by the Australian Labor Party with a massive swing of eleven per cent against the government. It was a result that could only be seen, as Colin Hughes commented, "as a censure of the government and a vote of confidence in" the new leader of the ALP, Gough Whitlam.[59] Rumours about the inadequacies of Holt's leadership began to pullulate in the alimentary tract of the Liberal Party. Meanwhile, storm clouds were gathering in Washington. The Joint Committee on Economic Affairs had reported to Congress on the same day as the Corio debacle that the war in Vietnam had cost so far an estimated $5.8 billion dollars, a figure twenty per cent higher than previously forecast, and that the actual costs might well exceed these figures. United States casualties were also rising as fighting intensified around the demilitarized zone. Ambassador Waller reported on 25 July a mood of increasing public scepticism about the war as a whole. He still doubted that the basic United States commitment to Vietnam was being called in question, but "he feared that if, following the United Kingdom's announced intention to withdraw from South East Asia, America's allies gave a negative response to proposals for more troops it would have a disproportionately adverse effect on United States opinion. Under these circumstances," the Ambassador considered, "Australia's response, as the most significant Western ally, was of particular importance."[60]

Hard on the heels of Waller's report came Maxwell Taylor himself, accompanied by Clark McA. Clifford, chairman of the president's Foreign Policy Advisory Council. They were a formidable duo and they were confronted with perhaps the most formidable task in the experience of Australian-American relations. It was the first time that a United States government had found itself in the position of pressing an Australian government for support which that government was seriously reluctant to provide. Even more ominous was the fact that the Australians seemed at last to have become prey to the kind of misgivings that had been troubling many senior United States officials for years. They told Taylor and Clark that "the relatively optimistic picture of the military situation given by the President to the Prime Minister contrasted with our own military assessments and with some private United States assessments . . . At the talks themselves, the Australian attitude was not to deny the substance of the United States view that there was a need for publicly declared allied solidarity and greater effort, but to bring into the equation the very considerable stretch already in Australia's military and economic effort, not only in Vietnam but elsewhere, and the new possibility in the light of recent British decisions that wider responsibilities would fall on us."[61]

No immediate decisions were called for or taken in the course of the Taylor-Clark mission. There could, however, be no doubt as to what Washington was hoping to get from Canberra. Nor was there any doubt that the growing mood of disillusionment in the United States was being replicated in Australia. Public relations officer for the Liberal Party in Victoria Murray Prior warned Howson with considerable understatement that there was "evidence of a bit of 'dissatisfaction' with the Vietnam war". Howson thought that "a better word is that there is a tiredness in the community because they can see no end in sight. There is no means of measuring how well or how badly the war is going in Vietnam, and therefore they cannot see how long this war may continue and what further sacrifices may be required of the Australian community. They are still resolved that it is necessary for us to be involved in the Vietnam fighting, but they would like to see some indication of the results of our efforts. I think this is a genuine feeling throughout the community."[62] It was also a genuine feeling throughout the United States community and also in Vietnam. Coincidentally, the *New York Times* reported forty-eight hours later that "in the opinion of most disinterested observers the war is not going well", and "victory . . . might be beyond our reach". It was noted that communist strength was higher than ever; that the North Vietnamese had committed only one-fifth of their military capacity; and that the allies by contrast were "reaching the bottom of their manpower pool".[63] What the *Times* really meant was that they were reaching the bottom of what was politically possible. The inequality of sacrifice was also becoming ever more conspicuous. In Vietnam, 11,099 Americans had been killed in action, along with a further 2,159 dead from accident or disease. Korean combat dead numbered 1,102 and Australian, 104. It would be difficult to argue that Australia should not be doing a little more, assuming that one thought that it should be doing anything at all.

Paul Hasluck had no doubt that everybody else should be doing more than they were doing. He deplored the fact that the United Kingdom, for example, "today sees her interests in a closer association with Europe more clearly than she sees her interests in participation in world affairs. This is a view," he asserted, "contrary to that of Australia." It was not indeed a case of Australia's taking over the former role of the United Kingdom but rather of "Australia also developing its own distinctive role". The problem, as ever for Paul Hasluck, was "the massive and persistent pressure of Communist China on the region and the declared policy of Communist China of overthrowing by subversion, by insurgency and by so-called wars of liberation the established regimes in the independent states of the region". It was a perception that had as little credibility in the existing circumstances as his further assertion that the "military outlook in Vietnam has shown steady and continued improvement since my last statement to the House ... it is clear," he concluded, "that the Vietnam allies must maintain their present efforts at every level of this complex and difficult conflict until the enemy comes to realize that he cannot achieve his objectives by force".[64]

This is the enemy was certainly not likely to do unless the allies were massively to expand their present efforts; but even Hasluck was reluctant to recommend a substantially augmented Australian commitment. Holt had once again on his own initiative proposed the dispatch of a third battalion. This prospect seemed to his advisers to be likely to create many and serious difficulties. They hesitated however as to "whether a positive recommendation against providing a third battalion should be made", on the grounds that there "could be an embarrassing situation ... if the Government were subsequently asked if it had acted upon the views of its official advisers".[65] This might suggest that the role of official advisers is to advise a government to do what they know it has decided to do anyway; but the government itself was divided. Holt was still holding out for the significant addition of a third battalion, but both Federal Treasurer McMahon and Defence Minister Fairhall agreed with Howson that the main task of cabinet would be "to achieve a reasonable balance" between Holt's desire and that of Treasury and most of the military "to keep the increased aid as low as possible".[66] A new factor had by then been introduced. The Thais were really coming at last. Prime Minister Kittikachorn farewelled 1,756 volunteers on 30 August in a ceremony invoking on their behalf the protection of the Triple Gem, the Emerald Budda and the Tutelary God.[67] There were apparently thousands more to come.

It was a fair question whether this sudden intervention by the Thais made an increased effort by Australia less necessary, if the purpose of the exercise were to support South Vietnam; or more necessary, if it were to pick up extra credit with the United States. Certainly, it did nothing to resolve the debate in Canberra. Even Paul Hasluck had now joined McMahon, Fairhall and Howson, as had Postmaster-General Sir Alan Hulme, in opposing the dispatch of a third battalion, arguing that it would mean "leaving ourselves with absolutely no room to manoeuvre in any other direction should the need arise". The only explanation that McMahon and Howson could think of was that "the PM has been mesmerized by the plea of President Johnson and is disposed to send every possible form of military aid to Vietnam whether or not it is going to be usefully used. I think he believes that, by doing this, we shall be able to get the Americans to look kindly on us with our requests that we may make to them in other directions . . . My own view is that this is unlikely to occur . . . Once again," he concluded, "I think we have another example of how military decisions are being made for political ends and not for genuine military reasons."[68]

Cabinet yielded to Holt's insistence on 6 September, agreeing in principle to the dispatch of a third battalion, though without setting a firm date for its departure. Holt himself was well aware of the problems. "We aren't going to sleep," he assured US Ambassador Clark, but went on to tell him of the difficulties and complexities in the way of augmenting the Australian involvement. By contrast, the Thais were positively pressing the United States to provide the technical assistance necessary to field a full Thai brigade group of 10,800 men, comprising three infantry battalions, an artillery battalion, an engineering battalion, and support troops as required. It was the one really encouraging gleam in an otherwise dispiriting global scene. "The predominant attitude in the Western Pacific towards the Vietnamese war," Senate Majority Leader Mike Mansfield summed up for Johnson's benefit, "appears to be indifference or perhaps more precisely, resignation. Except in Korea the war does not engender enthusiasm among the governments of the region . . . There are no indications," he continued, "which would lead us to expect any significant increase in the cooperation which we are presently receiving with respect to Viet Nam. There is, moreover, always the possibility that we could lose some of the support which we now have." Nor was the situation likely to improve in the foreseeable future. None of the governments in the region were offering ideas on how to end the war or formulas for opening negotiations, except for the Koreans, who wanted to enlarge the war. Mansfield was convinced that in spite of "assurances of progress in the war which I heard directly from General

Westmoreland ... there is no indication that a resolution of the conflict is to be expected in the near future".[69]

It was thus not surprising that the Americans should be turning with increasing impatience to the country which had consistently encouraged US intervention in Vietnam right from the outset with repeated assurances of support. However, the Holt government had just received another demoralizing blow at home, where Dr Douglas Everingham had retained the seat of Capricornia for Labor with a massive fifty-three per cent of the votes cast, improving on the support gained by a highly popular predecessor. Whatever had brought Holt triumph in the polls the year before certainly seemed to be failing him in 1967. McMahon had gone to Washington under strict instructions not to inform anybody that Australia would in fact be sending a third battalion. He loyally assured the Americans of Holt's leadership in "making clear to Ministers 'what the issues involved in Vietnam were ... and the critical importance of our association with the United States' ", despite his own reservations about where that leadership was taking the government. But Washington could not be appeased with only words this time. McMahon reported back to Canberra that the "pressure put upon him to have our decision indicated quickly to Johnson was 'extremely strong'." Nor could Ambassador Waller "remember stronger pressure being brought to bear".[70]

The Americans had never brought any pressure to bear before in any real sense. It had always been the Australians who had been encouraging, urging, hinting, and occasionally promising, while the Americans temporized, agonized, equivocated, and appreciated. The Australians could afford to be lavish with verbal support when the premiums for United States insurance were expected to remain low enough not to cause political or economic inconvenience, but now the rates seemed to be climbing disconcertingly. McMahon suggested that Holt tell Johnson personally and confidentially exactly what the Australian government proposed to do and what it could do. Holt instead called Prime Minister Holyoake of New Zealand to Canberra for urgent consultations. Both insisted beforehand that "they did not see their discussions as leading up to any immediate decisions" and said afterwards only that they were "in the process of reviewing their respective defence arrangements".[75] Two days later, Holt cabled Johnson that he would be increasing the Australian commitment to Vietnam by a further 1,700 troops, but that this would put the nation at the full strength of its present and planned military capacity. To go beyond that would involve decisions publicly unacceptable in the existing climate of opinion. Hotl had gone as far along the way with LBJ as he could go.

Holt moved with surprising slowness to implement the decision he had found it so hard to make. Ambassador Border was not told until 14 October to notify the Vietnamese of the increase, which was described as "having been taken in the light of previous requests by the Vietnamese Government for such military assistance as the Australian Government was able to provide". The Vietnamese of course had nothing to do with it, as was made clear when Holt told the House of Representatives on 17 October that Australia was "there because we believe in the right of people to be free . . . we are there because we do not believe that our great Pacific partner, the United States, should stand alone for freedom".[72] That was the reality. What he did not say was that the commitment represented the limit of the existing capability of the Australian Army. He was sending another 1,978 troops in all, with 26 *Centurion* tanks and 8 helicopters. It would give Australia a peak strength of 8,133 men in Vietnam, comprising 3 manoeuvre battalions. The Australian Army had raised only 8 battalions, of which 2 were in training and 4 would be overseas. Nothing more could be done unless the government were to raise the percentage of conscripts serving and it was not going to do that.[73] By contrast, the Koreans had peaked at 22 battalions and even the Thais would commit 6. Australia could not hope to pick up much credit in Vietnam against that kind of competition.

Credit, however, was the last thing that anybody looked like picking up in the last months of 1967. News of the increase in the Australian commitment was followed coincidentally by a wave of anti-war protests on an unprecedented scale throughout the Western world, from London to Tokyo, from Tel Aviv to West Berlin. A Los Angeles housewife burned herself to death on the steps of the Federal Building. Police used tear gas and clubs to disperse 2,500 students at the University of Wisconsin, protesting against recruitment programme by the Dow Chemical Company, which produced among other items napalm for use in Vietnam. At Brooklyn College 50 students protested against the presence on campus of US Navy recruiting agents, and 8,000 went on strike until the authorities agreed that "outside recruiters, including armed services and CIA, would have to conduct their business in an office and not in corridors, as hitherto". "It had become perilous," one commentator remarked, "for any government official to appear on a campus, where burning 'hawks', including Westmoreland, in effigy had become commonplace. Press and television gave every anti-war demonstration maximum coverage, and such unlikely foreign policy experts as movie stars, a prominent pediatrician, a Harvard economist, and several novelists, emerged as 'doves' or anti-war leaders." There had of course been a number of more convincingly credentialled people who had been arguing for years that the United States and its allies were not making the right decision about Vietnam. Johnson and his advisers had not been convinced by the counsel of the experienced and perceptive, however. They were more impressed by the antics of the irrational, the irresponsible and the plain crazy. Thirty-five thousand "doves" beseiged the Pentagon. One of their spokespeople outlined a strategy to "kidnap L.B.J. while wrestling him to the ground and pulling his pants off. We will attack with noisemakers, water pistols, marbles, bubble-gum wrappers and bazookas. Sorcerers, swamis, priests, warlocks, rabbis, gurus, witches, alchemists, speed freaks and other holy men will join hands and everyone will scream 'Vote for me!' "[74]

It achieved the desired result. Johnson told his family that he was going to retire from politics and would not be seeking a second term as president. Across the Pacific the shadows continued to darken over Harold Holt's leadership. Media opinion had swung temporarily in support of the government following Holt's speech on 17 October, but it fell again after Paul Hasluck had spoken with undaunted inflexibility in "total support" of the bombing offensive against North Vietnam. Columnist and former diplomat Bruce Grant attributed the slump in popularity of the most popular government in Australia history directly to "growing doubts about the Vietnam War".[75] But doubts about Vietnam meant doubts about the leadership that had taken the nation ever deeper into Vietnam. Liberal Party organizers were coming to view Holt as a problem, barely a year after he had led the party to a triumph that Menzies had never been able to achieve. Howson, Holt's own consultant Keith Sinclair, and federal party president Brigadier Sir John Pagan decided that one problem was that "the PM himself is not relaxing sufficiently — not taking enough time off to look at things in the broad. He gets too tied up with detail and doesn't have time to really look at the wider issues." They agreed that they would have to "try and find ways of getting the PM" to "rest and relax" over the coming weeks.

All this, if true, sounded most ominously like the first signs of an executive cracking up; and the problems of the government were getting worse. Oddly, support for both main parties fell in the Senate poll on 25 November, but support for the coalition fell from 45.2 per cent of the popular vote to 42.3 per cent, while that for the ALP declined only from 45.0 per cent to 44.7 per cent. The results were, Howson felt, "not nearly as good as we had hoped". Moreover, Federal Treasurer McMahon was not allegedly busy in Sydney "stirring up trouble not only between the Liberal and the Country Party but also within the Liberal Ministry itself". Chief Whip Dudley Erwin rang Howson, who had been conferring with the leaders of the party organization. They agreed that "the PM has concentrated too much on administration and not enough on politics this year, and that he needs more political advice, particularly from the party". He had "been too tired because he has taken too much on his own shoulders . . . he doesn't delegate sufficiently, and . . . is too surrounded by civil servants and not sufficiently by politicians . . . we must stress the need for working together as a team".[76] But there was a news flash from Portsea in the afternoon of 17 December. The prime minister had gone for a walk along the beach with two women friends. It was the most appropriate setting possible for the last scene of Harold Holt's life on earth. He told them that he was going for a swim and ran into the water, which was becoming alarmingly rough. They saw him raise his arm in which might have been a friendly wave, a farewell, or the gesture of a swimmer in difficulties. It was Harold Holt's last goodbye. It was goodbye also to a vision of regional defence and Pacific partnership that had led Australia into Vietnam.

Holt's end had at last been mercifully quick. Its circumstances also served to enhance a romantic fancy of dreams lost and hopes betrayed by fate. There was nothing quick or romantic about what fate had in store for the coalition or for South Vietnam. For both there would be a long drawn-out agony. John Grey Gorton became prime minister on 9 January 1968 after a bitter leadership crisis occasioned by John McEwen's refusal to serve under William McMahon. Gorton had barely assumed power when the North Vietnamese and Viet Cong delivered their greatest military effort of the war to date on 21 January, sweeping away all the illusions of allied progress sustained over the past three years. Negotiation became the only option for the United States. Johnson contracted the bombing offensive on 30 March and terminated it completely on 31 October, both times after Hasluck had insisted vehemently that the United States should do nothing of the kind. Hasluck himself quitted the portfolio of External Affairs in February 1969 to become one of Australia's most respected governor-generals. His successor, Gordon Freeth, lasted eight months, losing his seat in a federal election which saw the coalition's majority slashed to seven, down from the forty-one Gorton had inherited from Holt. Gorton attempted to secure his own leadership by pitchforking McMahon into External Affairs, in the hope that it would keep him out of the country too much to be able to establish an effective power base from which to challenge Gorton himself for the prime ministership. It was the sort of thing that Menzies was frequently accused of doing but in all probability never actually did, and it did not work. Gorton took himself gracefully out of office on 3 October 1969, yielding place to McMahon, who passed the External Affairs portfolio on to Leslie H. Bury. He lasted ten months during which time he failed totally to come to terms with the new United States strategy of detente with China — which the ALP Opposition came to terms with very effectively. Intelligent and enterprising salvage work by McMahon and Bury's able successor Nigel Bowen came too late. The last Australian troops left Vietnam in December 1971. Twelve months later, Gough Whitlam's narrow victory in the federal election ended twenty-three years of coalition rule. Communist forces captured Saigon on 30 April 1975. Australia's Vietnam adventure was over. The insurance premiums had been higher than anybody could have expected; and the policy seemed to have more fine print about it than ever.

Conclusion

Thirty-nine nations provided support in one form or another to South Vietnam in response to the Free World Assistance Program initiated by United States President Lyndon B. Johnson. Five sent military forces. Four actually committed them to combat. Two did so at their own expense. Australia was the first to send troops, the first to commit them to combat and the first to take casualties. It provided for some time the largest allied contingent in Vietnam and it lost the second largest number of combat dead. This is not indeed to say that very many Australians fought in Vietnam or that very many of those who fought there died there. United States forces in Vietnam numbered at their peak 542,000; Korean, 50,268; Thai, 11,568; Australian, 8,133; and New Zealand, 534. Over 56,000 Americans were killed in action, as were 4,208 Koreans, 472 Australians, 169 Thais, and 26 New Zealanders. In overall military term, Australia's effort could scarcely even be termed marginal. The Americans did not exactly do all the fighting but they did all that needed to be done.

This scarcely marginal military effort, however, was the cutting edge of a diplomatic effort which was absolutely crucial. The fact of the matter is that the Americans might not have been there at all if the Australians had not been there too. Australia was quite literally the only bona fide democratic government in the world, even including New Zealand, giving unconditional support to the strategy of United States military intervention in Vietnam. Australian ministers and their official advisers approved, incited and defended without qualification the most vigorous military measures being contemplated in Washington for the purpose of averting a communist victory in South

Vietnam. Menzies, Holt, Hasluck, Howson and Fairhall, Beale, Waller and Renouf pushed the hardest line of military intervention until Johnson himself unilaterally terminated the bombardment of North Vietnam in October 1968. They did so regardless of anything that was actually happening in Vietnam itself, politically, socially or militarily; regardless of mounting official and popular opposition to intervention within the United States; regardless of increasingly serious divisions within the Australian community on the issue; regardless of the absence of any material evidence whatever supporting the assumptions upon which their diplomatic initiatives were based; regardless of the fact that no other western-aligned government in the world was expressing the same perceptions with anything like the same degree of conviction; and regardless particularly of their own inability to mount a military effort remotely commensurate with that which they were urging the United States to exert. Paradoxically, they began to exhibit misgivings only when the Americans began for the first time to urge them to mount such an effort.

Even then, there was never any question of the Americans exerting anything that could sensibly be termed leverage upon their most reliably supportive Pacific partner. They had initially invited, encourage and appreciated. They occasionally discouraged. They finally requested. But it was on every occasion the Australian government itself which decided what it was going to send, when it was going to send it and finally that it was not going to send anything more. What the Vietnam experience showed most convincingly was indeed the total inability or unwillingness of the Americans to exert leverage upon even what would seem to be their most vulnerable allies, and perhaps especially upon their most vulnerable allies. Washington certainly pleaded with its "Free World" partners to show their flags in Vietnam, but it was a matter of pleading, not of pressure, and its pleas fell for the most part upon deaf or at best reluctant ears. No government decided to send combat troops to Vietnam in the first instance because it was directly asked to do so by the Americans. Korean offers were accepted only after prolonged negotiations and with the gravest reservations. Australia sent combat troops instead of the advisory and logistic support which the Americans actually wanted. New Zealand sent combat troops because Australia had decided to do so. And everybody, as always, left the Thais to make up their own minds in their own way and in their own time. There was indeed pressure being exercised during this initial period of decision. It was being exercised by Canberra upon Washington.

Australian pressure was exercised in pursuit of a wholly independent perception of Australian national interests, arrived at by the Australian government without the benefit of advice from anybody else. Basic to this perception was the concern about the hegemonic southward ambitions of the People's Republic of China, a concern shared with anything like comparable intensity at the time only by the government of North Vietnam. There was no question of Australia obsequiously following the guidance of great and powerful friends. What was being followed was a traditional Australian apprehension of a threat from Asia, which the Australian government sought to awaken in the minds of governments with vastly greater experience and understanding of Asian affairs. Nor was "All the Way with LBJ" in any sense a declaration of subservience. It was rather a triumphant recognition of the fact that the United States administration of Lyndon Johnson was going exactly where the Australian government wanted it to go. A shield of United States military power had been interposed between Australia and any possible threat from the north. The ultimate national security goal of Australian governments since federation seemed to have been attained. Harold Holt could feel that he had achieved what Alfred Deakin had sought without success.

One cannot of course calculate precisely how much this desired state of affairs had come about as a result of the efforts of the Australian government itself. There was no way that Australia could have compelled the United States to intervene militarily in Vietnam. What it could do was provide the element which successive administrations in Washington had described as the absolutely essential precondition for United States intervention. Eisenhower, Kennedy and Johnson had insisted alike that it was essential that South Vietnam should not be allowed to fall under communist control, but that it was also essential that the United States should not intervene unilaterally to prevent it from doing so. Appropriate regional support was indispensable, and this meant in practice support by a credible democratic government with recognized interests of its own in the region and with the capacity to act independently in support of them. There were very few credible democracies in the region with a capacity for independent action apart from Australia, and it would be very hard indeed to imagine any supporting military intervention by the United States in circumstances where Australia itself would be unwilling to provide such support. There would be a number of other regional countries which might be expected to lend their support once intervention had actually been initiated, but this could hardly occur without some measure of congressional support. Such support would not be forthcoming unless it could be shown that the United States would be acting in concert with a responsible ally with legitimate concerns in the region.

This meant Australia. It was Australia that Eisenhower first thought of in 1954 when it seemed virtually certain that the British would not participate in any military intervention in support of the French in Indochina. Plans for United States intervention were shelved when it became evident that Australia would not be participating either. Menzies, Hasluck, Waller and Renouf seized the critical moment ten years later to ensure that Johnson also would not feel required to abandon plans for intervention. It was not a matter of an Australian tail wagging the American dog. It was a matter of providing Johnson with an assurance of support that had not been available to Eisenhower, so that he would not feel required to draw back from the brink as Eisenhower had done. It was an assurance which could hardly have been provided in the circumstances by any other government. The British could not be expected to participate in intervention as they were co-chairmen of the Geneva Conference. Nor could the Canadians, as they were members of the International Control Commission set up by the Geneva Conference. The Taiwanese were unsuitable in every way. The Koreans were suspect. The Filipinos were unpredictable. The Thais would wait for the bandwagon to start rolling before they would come on board. The New Zealanders were too small and too peripheral. Australia might not have been the only regional country that could have provided the kind of credible support that would make United States military intervention politically possible; but it was the most desirable and the most certain.

There was a very cogent reason why the Australian government should have seized the opportunity to get the United States committed militarily to the Asian mainland. British disengagement from east of Suez was inevitable over time. All that was in question was how much time. There would then once more be nobody for Australia to turn to for protection in the region other than the United States. American assistance in the event of an attack on the Australian mainland itself was already provided for under the terms of ANZUS. But Australian governments naturally preferred that any threat to

Conclusion 169

their continent should be halted as far away from its shores as possible, and ideally while the threat was still potential rather than actual. It was not certain that the Americans would regard their obligations under ANZUS as extending quite that far. It was indeed all too easy to imagine how Australia might seem remote and even expendable from the perspective of Washington in any situation not directly involving the security of the United States itself. Australia does not cover the approaches to continental America; it is not on the way to anywhere else of strategic importance except perhaps Antarctica; it controls no choke points; its population is inconsequential; its productive capacity marginal; and its resources mainly supplementary to those of more conveniently situated or more reliable suppliers. Support from United States intervention in Vietnam was intended to resolve these problems, in the short run by establishing an American military presence across the approaches to Australia; and in the long run, by creating a new form of Pacific partnership between Canberra and Washington, committed permanently to preserving stability in the region. It was a purely Australian solution to an Australian problem based on Australian perceptions. What it tended to overlook was that other people had different problems, different solutions and different perceptions, and that Australia's capacity to influence their actions was necessarily limited. Twenty years later, the whole of Indochina is communist and Australia's security problems are more intractable than ever. Intervention in Vietnam was not the answer.

Notes to the Text

Abbreviations

AJPH	*Australian Journal of Politics and History*
CINFO	US Army Communication Division (Information)
CNIA	*Current Notes on International Affairs*
CSA	Controlled Source (American)
DDE	Dwight David Eisenhower
JCS	Joint Chiefs of Staff
LBJ	Lyndon Baines Johnson
NSC	National Security Council
NSF	National Security Files
PPP	Public Papers of the Presidents
SNIE	Special National Intelligence Estimate
USNA	United States National Archives

1 1954

1. Sir Keith Waller, Oral History Interview by Joe B. Frantz, 1 December 1969, Lyndon Baines Johnson Library, Austin, Texas, 12–13.
2. Sir Robert G. Menzies, Oral History Interview by Frantz, 25 November 1969, LBJ Library, 6–9.
3. Ronald H. Spector, *United States Army in Vietnam. Advice and Support: The Early Years, 1941–1960* (Washington: Center of Military History, United States Army, 1983), 211.
4. Phone Calls Series, 3 April 1954, John Foster Dulles Papers, Dwight D.

Eisenhower Library, Abilene, Kansas. The definitive study of this most enigmatic of presidents is by Stephen E. Ambrose, *Eisenhower* (London: George Allen & Unwin, 1984–). See also the series of *The Papers of Dwight David Eisenhower* (Baltimore: Johns Hopkins University Press, 1970–) and Robert H. Ferrell, ed., *The Eisenhower Diaries* (New York: Norton, 1981).

5. Senator Wiley telephone conversation, 7 April 1954, Phone Calls Series, Dulles Papers, DDE Library.
6. Dulles to AMEMBASSIES Paris 3476 and London 5175, 3 April 1954, Mike Gravel, ed., *The Pentagon Papers: the Defense Department History of United States Decision-Making in Vietnam. The Senator Gravel Edition* (New York: Beacon Press, 1971), 1: 460.
7. National Security Council, Action No. 1074-a, 5 April 1954, Gravel, *Pentagon Papers*, 1: 468–71; Stanley Robert Larsen and James Lawton Collins, Jr., *Vietnam Studies: Allied Participation in Vietnam* (Washington: Department of the Army, 1975), 120–21.
8. President Eisenhower's News Conference, 7 April 1954, United States National Archives, *Public Papers of the Presidents, 1954* (Washington: US Government Printing Office, 1958), 382.
9. Note by the Executive Secretary to the NSC on United States Objectives and Courses of Action with Respect to Southeast Asia, 11 January 1954, Gravel, *Pentagon Papers*, 1: 434–43; The President's News Conference, 7 April 1954, *PPP 1954*, 33.
10. The President's News Conference, 7 April 1954, *PPP 1954*, 382.
11. T.B. Millar, ed., *Australian Foreign Minister: The Diaries of R.G. Casey, 1951–60* (London: Collins, 1972), 7 April 1954, 124. The most perceptive and vigorous analysis of Casey's achievement in diplomacy is still Noela M. McKinnon, "Australian Foreign Policy, 1957–65: A Study of Four Foreign Ministers," Honours thesis, University of Queensland, 1975.
12. Michael G. Birgan, "Australian Attitudes and Reactions to the People's Republic of China, 1949–1972", Honours thesis, University of Queensland, 1972, 46. See also Eric M. Andrews, *Australia and China* (Carlton: Melbourne University Press, 1985) for the most recent and most authoritative analysis of the relationship between the two countries, and Gregory Clark, *In Fear of China* (Melbourne: Lansdowne Press, 1967), for a pioneering study in this field.
13. Great Britain, House of Commons, *Parliamentary Debates* 526, 13 April 1954, 969–75.
14. Senator Smith (NJ), telephone conversation, 19 April 1954, Phone Calls Series, Dulles Papers, DDE Library.
15. *Casey Diaries*, 18 April 1954, 133–34.
16. Ibid., 23 April 1954, 136–38.
17. Ibid., 26 April 1954, 139–40.
18. Dwight D. Eisenhower, *Mandate for Change* (Garden City: Doubleday, 1963), 351.
19. Dulles to Eisenhower, 25 April 1954, Gravel, *Pentagon Papers*, 1: 477–80.
20. DDE Diary, 27 April 1954, Eisenhower Papers, DDE Library.
21. Eisenhower, *Mandate*, 352–53.
22. Dulles to Eisenhower, 29 April 1954, Gravel, *Pentagon Papers*, 1: 481–82.
23. Walter Bedell Smith to Eisenhower, 29 April 1954; DDE to Smith, 30 April 1954, Eisenhower Papers, DDE Library.
24. *Casey Diaries*, 2 May 1954, 145–50.
25. Eisenhower to E.E. Hazlett, 23 October 1954, Eisenhower Papers, DDE Library.
26. Arthur W. Radford to Charles S. Wilson, 7 May 1954, Gravel, *Pentagon Papers*, 1: 501–3.
27. DDE Diary, Cabinet Minutes, 14 May 1954, Eisenhower Papers, DDE Library.

28. Eisenhower to Alfred M. Gruenther, 8 June 1954, Eisenhower Papers, DDE Library.
29. *Casey Diaries*, 4 June 1954, 151–52.
30. Telephone Call from Amb. Munro, 25 June 1954, Phone Calls Series, Dulles Papers, DDE Library.
31. *Casey Diaries*, 30 June 1954, 167–69.
32. Ibid., 29 July 1954, 172–73; see also Sir Alan Watt, *Australian Diplomat: Memoirs of Sir Alan Watt* (Sydney: Angus & Robertson, 1972), 217.
33. Australia, House of Representatives, *Parliamentary Debates*, 5 August 1954, 3 Eliz. II, 4: 63–69.
34. Telephone Call to Mr Merchant, 30 August 1954, Phone Calls Series, Dulles Papers, DDE Library.
35. *Casey Diaries*, 8 September 1954, 183–85.
36. Watt, *Diplomat*, 222–23.

2 1954–1962

1. Edward G. Lansdale to Maxwell D. Taylor, July 1961, "Resources for Unconventional Warfare, S.E. Asia", Gravel, *Pentagon Papers*, 1: 643–47; Neil Sheehan et al., eds., *The Pentagon Papers* (New York: Bantam, 1971), 54–60, 135–37; Larsen and Collins, *Allied Participation*, 52. The most comprehensive and stylish account of the role of Claire Lee Chennault in United States support of the Chinese Nationalists is in Christine A. Fegan-Will Ph.D., "Marriage of Convenience: Chinese Relations with the United Kingdom and the United States, 1940–45", University of Queensland, 1981. See also William M. Leary, *Perilous Missions: Civil Air Transport and CIA Covert Operations in Asia* (Birmingham: University of Alabama Press, 1984) and Sterling Seagrave et al., *Soldiers of Fortune* (Alexandria: TIME-LIFE Books, 1981).
2. Spector, *Advice*, 158–59, 225.
3. Denis Warner, *Reporting South-East Asia* (Sydney: Angus & Robertson, 1966), 10–11.
4. Spector, *Advice*, 278–81, 302.
5. Warner, *The Last Confucian* (New York: Macmillan, 1963), 71.
6. Terrence Maitland et al., *The Vietnam Experience: Raising the Stakes* (Boston: Boston Publishing Company, 1982), 63–65.
7. Spector, *Advice*, 223–24.
8. Note by the Executive Secretary to the National Security Council on US Policy in Mainland Southeast Asia, 25 Juy 1960, NSC 6012, DDE Library.
9. Spector, *Advice*, 355.
10. Ibid., 356.
11. Eldridge Burrow to Christian A. Herter, 7 March 1960, US Department of Defense, *United States — Vietnam Relations, 1954–1967* (Washington: USGPO, 1971), 10: 1254–57.
12. Harold Macmillan, *At the End of the Day* (London: Macmillan, 1973), 238–39.
13. Joint Chiefs of Staff to CINCPAC, 26 April 1961, *Vietnam: A History in Documents*, ed. Gareth Porter (New York: Meridian, 1979), 207.
14. Memo of Conversation, Department of State, 29 April 1961, *U.S.–Vietnam Relations*, 4: 64–66.
15. Lansdale, Memo, 8 May 1961, *US–Vietnam Relations*, 4: 107-10.
16. Lyndon B. Johnson to John F. Kennedy, 23 May 1961, "Mission to Southeast Asia, India and Pakistan", Vice President Security File, Vice Presidential Travel, LBJ Library.

Notes to pages 23-32   173

17. James Eayrs, *In Defence of Canada: Indochina: The Roots of Complicity* (Toronto: University of Toronto Press, 1983), 222–23, 243, 249.
18. Frederick E. Nolting, Jr., to Dean D. Rusk, 16 May 1961 and 21 June 1961, *Vietnam Documents*, 212–15.
19. NSC Action Memo No. 80, 29 August 1961, *US–Vietnam Relations*, 2: 247–48.
20. Harold Macmillant to Queen Elizabeth II, 15 September 1961, in Macmillan, *Day*, 239.
21. Memo from the JCS to Robert S. McNamara, JCSM-716-61, 9 October 1961, *Vietnam Documents*, 218–21.
22. Boswell Kilpatric, Memo for Record, 11 October 1961, *US–Vietnam Relations*, 4: 322–23.
23. The President's News Conference of 11 October 1961, *The Kennedy Presidential Press Conferences*, ed. George W. Johnson (New York: Coleman, 1978), 146–55.
24. Kennedy to Taylor, 13 October 1961, in Taylor, *Swords and Plowshares* (New York: W.W. Norton, 1972), 225–26.
25. Ibid., 240.
26. Ibid., 229.
27. Taylor to Kennedy, 1 November 1961, *US–Vietnam Relations*, 2: 331–36.
28. George W. Ball, *The Past Has Another Pattern: Memoirs* (New York: Norton, 1982), 366–67.
29. Robert H. Whitlow, *U.S. Marines in Vietnam: The Advisory & Combat Assistance Era, 1954–1964* (Washington: Department of the Navy, 1977), 43.
30. Australia, Department of Foreign Affairs, *Australia's Military Commitment to Vietnam*, 13 May 1975, 5.
31. Message from the President of the Republic of Viet-Nam (Diem) to the President of the United States (Kennedy), 7 December 1961, US Department of State, *Bulletin*, 1 January 1962, 13–14.
32. News Conference of the Secretary of State, 8 December 1961, US Department of State, *Bulletin*, 25 December 1961, 1053–58.
33. Macmillan, *Day*, 240.
34. Admiral Arleigh S. Burke, Oral History Interview by John T. Moore, Jr., 1972, John F. Kennedy Library, Point Columbia, Mass., 172.
35. Australia, Department of External Affairs, "Viet Nam: Documents on Communist Aggression", *Current Notes on International Affairs* (Canberra: Government Printer, 1965).
36. *Australia's Commitment*, 5.
37. Maitland et al., *Stakes*, 132.
38. Sir Robert Thompson, *No Exit From Vietnam* (New York: David MacKay, 1970), 123–24, 172–73.
39. Whitlow, *Marines*, 45.
40. Australia, Senate, *Parl. Deb.*, 30 March 1962, 21: 690.
41. Ngo Dinh Diem to Robert G. Menzies, 31 March 1962, *CNIA* 33: 6 (June 1962): 37–39.
42. Address by the United States Secretary of State, Dean Rusk, at a state dinner in Canberra on 9 May, 1962, *CNIA* 33: 5 (May 1962): 32–33.
43. Australia, H. of R., *Parl. Deb.*, 21 August 1962, 36: 581.
44. Menzies to Diem, 14 May 1962, US Department of State, *Bulletin*, 4 June 1962: 904–5.
46. Macmillan, *Day*, 242.
47. Press Statement by the Minister for Defence, 24 May 1962, *CNIA* 33: 5 (May 1962): 36.
48. Ian McNeill, *The Team: Australian Army Advisers in Vietnam, 1962–1972* (St Lucia: University of Queensland Press, 1984), 6.

49. Ibid., 7-8.
50. Ian Mackay, *Australians in Vietnam* (Adelaide: Rigby, 1968), 14.
51. Maitland et al., *Stakes*, 56.
52. State of the Union Address, 14 January 1963, USNA, *Public Papers of the Presidents: John F. Kennedy, 1963* (Washington: USGPO, 1964), 11-21.
53. *Australia's Commitment*, 14-15.

3 1963-1964

1. Don Aitkin, ed., *The Howson Diaries: The Life of Politics: Peter Howson* (Ringwood: Viking, 1984), 18 February 1963, 27.
2. Gregory Clark, "Vietnam, China and the foreign affairs debate in Australia: a personal account", in *Australia's Vietnam: Australia in the Second Indo-China War*, ed. Peter King (Sydney: Allan & Unwin, 1983), 18-35. See also Andrews, *Australia and China*; and Clark, *Fear*.
3. For a discussion of particular Australian concerns about the meaning of ANZUS at the time, see McKinnon, "Australian Foreign Policy", and Barclay, "In the Sticky Fly Paper: the United States, Australia and Indonesia, 1959-1964", *U.S. Naval War College Review*, 4: 286 (July-August 1981): 67-79.
4. McNeil, *Team*, 196.
5. See, inter alia, Menzies's reaction to the Korean Crisis in Barclay, *Friends in High Places* (Melbourne: Oxford University Press, 1985), 38-47.
6. Larsen and Collins, *Allied Participation*, 104-5.
7. Ball to Henry Cabot Lodge, 24 August 1963, *Vietnam Documents*, 204-10.
8. *Howson Diaries*, 27 August 1963, 53.
9. Lodge to Ball, 28 August 1963, in Ball, *Past*, 372-73.
10. Memo for Record of Meeting at State Department, 31 August 1963, Gravel, *Pentagon Papers*, 1: 202-5.
11. Report of the McNamara-Taylor Mission to South Vietnam, 2 October 1963, *US-Vietnam Relations*, 12: 554-73.
12. John A. McCone to Lodge, 6 October 1963, *Vietnam Documents*, 250-51.
13. CINFO to JCS, 2 December 1963, NSF, Country Files, Vietnam, LBJ Library.
14. CIA, Information Report, 16 December 1963, Vietnam, LBJ Library.
15. Whitlow, *Marines*, 121.
16. Warner, *South-east Asia*, 247-48.
17. McNamara to Johnson, 21 December 1963, NSF, Country Files, Vietnam, LBJ Library.
18. McCone, Highlights of Discussion in Saigon, 18-20 December 1963, 21 December 1963, Vietnam, LBJ Library.
19. McNamara to Johnson, 21 December 1963, Vietnam, LBJ Library.
20. United States Congress, House of Representatives, 88th Congress, 2nd Session, *Hearings on Military Posture and H.R. 9637, Before the Committee on Armed Services*, 27 January 1964, 6903-6.
21. Lodge to Rusk, 5 February 1964, Vietnam, LBJ Library.
22. William E. Colby, Memo for Distribution, 18 February 1964, "Appraisal of the Situation in South Vietnam", Vietnam, LBJ Library.
23. John T. McNaughton, "Draft Plan of Action for South Vietnam", 9 March 1964, Gravel, *Pentagon Papers*, 1: 559.
24. Johnson, *The Vantage Point: Perspectives of the Presidency, 1963-1969* (New York: Holt, Rinehart & Winston, 1971), 65-66.
25. Larry Berman, *Planning a Tragedy: The Americanization of the War in Vietnam* (New York: W.W. Norton, 1982), 28-29.

26. Larsen and Collins, *Allied Participation*, 115.
27. News Conference of the Secretary of State, 6 March 1964, US Department of State, *Bulletin*, 23 March 1964, 439–40, 442.
28. Rusk to Lodge, 17 March 1964, NSF, Country Files, Vietnam, LBJ Library.
29. Rusk to Lodge, 18 March 1964, Vietnam, LBJ Library.
30. Text of the Final Communique issued by the SEATO Council at the Conclusion of its Ninth Meeting, held in Manila, 13–15 April 1964, *SEATO Record*, 3: 3 (June 1964): 18–21.
31. *New York Times*, 24 April, 1964.
32. *Vietnam Documents*, 271–72; Chester L. Cooper, *The Lost Crusade: America in Vietnam* (New York: Dodd, Mead, 1970), 324–25.
33. W. Scott Thompson and Donaldson D. Frizzell, *The Lessons of Vietnam* (St Lucia: University of Queensland Press, 1977), 38–39.
34. Rusk to Lodge, 1 May 1964, NSF, Country Files, Vietnam, LBJ Library.
35. William E. Stevenson to Rusk, 2 May 1964, Vietnam, LBJ Library.
36. AMEMBASSY Manila to Rusk, 5 May 1964, Vietnam, LBJ Library.
37. Lodge to Rusk, 5 May 1964, Vietnam, LBJ Library.
38. Ball to Lodge and Stevenson, 8 May 1964, Vietnam, LBJ Library.
39. Rusk to Howard P. Jones, 9 May 1964, NSF, Country Files, Indonesia, vol. 2, LBJ Library; Jones to Rusk, 10 May 1964, Indonesia, LBJ Library.
40. Alan P. Renouf to Patrick Shaw, 11 May 1964, in Michael Sexton, *War For the Asking* (Melbourne: Penguin, 1982), 44–45.
41. Australia, H. of R., *Parl. Deb.*, 13 May 1964, 49: 1810.
42. McArthur to Rusk, 6 May 1964; McGhee to Rusk, 11 May 1964; Rusk to AMEMBASSIES, 18 May 1964, NSF, Country Files, Vietnam, LBJ Library.
43. *Australia's Commitment*, 9–10.
44. TIME Magazine, 29 May 1964, 21.
45. Lucius D. Battle to Rusk, 2 June 1964, NSF, Country Files, Vietnam, LBJ Library.
46. Rusk to Lodge, 4 June 1964, Vietnam, LBJ Library.
47. Rusk to McGhee, 8 June 1964, Vietnam, LBJ Library.
48. Rusk to Johnson, Memo for the President, "Third Country Aid to Viet Nam", 15 June 1964, Vietnam, LBJ Library.
49. *Australia's Commitment*, 10.
50. *Sydney Morning Herald*, 22 June, 1964.
51. Rusk to AMEMBASSIES, 2 July 1964, NSF, Country Files, Vietnam, LBJ Library.
52. Taylor to Rusk, 25 July 1964, Sheehan, et al. *Pentagon Papers*, 288–89.
53. Marshall Green to McGeorge Bundy, 7 November 1964, "Immediate Actions in the Period Prior to Decision", *Pentagon Papers*, 302–4.
54. *Howson's Diaries*, 31 July 1964, 105.

4 1964

1. Statement Read to Correspondents by the President, 3 August 1964, Department of State, *Bulletin*, 24 August 1964, 259.
2. William H. Sullivan, Oral History Interview by Paige E. Mulhollan, 21 July 1971, LBJ Library, 21–22. See also Michael Charlton and Anthony Moncrieff, *Many Reasons Why* (Harmondsworth: Penguin, 1979) for a detailed exposition of the case for presuming that no attack ever took place on 4 August. However, there is also no reason to doubt that the American sailors were genuinely under the impression at the time that they were being attacked. Mistakes of this kind do happen in war. Johnson unfortunately did not stop to consider the possibility that this might have been one.

3. Ball, *Past*, 379.
4. Lester B. Pearson, *Mike: The Memoirs of the Right Honorable Lester B. Pearson* (London: Victor Gollancz, 1975), 3, 137.
5. Message From the President to the Congress, 5 August 1964, Department of State, *Bulletin*, 24 August 1964, 261–63.
6. *The Times*, 6 August 1964; *New York Times*, 6 August 1964; *Sydney Morning Herald*, 6 August 1964.
7. Rusk to David K.E. Bruce, 6 August 1964, NSF, Country Files, United Kingdom, LBJ Library.
8. David K.E. Bruce, Oral History Interview by Thomas H. Baker, 9 December 1971, LBJ Library, 23.
9. Joint Resolution to Promote the Maintenance of International Peace and Security in Southeast Asia, *American Foreign Policy, 1950–1955: Basic Documents*, 1: 912–16.
10. Australia, H. of R., *Parl. Deb.*, 11 August 1964, 43: 20–22.
11. Rusk to AMEMBASSIES, 14 August 1964, NSF, Country Files, Vietnam, LBJ Library.
12. Thomas L. Hughes to Rusk, 28 August 1964, "Third Country Assistance to South Vietnam", Vietnam, LBJ Library.
13. *Howson Diaries*, 21 August 1964, 108.
14. Statement Made by Ambassador Taylor at a White House News Conference, 9 September 1964, Department of State, *Bulletin*, 21 September 1964, 433–34.
15. *Australia's Commitment*, 11.
16. CIA, SNIE 53–64; "Chances for a Stable Government in South Vietnam", 8 September 1964, NSF, Country Files, Vietnam, LBJ Library.
17. Ball to Rusk, 5 October 1964, Vietnam, LBJ Library.
18. JCS Comments, NSC Memo by William P. Bundy, 8 November 1964, "US Objectives and Stakes in SVN and SEA", Gravel, *Pentagon Papers*, 3: 625. The most comprehensive breakdown of casualty figures in the Korean War is in Robert Leckie, *Conflict: A History of the Korean War* (New York: G.P. Putnam & Sons, 1962). See also Gamal el-din Attia, *Les Forces armees des nations unies en coree et au moyen-orient* (Geneva: Plon, 1963).
19. Australia, H. of R., *Parl. Deb.*, 10 November 1964, 44: 2715–24.
20. Noela M. McKinnon, "Australian Foreign Policy, 1957–1965: A Study of Four Foreign Ministers", Honours thesis, University of Queensland, 1975, 151.
21. Memo of Conversation, 12 November 1964, NSF, Country Files, Australia, LBJ Library.
22. *Howson Diaries*, 24 November 1964, 124–25.
23. Press Statement by the Minister for External Affairs, Paul Hasluck in Washington, on 25 November, *CNIA* 35: 11 (November 1964): 33–35.
24. Taylor, *Swords*, 327.
25. Taylor, "The Current Situation in South Vietnam — November 1964", 27 November 1964, Sheehan et al., *Pentagon Papers*, 370–73.
26. William P. Bundy, Draft Position Paper on Southeast Asia, 29 November 1964, Gravel, *Pentagon Papers*, 3: 681.
27. *Australia's Commitment*, 11; Sexton, *War*, 54. Sexton claims that "it is obvious that at this stage the Americans had no thought of requesting units of combat troops from Australia. One reason was that they themselves had no thought yet of sending combat troops to Vietnam." The Americans had considered sending combat troops in 1954. Kennedy had proposed intervening in Thailand in 1961. Lansdale had proposed allied intervention in Vietnam at the same time. Taylor recommended the use of United States ground forces in Vietnam in 1961. McNamara indicated the necessity to commit ground troops in 1963. The issue of multilateral ground intervention had been discussed incessantly throughout 1964, in both

Washington and Canberra. In any case, William P. Bundy invited Australian participation in a multilateral ground force only four days later. It is not really clear what point Sexton is trying to make.
28. Rusk to AMEMBASSIES London, Canberra and Wellington, 4 December 1964, NSF, Country Files, Australia, LBJ Library.
29. CINCPAC to Rusk, "U.S. Aid to Britain to Assist Her in Meeting Commitments of Combined Interest Overseas", 6 December 1964, NSF, Country Files, United Kingdom, LBJ Library; Oral History Interview with David Bruce, 23; Richard Crossman, *The Diaries of a Cabinet Minister* (London: Hamilton & Cape, 1975), 11 December 1964, 84–95; Sir Harold Wilson, *The Labour Government, 1964–70: A Personal Record* (Harmondsworth: Penguin, 1974), 78–79.
30. McGeorge Bundy to LBJ, 10 December 1964, NSF, Country Files, United Kingdom, LBJ Library.
31. Michael V. Forrestal to LBJ, 8 December 1964, "Third Country Assistance to Vietnam", NSF, Country Files, Vietnam, LBJ Library.
32. *Howson Diaries*, 9–10 December 1964, 129–31; Taylor to Rusk, 11 December 1964, NSF, Country Files, Vietnam, LBJ Library; *Australia's Commitment*, 11–12.
33. Chester L. Cooper and McGeorge Bundy to LBJ, 22 December 1964, "Free World Assistance to South Vietnam (Special Report)", NSF, Country Files, Vietnam, LBJ Library.
34. Jerauld Wright to Rusk, 26 December 1964, Vietnam, LBJ Library.
35. Winthrop G. Brown to Rusk, 29 December 1964; Cooper to George E. Reedy, Jr., 29 December 1964, Vietnam, LBJ Library.
36. *Australia's Commitment*, 12.
37. Taylor to Rusk, 24 December 1964, NSF, Country Files, Vietnam, LBJ Library.
38. Whitlow, *Marines*, 166.

5 1965

1. Hasluck to Shaw, 5 January 1965, in Sexton, *War*, 90–91.
2. William P. Bundy to Rusk, 6 January 1965, NSF, Country Files, Vietnam, LBJ Library.
3. *Howson Diaries*, 6 January 1965, 136.
4. Waller, Oral History Interview, 13.
5. Waller to Hasluck, 7 January 1965, *Australia's Commitment*, 13.
6. Taylor to Rusk, 11 January 1965, NSF, Country Files, Vietnam, LBJ Library.
7. Carolyn O'Brien, "Australia's Achievement in Regional Defence Planning", Ph.D., University of Queensland, 1980, 298.
8. *Australia's Commitment*, 12–14.
9. Taylor to Rusk, 19 January 1965, NSF, Country Files, Australia, LBJ Library.
10. *Australia's Commitment*, 14.
11. Memo of Conversation, "Viet-Nam", 19 January 1965, NSF, Country Files, Vietnam, LBJ Library.
12. McGeorge Bundy to LBJ, 27 January 1965, in Johnson, *Vantage Point*, 122–23.
13. Hasluck to Menzies, 28 January 1965, *Australia's Commitment*, 15.
14. *SEATO Record* 4 (1965), 2, 40.
15. Waller to Hasluck, 2 February 1965, in Sexton, *War*, 102.
16. Memo by Taylor, 2 February 1965, NSF, Country Files, Vietnam, LBJ Library.
17. McGeorge Bundy to LBJ, 7 February 1965, Vietnam, LBJ Library.
18. Statement by the Australian Minister for External Affairs, Paul Hasluck, 8 February 1965, *CNIA* 36: 2 (February 1965): 3.
19. *Times of India*, 9 February 1965.

20. *Australia's Commitment*, 15.
21. *Howson Diaries*, 11 February 1965, 142.
22. *Le Monde*, 11 February 1965.
23. Wilson, *Record*, 115–17.
24. Bruce, Oral History Interview, 23; reproduced by permission of Mrs Evangeline B. Bruce.
25. *Crossman Diaries*, 11 February 1965, 156.
26. *New York Times*, 13 February 1965.
27. Statement by United Nations Secretary General U Thant, 12 February 1965, Australia, Department of External Affairs, *Select Documents on International Affairs, Viet Nam, First Half of 1965* (Canberra: AGPS, 1965), 9.
28. Statement by the International Commission for Supervision and Control in Viet Nam, 13 February 1965, *Select Documents*, 14–19.
29. William P. Bundy to LBJ, Memo for the President, 16 February 1965, NSF, Subject File, Vietnam, Vietnam Memos 28, LBJ Library; McGeorge Bundy to LBJ, 17 February 1965, NSF, Country Files, Vietnam, LBJ Library.
30. Hasluck to Rusk, 18 February 1965, *Australia's Commitment*, 15.
31. *Howson Diaries*, 22 February 1965, 143–44.
32. Jack W. Lydman to Rusk, 23 February 1965, Department of State Files, Australia, vol. 1, LBJ Library.
33. *Australia's Commitment*, 16.
34. Larsen and Collins, *Allied Participation*, 122.
35. Terrence Maitland et al., *The Vietnam Experience: Raising the Stakes* (Boston: Boston Publishing Company, 1982), 174–75.
36. Ray Bonds, ed., *The Vietnam War: An Illustrated History* (London: Salamander Books, 1979), 86.
37. Wilson, *Record*, 121.
38. *Globe and Mail* (Toronto), 9 March 1965.
39. Chester L. Cooper to LBJ, 11 March 1965, NSF, Subject File, Vietnam Memos, 31, LBJ Library.
40. CIA, "World Sitrep on Free World Assistance to Viet-Nam", 11 March 1965, Vietnam, LBJ Library.
41. Taylor to Rusk, 13 March 1965, Gravel, *Pentagon Papers*, 3: 445–47.
42. CSA Memo for Secretary of Defence and JCS, 14 March 1965, Gravel, *Pentagon Papers*, 3: 405.
43. *New York Times*, 22 March 1965.
44. Sharp to Sir Frederick Scherger, 22 March 1965, NSF, Country Files, Vietnam, LBJ Library.
45. *Australia's Commitment*, 21.
46. *New York Times*, 23 March 1965.
47. Wilson, *Record*, 122–23.
48. *New York Times*, 24 March 1965.
49. Australia, H. of R., *Parl. Deb.*, 23 March 1965, 45: 230–38.
50. *Howson Diaries*, 23 March 1965, 147–48.
51. Rusk to Mission Chiefs and CINCPAC, 24 March 1965, NSF, Subject File, Vietnam Cables 31, LBJ Library.
52. Joseph A. Medenhall, SCOPE Paper SEATO Meeting, London, 1 April 1965, 3–4 May 1965, NSF, Subject File, Vietnam, Memos 31, LBJ Library.
53. Great Britain, H. of C., *Parl. Deb.*, 1 April 1965, 709: 1865–68.
54. Pearson, *Memoirs*, 138–41.
55. NSC Meetings, 1–2 April 1965, Gravel, *Pentagon Papers*, 3: 403, 3: 453–57.
56. *Australia's Commitment*, 16.
57. Rusk to Taylor, 10 April 1965, Country Files, Vietnam, LBJ Library.

58. Taylor to Rusk, 17 April 1965, Gravel, *Pentagon Papers*, 3: 704–5.
59. Australia's Commitment, 16.
60. Rusk to Taylor, 12 April 1965, NSF, Country Files, Vietnam, LBJ Library.
61. Rusk, Memo of Conversation, 13 April 1965, NSF, Country Files, Australia, LBJ Library.
62. Taylor to Rusk, 17 April 1965, Gravel, *Pentagon Papers*, 3: 704–5.
63. Gregory Clark, "Vietnam, China and the foreign affairs debate in Australia: a personal account", in Peter King, ed., *Australia's Vietnam: Australia in the Second Indochina War* (Sydney: George Allen & Unwin, 1983), 26.
64. *Howson Diaries*, 22 April 1965, 151.
65. Australia's Commitment, 18.
66. Rusk to Taylor, 28 April 1965, NSF, Country Files, Australia, LBJ Library.
67. Ibid.
68. Australia, H. of R., *Parl. Deb.*, 29 April 1965, 45: 1060–61.
69. *Howson Diaries*, 29 April 1965, 154.

6 1965–1966

1. Wilson, *Record*, 139.
2. SEATO Ministerial Council Meeting, London, 3–5 May 1965, Background Paper, "The Future of SEATO", 28 April 1965, NSF, International Meetings and Travel File, SEATO Meeting, May 1965, LBJ Library. Secretary Rusk was referring to Article 8 of the ANZUS Treaty.
3. Rusk to Bruce, 29 April 1965, NSF, Country Files, United Kingdom, LBJ Library.
4. Taylor to Rusk, 29 April 1965, NSF, Country Files, Vietnam, LBJ Library.
5. Great Britain, H. of C., *Parl. Deb.*, 3 May 1965, 712, 709–14.
6. The *Dominion* (Wellington), 28 May 1968, 11.
7. Doyle et al., *America Takes Over*, 11.
8. Johnson, *Vantage Point*, 142–43.
9. Lydman to Rusk, 4 June 1965, NSF, Country Files, Australia, LBJ Library.
10. Address by the prime minister, Sir Robert Menzies, to the Australian-American Association in Washington on 11 June 1965, *CNIA* 33: 6 (June 1965): 339–43.
11. W. Scott Thompson and Donaldson D. Frizzell, eds., *The Lessons of Vietnam* (St Lucia: University of Queensland Press, 1977), 12–13.
12. Jack J. Valenti, *A Very Human President* (New York: Norton, 1975), 114–15.
13. Taylor, *Memoirs*, 349.
14. Wilson, *Record*, 150–51.
15. Memo of Conversation, "Commonwealth Initiative in Vietnam", 15 June 1965, NSF, Country Files, United Kingdom, LBJ Library.
16. *Crossman Diaries*, 15 June 1965, 250; 17 June 1965, 252.
17. Wilson, *Record*, 153.
18. Taylor to Rusk, 19 June 1965, NSF, Subject Files, Vietnam Cables (a), 35, LBJ Library.
19. The *Australian*, 19 June 1965.
20. *Howson Diaries*, 23 June 1965, 162.
21. Communique issued at conclusion of Commonwealth Prime Ministers' Conference, 25 June 1965, *Selected Documents*, 76–77.
22. Note by the Communist Chinese Authorities Concerning the Commonwealth Mission, 25 June 1965, *Select Documents*, 75–76.
23. Ball to LBJ, 1 July 1965, Gravel, *Pentagon Papers*, 4: 618–19.
24. *Howson Diaries*, 7 July 1965, 162–63.

25. John T. McNaughton to General Goodpaster, "Forces Required to win in South Vietnam", 14 July 1965, Gravel, *Pentagon Papers*, 4: 291–93.
26. McNamara to LBJ, 20 July 1965, *Vietnam Documents*, 317–20.
27. Rusk to Lydman, 26 July 1965, Department of State Files, Australia, vol. 1, LBJ Library.
28. Johnson, *Vantage Point*, 153.
29. Australia's Commitment, 23–26.
30. *SEATO Record*, 4 (1965), 18 August 1965, 5, 22.
31. *Howson Diaries*, 19 August 1965, 169–70.
32. Waller, Oral History Interview, 19–20.
33. See Andrews, *Australia and China*; also United States, Foreign Affairs Division, Congressional Research Services, "Chronology of Sino-Soviet Relations, 1965–1974"; *People's Daily*, 2 September 1965; J.Y. Cheng, "China's Foreign Policy — Continuity and Change", *Asian Quarterly*, 4 (1976): 296–326; Wang Gungwu, *China and the World Since 1949* (London: Macmillan, 1977).
34. McNamara to LBJ, 30 November 1965, *Vietnam Documents*, 322–24.
35. Joint State-Defense Outgoing Telegram Canberra No. 432, 3 December 1965, Department of State Files, Vietnam, vol. 15, LBJ Library.
36. Lydman to Rusk, 9 December 1965, Vietnam, LBJ Library.
37. Barclay, "Friends in Salisbury: Australia and the Rhodesian Unilateral Declaration of Independence, 1965–72", *Australian Journal of Politics and History* 29: 1 (1983): 38–49.
38. *Australia's Commitment*, 26–27.
39. Australia, H. of R., *Parl. Deb.*, 10 December 1965, 49: 3916.
40. Michael Fogarty, "Ted Serong: An Army Career", *Defence Force Journal* 56 (January/February 1986): 4–15.
41. Wilson, *Record*, 244–45.
42. *Crossman Diaries*, 21 December 1965, 418.
43. McNaughton to LBJ, "Some Paragraphs on Vietnam," 19 January 1966, Sheehan et al., *Pentagon Papers*, 491–93.
44. *Howson Diaries*, 31 December 1965, 194.
45. Canada, H. of C., *Parl. Deb.*, 20 January 1966, 1: 62–63.
46. Pearson, *Memoirs*, 144–45.
47. *The Times*, 1 February 1966.
48. Wilson, *Record*, 266–68; Great Britain, H. of C., *Parl. Deb.*, 8 February 1966, 724: 258–62.
49. "Resumption of Bombing in North Viet Nam", 1 February 1966, *CNIA* 37: 2 (February 1966): 76–77.
50. *Howson Diaries*, 3 February 1966, 206.
51. "United Kingdom/Australia Defence Talks", *CNIA* 37: 2 (February 1966): 77–80.
52. Waller, Oral History Interview, 4–5.
53. *Howson Diaries*, 19 February 1966, 207.
54. "Visit of Vice-President Humphrey to Australia", *CNIA* 37: 2 (February 1966): 82–90.
55. George S. Moore to Jack J. Valenti, 4 March 1966, LBJ Subject File, CO18 Australia, LBJ Library.
56. *Howson Diaries*, 24 February 1966, 208.
57. *People's Daily*, 2 February 1966.
58. *Australia's Commitment*, 27.
59. Ibid., 28.
60. Nguyen Cao Ky to Harold E. Holt, 7 March 1966, *Vietnam News* 1 (1966), 4, 47–48.
61. Australia, H. of R., *Parl. Deb.*, 8 March 1966, 50: 22–35.

62. Ibid., 15 March 1966, 50: 245–49.
63. *Howson Diaries*, 8 March 1966, 210.
64. Ibid., 23 March 1966, 213.
65. Ruth Bacon, "Free World Attitudes on Viet-Nam", 25 March 1966, NSF, Country Files, Vietnam, LBJ Library.
66. LBJ to Wilson, 1 April 1966, White House Central Files, Subject Files, CO35, United Kingdom, LBJ Library.

7 1966–1967

1. Cyrus R. Vance to LBJ, 8 April 1966, NSF, Country Files, Vietnam, LBJ Library.
2. Sheehan et al., *Pentagon Papers*, 474–75.
3. *Howson Diaries*, 11 April 1966, 216.
4. *People's Daily*, 1 May 1966.
5. Wallace Brown, "A World Trip With Voters in Mind", *Courier-Mail* (Brisbane), 26 April 1986.
6. *Howson Diaries*, 3 May 1966, 219; 19 May 1966, 223.
7. Edward Doyle et al., *The Vietnam Experience: America Takes Over* (Boston: Boston Publishing Company, 1982), 76.
8. *The Times*, 16 June 1966.
9. Wilson, *Record*, 321.
10. Cecil King, *The Cecil King Diary, 1965–1970* (London: Jonathan Cape, 1972), 5 July 1966, 76.
11. *Howson Diaries*, 1 July 1966, 228.
12. *King Diary*, 16 July 1966, 78–79.
13. Address by the Prime Minister, Harold Holt, to the National Press Club in Canberra, 18 July 1966, *CNIA* 37: 7 (July 1966): 451–61.
14. Rusk to LBJ, Memorandum for the President, 22 July 1966, NSF, Country Files, United Kingdom, LBJ Library.
15. Wilson, *Record*, 341.
16. Australia, H. of R., *Parl. Deb.*, 18 August 1966, 52: 215–26.
17. Lex McAulay, *The Battle of Long Tan* (Melbourne: Hutchinson, 1986), passim.
18. Thompson, "America Fights the Wrong War", the *Spectator*, 12 August 1966.
19. Institute for Defense Analyses, "The Effects of U.S. Bombing on North Vietnam's Ability to Support Military Operations in South Vietnam: Retrospect and Prospect", 29 August 1966, Sheehan et al., *Pentagon papers*, 502–9.
20. *King Diary*, 8 September 1966, 89–91.
21. Address by the Minister for External Affairs, Paul Hasluck, to the United Nations General Assembly, 27 September 1966, *CNIA* 37: 9 (September 1966): 531–40.
22. Walt Whitman Rostow, Memo for the President, 3 October 1966, NSF, Manila Conference, LBJ Library.
23. McNamara, Memo for the President, "Actions Recommended in Vietnam", 14 October 1966, Sheehan et al., *Pentagon Papers*, 542–51.
24. Marshall Wright, Paul S. Garvey, and C. Richard Spurgin, "Presidential Decisions, the Seven-Nation Manila Conference and the President's Asia Trip, Oct. 17–Nov. 2, 1966", NSF, Manila Conference, LBJ Library.
25. Frank Galbally to LBJ, 24 October 1966, TR100, Johnson Papers, LBJ Library.
26. Wright, Garvey and Spurgin, "Presidential Decisions", LBJ Library.
27. E.M. Cronk, Memorandum of Conversation, "Viet-Nam and Related Matters", 21 October 1966, LBJ Library.
28. Harry McPherson, *A Political Education* (Boston: Little, Brown & Co., 1972), 306–7.
29. "Visit of President Johnson to Australia", *CNIA* 37: 10 (October 1966): 595–603.

30. *Howson Diaries*, 21 October 1966, 244–45.
31. Larsen and Collins, *Allied Participation*, 23. The New Zealander had a battery of artillery in Vietnam, but their contingent of 155 men did not constitute a manoeuvre battalion.
32. McPherson, *Education*, 313–14.
33. Chester L. Cooper, *The Lost Crusade: America in Vietnam* (New York: Norton, 1972), 266–67.
34. *Sydney Morning Herald*, 9 November 1966.
35. Ibid., 10 November 1966.
36. LBJ to Holt, 28 November 1966, NSF, Subject File, CO10, Australia, LBJ Library.
37. *Australia's Commitment*, 29.
38. *Howson Diaries*, 13 December 1966, 251–52; 14 December 1966, 253.
39. *Australia's Commitment*, 30–31.
40. *Howson Diaries*, 20 January 1967, 262–63.
41. *Age* (Melbourne), 9 January 1967.
42. *Howson Diaries*, 19 January 1967, 261–62.
43. Harry G. Gelber, "Problems of Australian Foreign Policy, Jan–Jun 1967", *Australian Journal of Politics and History* 13: 3 (December 1967): 313–22.
44. Colin A. Hughes, "Australian Political Chronicle, Jan–Apr, 1967", *AJPH* 13: 2 (August 1967): 251–55.
45. *Howson Diaries*, 20 January 1967, 262–63.
46. New Zealand, Department of External Affairs, *External Affairs Review* 18 (1967): 3, 40.
47. William and Sonia McMahon to LBJ and Lady Bird Johnson, 5 April 1967, NSF, Subject File, CO18, Australia, LBJ Library.
48. *Australia's Commitment*, 32.
49. "Notes on Johnson Discussion with Wheeler and Westmoreland", 27 April 1967, Sheehan et al., *Pentagon Papers*, 567–69.
50. "SVN Troop Deployments in Relation to Population", 4 May 1967, Gravel, *Pentagon Papers*, 4: 470.
51. Hughes, "Chronicle, May–Aug, 1967", *AJPH* 13: 3 (December 1967): 405–11.
52. Aitkin, *Howson Diaries*, 257.
53. "Visit to the United States, Canada and Britain by the Prime Minister", *CNIA* 38: 6 (June 1967): 245–53.
54. "Australia–New Zealand Relations", *CNIA* 38: 6 (June 1967): 253–58.
55. "Visit to the United States", *CNIA* 38: 6 (June 1967): 245–53.
56. LBJ to Holt, 11 July 1967, NSF, Subject File, CO18, Australia, LBJ Library.
57. William P. Bundy to Rusk, McNamara, Rostow and Katzenbach, 13 July 1967, "Messages to Manila Nations and Possibilities for Additional Troop Contributions", Gravel, *Pentagon Papers*, 4: 523–24.
58. "British White Paper on Defence", *CNIA* 38: 7 (July 1967): 295–96.
59. Hughes, "Chronicle": 411. Don Aitkin thought that Holt's domestic setbacks were "inexplicable", and that it was "not that the Labor Party was putting pressure on the government". Aitkin, *Howson Diaries*, 257.
60. *Australia's Commitment*, 32.
61. Ibid., 32–33.
62. *Howson Diaries*, 4 August 1967, 315–16.
63. *New York Times*, 6 August 1967.
64. Australia, H. of R., *Parl. Deb.*, 17 August, 1967, 56: 206–17.
65. *Australia's Commitment*, 33.
66. *Howson Diaries*, 21 August 1967, 319.
67. Thailand, Ministry of Foreign Affairs, *Foreign Affairs Bulletin* 7 (1967): 102.
68. *Howson Diaries*, 6 September 1967, 325–26.

69. Mike Mansfield to LBJ, 19 September 1967, White House Central Files, CO1-3, LBJ Library.
70. *Australia's Commitment*, 34.
71. "Australia–New Zealand Relations", *CNIA* 38: 9 (September 1967): 443.
72. Australia, H. of R., *Parl. Deb.*, 17 October 1967, 57: 1855–58.
73. Peter G. Hughes, "The Pattern of Australia's Defence, 1963–1971", Honours thesis, University of Queensland, 1972, 120–21.
74. Bonds, *Vietnam*, 144; "The Banners of Dissent", *TIME Magazine* 90: 17 (October 1967), 9–15.
75. *Age* (Melbourne), 2 November 1967.
76. *Howson Diaries*, 16 November 1967, 351; 22 November 1967, 354; 27 November 1967, 355; 13 December 1967, 361.

Glossary

ADF	Australian Defence Force
ANZUS	Australia, New Zealand, United States Tripartite Security Pact
APC	Armoured Personnel Carrier
ARVN	Army of the Republic of Vietnam (South Vietnam)
CAS	Chief of Air Staff
CAT	Civil Air Transport
CINCPAC	Commander in Chief Pacific Fleet
DRV	Democratic Republic of Vietnam (North Vietnam)
FLN	Front de Liberation nationale
GNZ	Government of New Zealand
GOA	Government of Australia
GOP	Government of the Philippines
GRC	Government of the Republic of China (Taiwan)
GVN	Government of Vietnam (South Vietnam)
ICC	International Commission for Supervision and Control in Vietnam
JCS	Joint Chiefs of Staff
LST	Landing Ship (Tank)
MAAG	Military Assistance Advisory Group
MAC	Military Assistance Command
MACV	Military Assistance Command (Vietnam)
MAP	Military Assistance Program
NSC	National Security Council
NVN	North Vietnam
PRC	People's Republic of China

Glossary

ROK	Republic of Korea (South Korea)
SAS	Special Air Service
SEATO	Southeast Asia Treaty Organization
SMM	Saigon Military Mission
SVG	South Vietnamese Government
SVN	South Vietnam
USAF	United States Air Force
USG	United States Government
USMC	United States Marine Corps
VNAF	Vietnamese Air Force

Bibliography

A. Primary Sources (Unpublished)

1. Private Papers

Dulles, John Foster. Papers. Phone Calls Series, Dwight D. Eisenhower Library, Abilene, Kansas.
Eisenhower, Dwight D. Papers. DDE Library.
Johnson, Lyndon B. Papers. Lyndon B. Johnson Library, Austin, Texas.

2. Documents

AUSTRALIA

Department of Foreign Affairs, *Australia's Military Commitment to Vietnam*.

UNITED STATES OF AMERICA

Department of State Files, Australia, United States, National Archives.
Department of State Files, Vietnam Cables, USNA.
Department of State Files, Vietnam Files, USNA.
National Security Files, Country Files, Australia, LBJ Library.
National Security Files, Country Files, Indonesia, LBJ Library.
National Security Files, Country Files, United Kingdom, LBJ Library.
National Security Files, Country Files, Vietnam, LBJ Library.

Bibliography 187

National Security Files, International Meetings and Travel File, Manila Conference, LBJ Library.
National Security Files, Vice Presidential Security File, Vice Presidential Travel, LBJ Library.
White House Central Files, Subject Files, CO18 Australia, LBJ Library.
White House Central Files, Subject Files, CO35, United Kingdom, LBJ Library.

3. Oral History Interviews

Burke, Admiral Arleigh S. Interview by John T. Moore, Jr. John F. Kennedy Library, Boston, Massachusetts.
Bruce, Ambassador David K.E. Interview by Thomas H. Baker. LBJ Library.
Menzies, Sir Robert G. Interview by Joe B. Frantz. LBJ Library.
Sullivan, Admiral William H. Interview by Paige E. Mulhollan. LBJ Library.
Waller, Ambassador Sir Keith. Interview by Joe B. Frantz. LBJ Library.

B. Primary Sources (Published)

1. Private Papers

Aitkin, Don, ed. *The Howson Diaries: The Life of Politics: Peter Howson.* Ringwood: Viking, 1984.
Crossman, Richard. *The Diaries of a Cabinet Minister.* London: Macmillan and Cape, 1975.
King, Cecil. *The Cecil King Diary, 1965–1970.* London: Jonathan Cape, 1972).
Millar, T.B., ed. *Australian Foreign Minister: The Diaries of R.G. Casey, 1951–60.* (London: Collins, 1972).

2. Documents

AUSTRALIA

Department of External Affairs. *Current Notes on International Affairs.*
Department of External Affairs. *Select Documents on International Affairs: Vietnam, First Half of 1965.* Canberra: AGPS, 1965.

Department of External Affairs. *Viet Nam: Documents on Communist Aggression.*

NEW ZEALAND

Department of External Affairs. *External Affairs Review.*

SEATO

SEATO Record.

THAILAND

Ministry of Foreign Affairs. *Foreign Affairs Bulletin.*

UNITED STATES OF AMERICA

Congress, House of Representatives, 88th Congress, 2nd Session. *Hearings on Military Posture and H.R. 9637, Before the Committee on Armed Services.* 27 June 1964.

Department of Defense. *United States–Vietnam Relations, 1954–1967.* Washington: USGPO, 1971.

Department of State. *American Foreign Policy, 1950–1955: Basic Documents 1.* Washington: USGPO, 1957.

Department of State. *Bulletin.*

Gravel, Mike, ed. *The Pentagon Papers: the Defense Department History of United States Decision-Making in Vietnam. The Senator Gravel Edition.* New York: Beacon Press, 1971.

Johnson, George W., ed. *The Kennedy Presidential Press Conferences.* New York: Coleman, 1978.

National Archives and Records Service. *Public Papers of the Presidents: Dwight D. Eisenhower, 1954.* Washington: USGPO, 1958.

National Archives and Records Service. *Public Papers of the Presidents: John F. Kennedy, 1963.* Washington: USGPO, 1964).

Porter, Gareth, ed. *Vietnam: A History in Documents.* New York: Meridian, 1979.

Sheehan, Neil, et al., eds. *The Pentagon Papers.* New York: Bantam, 1971.

VIETNAM (REPUBLIC OF VIETNAM)

Department of Foreign Affairs. *Vietnam News.*

3. Memoirs

Ball, George W. *The Past Has Another Pattern*. New York: Norton, 1982.
Eisenhower, Dwight D. *Mandate for Change*. Garden City: Doubleday, 1963.
Johnson, Lyndon B. *The Vantage Point: Perspectives of the Presidency, 1963–1969*. New York: Holt, Reinhart & Winston, 1971.
Macmillan, Harold. *At the End of the Day*. London: Macmillan, 1973.
McPherson, Harry. *A Political Education*. Boston: Little, Brown & Co., 1972).
Pearson, Lester B. *Mike: The Memoirs of the Right Honorable Lester B. Pearson*. London: Victor Gollancz, 1975.
Taylor, Maxwell D. *Swords and Plowshares*. New York: Norton, 1982.
Watt, Sir Alan. *Australian Diplomat: Memoirs of Sir Alan Watt*. Sydney: Angus & Robertson, 1972.
Wilson, Sir Harold. *The Labour Government, 1964–70: A Personal Record*. Harmondsworth: Penguin, 1974.

4. Official Histories

Eayrs, James. *In Defence of Canada: Indochina: The Roots of Complicity*. Toronto: University of Toronto Press, 1983.
Larsen, Stanley Robert, and James Lawton Collins, Jr. *Vietnam Studies: Allied Participation in Vietnam*. Washington: Department of the Army, 1975.
Spector, Ronald H. *United States Army in Vietnam. Advice and Support: The Early Years*. Washington: Center of Military History, United States Army, 1983.
Whitlow, Robert H. *U.S. Marines in Vietnam: The Advisory & Combat Assistance Era, 1954–1964*. Washington: Department of the Navy, 1977.

5. Parliamentary Debates

Australia, House of Representatives, 1954–1967
Australia, Senate, 1962
Great Britain, House of Commons, 1954–1967

6. Newspapers and Periodicals

Age (Melbourne)
Courier-Mail (Brisbane)
Dominion (Wellington)
Globe and Mail (Toronto)
Le Monde
New York Times
People's Daily
Spectator
Sydney Morning Herald
The Times
Times Magazine
Times of India

C. Secondary Sources (Unpublished)

Birgan, Michael J. "Australian Attitudes and Reactions to the People's Republic of China, 1949–1972". Honours thesis, University of Queensland, 1972.

Fegan-Will, Christine A. "Marriage of Convenience: Chinese Relations with the United Kingdom and the United States". Ph.D., University of Queensland, 1981.

Hughes, Peter G. "The Pattern of Australia's Defence, 1963–1971". Honours thesis, University of Queensland, 1972.

McKinnon, Noela M. "Australian Foreign Policy, 1957–65: A Study of Four Foreign Ministers". Honours thesis, University of Queensland, 1975.

O'Brien, Carolyn A. "Australia's Achievement in Regional Defence Planning, 1919–1914. Ph.D., University of Queensland, 1980.

D. Secondary Sources (Published): Select List

1. Articles

Barclay, Glen St J. "In the Sticky Fly Paper: the United States, Australia and Indonesia, 1959–64". *U.S. Naval War College Review* 4: 286 (July–August 1981).

_____. "Friends in Salisbury: Australia and the Rhodesian Unilateral Declaration of Independence, 1965-72". *Australian Journal of Politics and History* 29: 1 (1983).

Fogarty, Michael. "Ted Serong: An Army Career". *Defence Four Journal* 56 (January-February 1986).

Gelber, Harry G. "Problems of Australian Foreign Policy, Jan-Jun 1967". *AJPH* 13: 3 December 1967.

Hughes, Colin A. "Australian Political Chronicle, Jan-Apr 1967". *AJPH* 13: 2 August 1967.

O'Brien, Carlyn A. "Oceans Divide, Oceans Unite: The Concept of Regional Security in Australian Defence Planning". *AJPH* 25: 2 (July 1979).

2. Books

Ambrose, Stephen E. *Eisenhower the Soldier, 1890-1952*. London: George Allen & Unwin, 1984.

Andrews, Eric M. *Australia and China*. Carlton: Melbourne University Press, 1985.

Attia, Gamal el-din. *Les Forces armees des nations unies en coree et au moyen-orient*. Geneva: Plon, 1963.

Barclay, Glen St J. *Friends in High Places: Australian-American Diplomatic Relations Since 1945*. Melbourne: Oxford University Press, 1985.

Berman, Larry. *Planning a Tragedy: The Americanization of the War in Vietnam*. New York: W.W. Norton, 1982.

Bonds, Ray, ed. *The Vietnam War: The Illustrated History of the Conflict in Southeast Asia*. London: Salamander, 1979.

Clark, Gregory. *In Fear of China*. Melbourne: Lansdowne Press, 1967.

Cooper, Chester L. *The Lost Crusade: America in Vietnam*. New York: Dodd, Mead, 1970.

Doyle, Edward, et al. *The Vietnam Experience: America Takes Over*. Boston: Boston Publishing Company, 1982.

King, Peter, ed. *Australia's Vietnam: Australia in the Second Indo-china War*. Sydney: George Allen & Unwin, 1983.

Leary, William M. *Perilous Missions: Civil Air Transport and CIA Covert Operations in Asia*. Birmingham: University of Alabama Press, 1984.

Leckie, Robert. *Conflict: A History of the War in Korea*. New York: G.P. Putnam & Sons, 1962.

McAulay, Lex. *The Battle of Long Tan*. Melbourne: Hutchinson, 1986.

McNeill, Ian. *The Team: Australian Army Advisers in Vietnam, 1962–1972*. St Lucia: University of Queensland Press, 1984.
Maitland, Terrence, et al. *The Vietnam Experience: Raising the Stakes*. Boston: Boston Publishing Company, 1982.
Moncrieff, Anthony. *Many Reasons Why*. Harmondsworth: Penguin, 1979.
Race, Geoffrey. *War Comes to Long An*. Berkeley: University of California Press, 1972.
Seagrave, Sterling, et al. *Soldiers of Fortune*. Alexandria: TIME-LIFE Books, 1981.
Sexton, Michael. *War For the Asking*. Melbourne: Penguin, 1982.
Thompson, Sir Robert. *No Exit From Vietnam*. New York: David Mackay, 1970.
Thompson, W. Scott, and Donaldson D. Frizzell, eds. *The Lessons of Vietnam*. St Lucia: University of Queensland Press, 1977.
Trullinger, James W. *Village at War*. New York: Longmans, 1980.
Valenti, Jack J. *A Very Human President*. New York: Norton, 1978.
Warner, Denis. *The Last Confucian*. New York: Macmillan, 1963.
———. *Reporting South-East Asia*. Sydney: Angus & Robertson, 1966.

Index

"all the way with LBJ", 138, 167
Anderson, Harold D.
  audience with Quat, 104
  awaiting request from Quat, 102
  embarrassed by confusing instructions, 54
  offers token assistance, 28
  suggests symbolic gestures, 81
  tells Westmoreland about Australian combat support, 107-8
  US approach to, 34
  urges prior consultation with Vietnamese, 130
anti-war movement, 100, 113, 119, 137, 161
ANZUS (Australia, New Zealand, United States, Tripartite Security Pact)
  application to confrontation with Indonesia, 49
  Dulles calls meeting, 7-8
  Eisenhower considers as base for intervention, 2
  Howson's views on, 118
  proposals for enlarged ANZUS, 107
  Renouf opposes NZ plan for meeting in Washington, 92-93
  uncertainty about US obligations under, 35-36, 67, 78
Arellano, Oscar, 14
Argentina, 73, 94
ARVN (Army of the Republic of Vietnam)
  breakdown of combat capabilities of, 16-17
  coup against Diem, 38
  defeat at Ap Bac, 33-34
  defeat at Qui Nhon, 86
  defeat by Viet Cong (VC), 42, 56
  Serong's views on, 33
  training in jungle warfare, 20, 45
Ball, George W.
  fears Australian enthusiasm could be dampened, 52
  proposes peace conference, 115
  thinks no attractive options open, 134
  thinks situation hopeless, 64
  urges political solution, 63-64
  warns JFK against involvement in Vietnam, 26
  says South Vietnamese losing war, 114
Barwick, Sir Garfield, 27, 30, 35
Battle, William C., 52, 110
Beale, Sir Howard, 26, 28
Belgium, 50
Binh Gia, 78-79
Border, Sir Louis, 149, 161
Bowen, Sir Nigel, 164
Brazil, 73, 94
British Advisory Mission, 28, 39, 45
British White Paper on Defence, 155
Brown, Wallace, 135
Brown, Winthrop, 76
Bundy, McGeorge, 71, 83-84
Bundy, William P.
  approaches Australia, NZ, UK, 70
  assesses UK, India, Canada, 88-89

Index

examines prospects for increased allied support, 155
fears political cost of war, 135
prepares plans for flexible response, 69
talks with Renouf, 79
talks with Waller, 82
Burke, Arleigh J., 27, 33
Burrow, Eldridge, 20
Butler, R.A., 60

Calwell, Arthur A., 123, 150
Canada, 22-23, 51-52, 69
Capricornia by-election, 160
Casey, Richard G.
 conceals misgivings from Americans, 9
 dealings with Dulles, 6-8
 doubts on supporting US in Indo-China, 4
 embarrassed by minimal Australian defence effort, 10
 problems with Dulles over SEATO, 11-12
 views on Nehru, 5
CAT (Civil Air Transport), 16
Chennault, Claire Lee, 16
Chiang K'ai-shek, 16, 44, 72
Chiefs of Staff (Australian), 62, 80
China, People's Republic of,
 analyses waging of peoples' wars, 120
 Australia needs bastion against, 35
 Beijing-Jakarta Axis, 121
 buys wheat from Australia, 121
 Casey's views on expansionist threat of, 4
 foreign policy of, 121
 Hasluck's fears of expansionism of, 97
 Menzies's fears of expansionism of, 105
 North Vietnam's fears of expansionism of, 111
 rejects Commonwealth Peace Mission, 114
 Split with Russia, 97, 119-20
Churchill, Sir Winston S., 2
CIA (Central Intelligence Agency)
 advises LBJ on British effort in Malaysia, 71
 appreciates Australian commitment in Vietnam, 93
 Civil Air Transport, 16
 consultations with Canadians, 23
 doubts possibility of stable government emerging, 63
 observes lack of forward motion in Vietnam, 38
 Operation Brotherhood, 15
 reports on Duong Van Minh, 38
 sees no organized government in Vietnam, 39
Clark, Ed, 119
Clark, Gregory, 35
Clifford, Clark McA., 156
Cooper, Chester L., 92
Corio by-election, 156
Crossman, Richard, 87, 112

Da Nang, 91-92, 103
defence spending (Australia), 10, 66
De Gaulle, Charles, 137
Denmark, 132
Diem, Ngo Dinh, 14, 17, 26, 29, 43
domino principle, 3, 22, 65
Dove Unit, 91
Dulles, John Foster, 2, 7, 9, 11-12

Eden, Sir Anthony, 5, 9
Eisenhower, Dwight D., 2, 6-8, 121

Fairhall, Sir Allen, 131
Felt, Harry D., 21, 29
Forbes, Alexander J., 66
Forrestal, Michael V., 72-73, 84
France
 civil aid to Vietnam, 71, 93
 facing defeat at Dien Bien Phu, 2
 offers assistance to US, 46
 opposes bombing of North Vietnam, 126
 Ky breaks diplomatic relations with, 114

Gelber, Harry G., 150
Germany, Federal Republic of, 46, 50, 64, 94
Gorton, Sir John Grey, 29, 164
Greece, 52
Gurr, Robert M., 36

Hancock, Sir Valston, 79
Harkins, Paul D., 31, 33, 38
Harriman, Averill, 85
Hasluck, Sir Paul C.

Index 195

asks Waller to report on US
    involvement, 148
concerned about US intentions in
    Vietnam, 77, 101
condemns British inactivity
    in Southeast Asia, 139, 157
discusses new role for Australia in
    region, 157-58
opposes sending third battalion, 159
supports bombing of North
    Vietnam, 163-64
pleased with British Labour
    Government, 115
promises Australian support for
    US, 50
receives news of Binh Gia, 79
supports air attacks on North
    Vietnam, 70
talks with McNamara, 151-52
tells LBJ Australia sending
    battalion, 101
urges Menzies to support US, 83
visits Washington, 67-68
warns of Chinese aggression,
    54-55, 142, 153, 157-58
Healey, Denis, 139-40
Hicks, Sir Edwin, 149
Holt, Harold E.
    advisors concerned about, 162-63
    "all the way with LBJ", 138
    applauds Chinese realism, 153
    Capricornia by-election, 160
    death of, 163
    decides to send third battalion, 149,
        153, 159
    decides to send task force, 129-30
    election campaign, 146-47
    election victory, 148
    Harold Wilson on, 141
    Johnson visit, 144-45
    meets with Hubert H. Humphrey,
        127-28
    meets with Lester Pearson, 154
    personal style, 124-25, 128, 152
    political problems of, 152-53
    regrets British withdrawal from
        east of Suez, 155
    suggests British support
        Australian position, 127
    supports bombing of North
        Vietnam, 126
    talks of Australian
        partnership with US, 127, 139
    tells Johnson reached limit of
        Australian commitment, 160-61
    thinks Australian people questioning
        link with UK, 140
    warns of Chinese expansionism, 131
Holyoake, Sir Keith J.
    at ANZUS Meeting, 92
    decides to augment NZ
        commitment, 151
    Harold Wilson on, 141
    meeting with Holt, 160
    sends detachment to Vietnam, 109
    supports bombing of North
        Vietnam, 60
Howson, Peter
    considers chances of snap
        election, 105, 145
    dissatisfied with progress of war,
        157
    "Fortress Australia", 113
    hopes for a reasonable solution
        in Vietnam, 124
    pushes hard line in Washington,
        67-68
    puzzled by Holt's decision to
        send extra battalion, 149
    worried about Holt, 162-63
Hughes, Colin A., 150, 152, 156
Hughes, Sir Wilfrid Kent, 36
Hulme, Sir Alan, 159
Humphrey, Hubert H., 127-29
Huong, Tran Van, 75, 83

ICC (International Control
    Commission), 73, 87-88
Indonesia, 51, 121
Israel, 132
Italy, 51

Japan, 89, 93
Johnson, Lyndon B.
    asks where will it all end, 152
    Australian visit, 143-45
    decides to retire from politics, 162
    election victory, 65
    Korean visit, 145
    and Michael Stewart, 96
    mission to Saigon, 22
    and Lester Pearson, 100
    reacts to Pleiku, 85
    reacts to Tonkin Gulf, 59-60
    sends Air Mobile Division, 117
    sends directive to US ambassadors,
        55

Index

seeks further Australian support, 154-55
and Harold Wilson, 86-87, 123-24, 133, 139
Johnson, U. Alexis, 81
Joint Chiefs of Staff (US), 63, 65, 68, 95

Kennedy, John F.
  considers invoking SEATO in Laos, 24
  consults with Harold Macmillan about Laos, 21
  sends Taylor to Southeast Asia, 25
  State of the Union address, 34
  tells Ball he's crazy, 26
  would not thwart change of government in Vietnam, 38
Khanh, Nguyen, 41, 56, 62, 77, 90
Khoman, Thanat, 74
King, Martin Luther, Jr, 95
Korea
  Dove Unit arrives in Vietnam, 91
  forces in Vietnam, 93
  Forrestal hopes for help from, 73-74
  JCS seeks division from, 95
  LBJ visits, 145-46
  massive increase in commitment to Vietnam, 133
  offer of combat forces rejected, 76
  offers military aid to Vietnam, 45
  US sees no useful role for, 72
Ky, Nguyen Cao,
  attacks Chap Le, 85
  becomes Premier, 113
  breaks diplomatic relations with France, 114
  personal style, 56
  political problems of, 131-32
  prospects for survival of, 134
  threatens use of armed force against Buddhists, 134
  visits Australia, 149-50

Laking, George, 76, 101
Lang, Kam Dang, 74, 76
Lansdale, Edward G., 14-16, 20-21
Laos, 18, 24
LeMay, Curtis, 67
Lodge, Henry Cabot, 37, 41, 48, 103, 108
Long Tan, 141

Loomis, Alan, 74
Lydman, Jack L., 91

McEwen, Sir John, 147-48
McKinnon, Noela M., 67
McMahon, Sir William, 151, 158, 160, 163
Macmillan, Harold
  considers sending token force to Thailand, 31
  consults with Kennedy, 21, 43
  establishes British Advisory Mission, 28
  on US involvement in Vietnam, 27
  warns about involvement in Vietnam, 24
McNamara, Robert S.
  advocates expansion of US involvement, 116
  hopes for additional allied effort, 127
  seeks Australian support, 122
  seeks extra Australian battalion, 152
  seems to be in despair, 142
  urges US support for Vietnam, 42
  warns LBJ about Vietnam, 39-41
McNaughton, John T., 42, 115, 124, 136
Makins, Sir Roger, 5
Malayan Jungle School, 20
Mansfield, Mike, 159
Marcos, Ferdinand, 75, 132, 142
Martin, Paul G., 92
Menzies, Sir Robert G.,
  advocates forward defence strategy, 11
  decides not to plan for any increase in Australian commitment, 117, 122
  decides to support Thailand, 31
  delays sending military personnel to Vietnam, 29
  directs Casey on SEATO, 12
  had no hesitations about Australian involvement in Vietnam, 1
  increases Australian defence spending, 66-67
  offers combat advisors, 30
  offers token support for Vietnam, 26
  on Commonwealth Peace Mission, 112

retires from politics, 123
  tells Parliament about decision to send combat troops, 105
  unable to provide assistance requested, 76
  warns against Chinese expanionism, 110
Mexico, 61
Military Assistance Command, 28
Minh, Duong Van, 38, 62
Munro, Sir Leslie K., 9
Murville, Couve de, 86, 100

Nehru, Jawaharlal, 5
Netherlands, the, 53
New Zealand,
  commitment to Vietnam of, 93
  considers sending noncombatants, 51
  Dulles attempts to intimidate, 9
  indicates reservations about US policy, 101
  seems less forthcoming than Australia, 73, 90
  sends combat troops, 109
  sends staff officer to Saigon, 36
  US seeks battery from, 103
  US seeks combat troops from, 100
  US seeks marked increase in commitment of, 70
Nhu, Madame, 37
Nolting, Frederick E., Jr, 21-22

Oanh, Nguyen Xuan, 62
O'Brien, Carolyn A., 80
Operation Brotherhood, 15

Pagan, Sir John, 162
Pakistan, 132
Paltridge, Shane, 79, 83
Park, Chung Hee, 129
Pearson, Lester B.
  Bundy thinks not easy to control, 89
  concerned about stamina of LBJ, 100
  opposes intervention in Indo-China, 5
  recommends bombing pause, 99
  regrets resumption of bombing, 126
  talks with Holt, 154
Philippines
  considers sending task force, 75

  Humphrey abused in, 129
  political problems with, 90
  proposals for involvement of, 72-73
  role in covert operations, 15
  Vietnamese approaches to, 47-48, 69
Pleiku, 85
Pompidou, Georges, 86
Quat, Phan Huy, 90-91, 102-4
Qui Nhon, 86

Reid, Allan, 104
Renouf, Alan P.
  advises blockade of North Vietnam, 92
  is annoyed with New Zealand over ANZUS meeting, 92-93
  sees Bundy, 79
  suggests Australia would send combat troops, 101
  urges prompt and positive Australian response, 49-50
Ridgway, Matthew B., 18
Rostow, Walt Whitman,
Rusk, Dean D.
  advises Vietnam ask for Australian support, 101
  considers possible allies in Laos, 21
  pleased with Australian and New Zealand support, 98
  reacts to Tonkin Gulf, 60-61
  reports on "more flags" campaign, seeks more help from Australia, 116-17
  talks with Holt about Commonwealth link, 140
  thanks Australia for combat troops, 102
  urges Felt accept token Australian support, 30
  wants Taiwan kept out of Vietnam, 44-45

San Juan, "Frisco" Johnny, 15
Scherger, Sir Frederick R., 95
Seaborn, Blair, 88, 92
SEATO (Southeast Asia Treaty Organization)
  as base for support to Laos, 21, 24
  as base for support to Vietnam, 19, 44, 60-61, 106, 118
  Casey argues with Dulles about, 12

Index

Dulles
  has great reservations about, 11
  Johnson thinks not the answer, 22
  supports allied involvement in Vietnam, 108
  and Tonkin Gulf, 61
  US and Australian allies in, 96
Serong, F.P., 31-33, 36, 48
Shaw, Sir Patrick, 79
Smith, Walter Beddell, 7
SMM (Saigon Military Mission), 14
Stevenson, William E., 47
Stewart, Michael
  consults with Johnson about use of gas in Vietnam, 96-97
  consults with Rusk, 95
  Crossman regards as 100 percent Anglo-American, 112
  defends US action in House of Commons, 99
  defends US raids after Pleiku, 85
  Hasluck displeased with, 139
  tells House about Commonwealth Peace Mission, 108
Strategic Hamlet Program, 29, 41
Suphamongkhon, Konthi, 74

Taiwan, 3, 16, 44, 72
Taylor, Maxwell D.
  believes US morally committed after coup, 43-44
  confrontation with Vietnamese leaders, 77-78
  fears collapse of morale in Vietnam, 25
  has hopes of Khanh, 63
  mission to Saigon, 24
  never thought of withdrawal from Vietnam, 68
  puzzled about Australian intentions in Vietnam, 108
  recommends change of government in Vietnam, 37-38
  sees no limit to possible escalation, 96
  sees problems with use of ground forces, 95
  suggests US look for excuse for air strikes, 80
  visits Australia, 156
Thailand
  assessing situation in Vietnam, 74
  covert support for Laos, 74
  Eisenhower expects to resist Communist threat, 3
  fear of Vietnam war spreading, 89
  flying combat missions in Vietnam, 93
  JCS concerned to defend frontiers of, 24
  Kennedy and Macmillan discuss, 21
  sends forces to Vietnam, 158-59
  showing statesmanship in region, 9
  wants US to send combat troops, 25
Thant, U, 87, 125, 137
Thieu, Nguyen Van, 118
Thompson, Sir Robert G., 28, 31, 33, 141
Tonkin Gulf, 58-59
Townley, Athol, 31

Unger, Leonard, 82, 101

Vance, Cyrus R., 93
Voyager, 153
Vung Tau, 110

Walker, Patrick Gordon, 99
Waller, Sir Keith
  explains Australian attitude toward Commonwealth Peace Mission, 112
  Hasluck asks to report personally on American thinking, 148
  keeps up pressure on Americans, 83
  reports increasing public scepticism in US, 156
  seeks formal invitation from Rusk, 102
  supports US action, 99
  talks with Unger and Bundy, 82-83
  tells Rusk of Australian military build-up, 67
  told to be tactful with Americans, 81-82
  under unprecedented pressure in Washington, 160
  unsure about requests for Australian aid, 1
Warner, Denis, 17, 21, 39
Westmoreland, William C.
  looks forward to Australian team, 95
  needs 459,000 troops, 125
  praises Australians, 137
  praises Koreans, 116

thinks moral commitment to
  Vietnam after coup, 42-43
wants additional allied forces, 109
wants 665,000 troops, 152
Wheeler, Earle G., 111
Whitlam, E. Gough, 156
Willesee, Mike, 151
Wilson Sir Harold
  angry with FO over support for
    air strikes, 126
  announces withdrawal from east
    of Suez, 137
  Crossman and Bundy find amusing,
    71
  LBJ disappointed with, 144
  LBJ seeks support from, 69
  LBJ advises not to tell US how
    to run Vietnam, 86-87
  LBJ tired of advice from, 100
  meets with Holt, 154
  meets with Paul IV, 105-6
  plans Commonwealth Peace
    Mission, 111-13
  reassures Cabinet about British
    commitment, 70-71
  regrets bombing of Hanoi, 137
  sees Menzies, 112
  under pressure from Left, 88-89,
    92, 124
  views on Holt and Holyoake,
    140-41
  warns LBJ about air strikes,
    123-24

Youngsdale, Carl, 78

Zhou, Enlai, 121, 135
Zuckert, Eugene M., 67